Pelé

Pelé

The Autobiography

with **Orlando Duarte** *and* **Alex Bellos**

Translated from the Portuguese by
Daniel Hahn

POCKET
BOOKS

LONDON • SYDNEY • NEW YORK • TORONTO

First published in Great Britain by Simon & Schuster UK Ltd
in 2006
This edition published by Pocket Books in 2007
An imprint of Simon & Schuster UK Ltd
A CBS COMPANY

5 7 9 10 8 6

Simon & Schuster UK Ltd
1st Floor
222 Gray's Inn Road
London WC1X 8HB

Simon & Schuster Australia
Sydney

www.simonandschuster.co.uk

A CIP catalogue for this book is available
from the British Library.

ISBN-13: 978-1-84739-681-5

Plate sections designed by Tina Steadman
Typeset in Palatino by M Rules
Printed and bound in Great Britain by
CPI Group (UK) Ltd, Croydon, CR0 4YY

Para minha família

CONTENTS

	Preface: Planet Football	3
1	The Boy from Bauru	9
2	The Beautiful Game	31
3	From Santos to Sweden	59
4	Joy and Pain	101
5	Target Man	133
6	Glory	155
7	The First Farewells	191
8	Cosmonaut	217
9	Citizen of the World	235
10	Family	263
11	Icon	279
	Appendix: Pelé's Goalscoring Career	307
	Picture Credits	343
	Index	345

OBRIGADO

I want to thank:

FIFA, especially Sepp Blatter and Jerome Champagne, for suggesting that I write this book;

DUET, Henry Gabay and Alain Schibl, and also Jonathan Harris, for their help in bringing the autobiography to life;

Simon & Schuster UK and Andrew Gordon, for their extraordinary contribution;

Celso Grellet and José 'Pepito' Rodrigues, who helped a lot;

Orlando Duarte and Alex Bellos, the writers;

my family, for their support during my career;

all the players who have passed away and who opened the door for me, in the name of my father, Dondinho;

and God, who gave me the gift to play football.

PREFACE

Planet Football

I'm able to say that I'm a happy man, because I've had the support of so many of you to help me reach where I am today. And it is because of football that I have achieved whatever I have achieved. Every goal I scored, every goal we celebrated, was intensely felt – whether the first or the thousandth.

I'm happy because I've shared football pitches, and shots, and indeed much of my life, with players like Tostão, Garrincha, Clodoaldo, Pepe, Rivelino, Gilmar, Bellini, Jairzinho, Zagallo and so many others. I have lived through football's golden years; the Brazil teams of 1958, '62 and '70 brought football to the whole world, made people fall in love with it. Our joyful way of playing gave the rest of the world a taste for this marvellous sport. In that time we spread a real passion for football – a passion that seems to be passed on in the genes, as children are born with a love for this game already in their hearts.

A boy who played with a ball made of socks, who moved on to play with a professional ball, on professional pitches, in teams that made history. I saw the world, met great people – wonderful people. I never expected to fly so high.

I'll never forget my team-mates from the national squad or

my domestic club, Santos. Our time was a pure one, innocent, almost rough-and-ready, in the sense of the simplicity which was within our reach, before technology invaded our lives. There was nothing modern in our day. Our strip was made of coarse cotton, our shorts were short and our boots heavy. Those shorts – I think it's funny watching old games where players have their whole legs and thighs showing; it's all so much more elegant today. Football itself has changed too, with time, and there have been many improvements to the rules.

But the rules would mean nothing without all those idols who have to interpret them on the pitch; without whom we wouldn't have the spectacle that football has come to represent. To our mind, Brazil had – and still has nowadays – a special place in the world of football, a special brand, owing to being five-times World Champions, and having had so many brilliant players. Again I must acknowledge the privilege I've felt in being able to play with them, my friends and team-mates, in so many of those great victories.

Football is special. You play in a group, you can't play it alone – there is something magical in the absolute harmony that exists among team-mates. A ball passed well to a striker is every bit as important as the goal itself. When it's well tuned, it all comes out beautifully, as though we were taking part in a cleverly choreographed dance. And it really thrills the audience when this happens, they can appreciate the tone of the game, its beauty. I feel the spectators should be like the twelfth player on a team, so important are they in the spectacle as a whole. And the spectators, the fans, must be aware that there are rules for them too – respect for the club, for your opponents, for the players on the pitch, for the women in the stadium, for the children who will ensure that football won't die out in the future. They should have the right to be exuberant, to burst with music, songs, banners and much more, as long as they don't offend anybody. Aggression is the one thing that is inexcusable.

As players we get to befriend players from other clubs. Real friends. We're often invited to their homes, we get to know their families, and we are constantly searching for ways of improving football as a whole. The ambition should always be to play an elegant game. Because from that nucleus emerges an example that reaches everyone, in Brazil and beyond. This is what counts. We have to be worthy and competent to show the world that we're not *just* five-times champions, but also people with feelings and manners, obeying the number-one rule of every sport, and of life – to know how to lose.

I hope that this book, in which I talk about my life, might at some points serve as an example of what football has done for me, of what it means to me, and as a demonstration of the fact that if you want to succeed, you have to know how to face the challenge. In sport as in life: there are defeats, and there are victories.

EDSON ARANTES DO NASCIMENTO
May 2006

1

The Boy from Bauru

'The greatest goal I scored was a one–two with Celeste: we named him Edson Arantes do Nascimento: Pelé'

DONDINHO, PELÉ'S FATHER

However long we may live, we never forget the time when we were young. Memory is like a film which we alone can watch. For me, childhood is the best part of that film: time and again my thoughts return to my experiences, the innocence and mischief of that time, and the dreams and nightmares too.

I was born in Três Corações in Minas Gerais, a state in the south-east of Brazil just to the north of Rio de Janeiro. It is an area very rich in minerals, especially gold – the early Portuguese explorers were thrilled at the abundance and brilliance of that rich yellow mineral and settled there to exploit it. Among them was a farmer. He was a responsible man, a hard worker, and was dedicated to the land he'd acquired on the banks of the Rio Verde. He asked his superior for permission to build a chapel there, and permission was granted; when it was ready he named it the Holy Hearts of Jesus, Mary and Joseph. The name he gave the chapel was in tribute to the three Sacred Hearts in which the farmer had such faith, and which in turn became the name of the place – Três Corações, the three hearts.

Brazil, though, is a land of stories, and as you will discover throughout this book, a story in Brazil isn't worth telling unless there are alternative versions to call upon. And the three hearts are no different: some have it that the name refers to the love of three cowboys who were prevented from marrying three local girls; others hold that it is related to the fact that as the Rio Verde approaches the town it forms little curves like three little hearts. I'm sticking with the farmer, though – it's the story I was brought up with, and one that has always appealed to me.

The first records of the current town date from 1760, with the foundation of the chapel of the Sacred Hearts. But for some reason there was a problem with the land deeds, and the area on which the chapel was built was sold. The chapel itself was destroyed, and it wasn't until the end of the eighteenth century that a replacement was built, when a Captain Antônio Dias de Barros provided a new one. The then village of Rio Verde which was developing around it was established as a parish, and renamed Três Corações do Rio Verde. In 1884, after a visit from Brazil's last emperor, Dom Pedro II, and his family, and the opening of a rail link to the city of Cruzeiro in Minas Gerais, Três Corações became a town.

Even though I only lived there a couple of years it remains a village in my memory, and whatever the legends that people spread about the name, there's one thing I feel sure of – it feels completely natural to me, it makes complete sense, that I should have been born in a place called 'three hearts'. Looking back on my life for this book has revealed to me many occasions of confusion and uncertainty, but what has also become clear is an underlying coherence to my life, and I think it can be seen here too, for this name Três Corações has always been an important signpost for me. I feel it above all in relation to my religion, because within it beat those three sacred hearts that are so beloved and revered by all of us who are Catholics. But I see it too in the other places that informed my upbringing and whatever I went on to achieve in the world – in Bauru, deep in the middle of the state of São Paulo, where my family moved and where my love of football was born; and in Santos, along the coast from Rio, where I experienced such happiness as a player and won so many championships. The places where I was born, where I grew up and where I played football – they have given me three hearts too.

★

It has now been more than sixty-five years since I came into the world, on 23 October 1940, in Três Corações. My journey has been a long one, but strangely there's almost nothing about it that I cannot remember. I was born poor, in a small house built from second-hand bricks, but although this makes it sound sturdy, from the outside you could tell how ramshackle it really was. Although I'm honoured that the street has been named after me and there's even a plaque on that house saying that's where I was born, it hasn't changed much and still looks pretty run-down. Perhaps the plaque even helps hold the thing together. When I went back to visit this house later in life it brought to mind vividly what the scene of my birth must have been like – a scene that has been described to me by my grandmother, Ambrosina, who was there to help my young mother Celeste through the pains and stresses of childbirth. Eventually, the tiny wriggling infant that was me was held up to the world, prompting my uncle Jorge to exclaim, 'He's certainly black enough!' – perhaps this answered my father's first question about whether I was a boy or a girl. Apparently pleased at the knowledge of my sex my father prodded my scrawny legs and said, 'This one will be a great footballer.' My mother's reaction is not recorded, although I can imagine she was none too pleased with this prediction.

My mum, Celeste, was a local girl, the daughter of a cart-driver. She was petite, with a glistening head of hair and a beautiful smile. My dad, João Ramos do Nascimento – everyone knows him as Dondinho – was from a small town about sixty miles away. He was doing military service in Três Corações when they met. He was also centre-forward for Atlético of Três Corações. It wasn't a properly professional club and it hardly made him any money. There were no victory bonuses or anything like that. And in those days being a footballer meant you had a kind of reputation, it gave you – how shall I say – a certain notoriety. Anyway, my parents married when she was fifteen and by sixteen she was pregnant with me.

Shortly before I came along, there was another arrival in Três Corações: electricity. In order to celebrate this great improvement to our daily lives, Dondinho named me Edson, a tribute to Thomas Edison, the inventor of the light bulb. In fact, on my birth certificate I am actually called Edison with an 'i', a mistake that persists to this day. I'm Edson with no 'i', but to my eternal annoyance quite often the 'i' appears on official or personal documents and time after time I have to explain why. As if that wasn't confusing enough, they got the date wrong on my birth certificate as well – it says 21 October. I'm not sure how this came about; probably because in Brazil we're not so fussy about accuracy. This is another mistake that carries on to this day. When I took out my first passport, the date was put in as 21 October and each time I have renewed it the date has stayed the same.

Life wasn't easy in Três Corações and soon there were more mouths to feed. My brother Jair, known as Zoca, was born in the same house I was. I'm sure my mother was thinking, 'I hope neither of my sons decides to become a footballer. There's no money in it. A doctor, perhaps? Now there's a sensible job!' Well, we know what happened. I would grow to love the game as my father did – it was the thing he knew best and he hoped, like tens of thousands of other footballers in Brazil, that one day he would get the break that meant he could finally support us through scoring goals.

And it almost happened. In 1942 he was called up to play for Atlético Mineiro, the biggest club in the state, based in the capital Belo Horizonte. It seemed that this was the stroke of luck he needed. This was a proper professional club that was known nationally, not like its much poorer namesake Atlético of Três Corações. Atlético played against strong teams. His first try-out was a friendly against the Rio team São Cristóvão. They had a defender, Augusto, who would later get a national call-up and captain Brazil in the 1950 World Cup. Unfortunately, Augusto became known in our family for another reason: in a collision with Dondinho during the match, my dad came off the worst. He damaged his knee – ligaments, I think. He was unable to play the next game and his flirtation with the big time was over.

Back he came to Três Corações and his journeyman career. We also lived in the nearby towns of São Lourenço and Lorena, where he played for the clubs Hepacaré and Vasco – not the famous Rio club, but one named after it. In Lorena, a moutain-side spa resort, my sister Maria Lúcia was born.

Dondinho was a good player. He was a striker, a big guy – almost six foot – and was a great header of the ball. Usually this sort of player would, typically, be English, but at that time Brazil had a footballer who scored some amazing headers called Baltazar. Everyone said that my dad was the 'up-country

Baltazar'. I think that football already ran in the family. He had a brother, Francisco, who I never met because he died young, who was also a striker and who was apparently even better than he was.

It was said that Dondinho once headed five goals in the same match. It happened when I was too young to remember. Later in my career, when I reached a thousand goals, some journalists started to research this claim to see if it was true or not. And it was – they reported that the only goal-scoring record that didn't belong to Pelé belonged to his own father! Now only God can explain that one . . .

✯

It was in São Lourenço in 1944 that something happened that would change all our lives – mine especially. My father received an invitation from the football club in Bauru, north-west of São Paulo, to play there but also, crucially, to take on a job as a local government functionary. He went to Bauru to find out more about the city and the proposal. He liked it, and my mother was delighted at the prospect of the non-football job, which would bring the family some security and improve our financial circumstances. We would finally, she hoped, be able to escape from the suffocation of near-destitution. Things look different to children, though – we knew nothing, life just carried on as normal. Zoca, Maria Lúcia and I were still very young.

My father managed to convince my mother. We sent on ahead what little luggage we had. The people from Bauru sent us our tickets, and off we went. I found the train journey completely exhilarating: in many ways it is my first real memory – at the age of four the happiness that train journey gave me is engraved on my mind. I spent almost the whole journey glued to the window, transfixed by the constantly changing view. The train went slowly but that was fine by me: all the more time to take in the scenery. It was the first time I was really aware of what my country looked like; or at least, that part of it. In those days the nearest we had to air-conditioning was to open the big windows on either side of the carriage, and on one long corner I was so curious to see the front of the train and the plume of smoke from the engine that I leaned out too far and would have fallen had it not been for my father. He yanked me back to safety, under a gaze from my mother that reproached me for my irresponsibility. My time on this earth could have ended right there. But God was keeping an eye on me . . . Sitting between them for the remainder of the journey I didn't take any more risks.

We arrived on 15 September 1944, full of optimism about the future – now my father would prove himself as a footballer, and with money worries put aside he would shine even more brightly. We stayed initially in the Station Hotel, on Rodrigues Alves Avenue, by the corner with Alfredo Ruiz; then we rented a house on Rubens Arruda Street, right alongside the Barone family. One of the children of this family would turn into Baroninho, who would play for Noroeste (another Bauru club), Palmeiras and Flamengo. The people living next-door to us were only Baroninho's grandparents, but it promised well.

And Bauru itself felt like the centre of the world: much bigger than anywhere I had lived up to that point, with all the trappings of a big city, or so I imagined: shops, a cinema and hotels. Even then it was one of the larger cities in the interior of Brazil, with a population of about 80,000, and something of a transport hub, with three of the main rail lines passing through it. It felt like a new beginning, and the kind of place where fortunes could be made.

But there was a complication immediately, in that the club that had proposed the contract with my father, Lusitana, had changed into the Bauru Athletic Club (BAC), and new bosses were in place, with new opinions and new obligations. They were prepared to honour the football part of the contract – Dondinho was a good player, remember, despite his suspect knee – but of the main reason we had gone to Bauru in the first place, the job as a functionary, there was no mention. So it seemed we were back to square one, and with an even larger family to support than in Três Corações. As well as my parents Dona Celeste and Dondinho, my brother, sister and uncle Jorge, we also had my grandmother on my father's side, Dona Ambrosina, living with us.

Thankfully, his knee held out to begin with. In 1946 Bauru won the São Paulo 'countryside championship' of the best teams in the interior of the state. My father was the best player and he scored loads of goals. He became well-known around town. Yet success was fleeting because his knee was in a real state. I remember him stuck in the house in the evenings, just sitting there with his swollen knee. There wasn't much medical attention in Bauru at the time and I used to fetch him ice and then help him put it on his knee. Doctors at the time probably wouldn't have been able to pronounce the word 'meniscus', let alone know how to operate on one. Dondinho was able to play less and less until eventually, after eight years at BAC, he gave it up completely.

During the periods when my dad was sidelined from football through injury, the family really struggled. Zoca, Maria Lúcia and I were always barefoot and wore only cast-off clothes. The house was small and overcrowded with a leaky roof. With no regular source of income, I remember that on several occasions the only meal my mum had for us was bread with a slice of banana. We never went without food – like many people worse off than us in Brazil – but for my mother it was a life governed by fear, a fear of not being able to provide. And one of the things that I have learned in my sixty-five years is that fear of life is fear of the worst kind.

Members of the family chipped in, of course. My uncle Jorge took a job as a delivery man for the Casa Lusitana. He would work there for nineteen years, and his dedication (which was his great forte) would help him to rise through the ranks, while his salary helped us eat. And my aunt Maria, my father's sister, used to bring us food and sometimes clothes when she visited us on her day off from her job in São Paulo.

It was also up to me to help. I was the eldest child, after all, and so I decided to do my bit. I must have been about seven when – thanks to Jorge – I scraped together enough money to assemble some shoe-shining kit, and planned to hang out in the more salubrious corners of Bauru making a mint from shining already-shiny shoes. But my mother was far more democratic and insisted I begin closer to home, getting business from our near neighbours. As half the people on our street wandered around barefoot I remember thinking this was not such a good idea, but Dona Celeste was not the kind of woman you disagreed with, and so I dutifully knocked on all the doors on Rubens Arruda Street asking people if they wanted their shoes shined. They were kind, but I only got one sale, and even then I didn't know how much to charge. Early lessons in business, which I wasn't always to heed: find out where the customers are, and know your price.

Nor, I realised, was I very good at the shining itself, and so some practice was required. I polished my father's football boots and also did my own one pair of shoes – a smart pair my aunt Maria had brought on one of her visits one day, which used to belong to her boss's son. I only wore them on special occasions and they lasted a while until – perhaps this was the most special occasion of them all – I decided to find out what it was like to kick a football in shoes rather than my usual bare feet, and ruined them.

Eventually I persuaded Dona Celeste that there was no point in trying to get shoe-shine work in our poor neighbourhood, and grudgingly she agreed that I could accompany my father to the Bauru Athletic Club stadium on match days, where at least there would be lots of shoes and Dondinho could keep an eye on me. He was too busy working to bother with that, but the presence of so much potential business for me meant I couldn't fail, and when we went home that day together I had two cruzeiros in my pocket. After this early success my mother became a little more lenient and allowed me to go and shine shoes at the railway stations in town, too – there was more competition there, as other boys like me had the same idea, but at least I was making a little money.

About a year later things picked up at home when my father finally managed to land a job working in a health clinic. It was pretty menial stuff – cleaning, fetching and carrying, mostly, but because the job was funded by the local government it felt much more secure than any of the other part-time work he did, and for the first time in years the shadow of poverty was lifted – not removed, but at least lifted – from our house.

*

And meanwhile, of course, there was the small matter of my education to deal with. My mother was adamant that I should go to school and get the best out of what it had to offer, and so I was duly enrolled in the Ernesto Monte primary school in Bauru. In theory I would stay there for four years and then go to secondary school for another four years. After that, if you were diligent or clever or lucky enough, there was *colegial*, or prep school, for three more years before entering university. At the age of eight, though, that seemed a long way away.

The process of preparing a poor boy for school in those days was odd. My mother and grandmother sewed up my torn shorts. I wore shirts made from the material used for transporting wheat (although it was good fabric, pure cotton). In fact at first I was pleased to be going to school. They gave me a case with coloured pencils which I used up right away, painting everything I could. It was my father who took me on the first day, and my behaviour to begin with was exemplary. But I soon became the class chatterbox, and trouble.

I remember my first teacher well – her name was Dona Cida. She brooked no argument and was a harsh disciplinarian – she wouldn't stand for any misbehaviour. I was often punished by being made to kneel on a pile of dried beans, hard as little stones – maybe that helped to strengthen my knees for the work they had ahead . . .

I wasn't a great student, although at first things weren't so bad – I could be a bit of a brat at times but Dona Cida wasn't as strict as some of my later teachers and a couple of the assistants in that first year liked me, despite my occasional misbehaviour. I wanted to learn, and I don't think I was stupid, but I didn't really get on with school. I look back now and it seems strange, not just because I now know how important education is, but because I had a good motive for doing well – at around this time, seven or eight years old, I had a passion for aeroplanes and dreamed of becoming a pilot. I would go down to the Aero Club to watch planes and gliders doing manoeuvres. I was desperate to be a pilot, and whenever I could I would scoot off, even skip school, to head down to the airfield and marvel at the planes being readied for take-off or coming in to land, and the pilots going about their business. It seemed an impossibly romantic way to earn a living – to live – and I was in its thrall.

I remember talking to my father about it and being surprised that he thought it was a good enough ambition: I expected him to dismiss the idea, but instead he cleverly reminded me of all the skills I would need to acquire in order to achieve this goal – reading, writing, navigating and the rest. It was one of the first times I recall him treating me like a man, and taking me seriously, and it made a big impression. As well as being a footballer he had a good head on his shoulders – he was always the one to rein in Dona Celeste's fireworks – and I knew instantly that I should listen to what he was saying. It made school seem more relevant, more useful. Even when skipping school I knew that I'd have to get some sort of education to be able to fly. But one day all that changed.

We were all hanging out after school one afternoon, probably kicking a ball about, when someone shouted that there was a dead guy in the morgue, a pilot who had crashed his glider. We were just boys, and lots of my friends and I found this really exciting. A dead guy! And a pilot! I went to look at the scene of the accident close-up, naughty and curious, eager not to miss anything. As if that wasn't enough, my friends and I then went over to the hospital where the autopsy was taking place, and saw the dead pilot laid out on the slab though a dirty window.

I was fascinated at first – I think it was probably the first time I had seen a dead body – but then the mortuary attendant or doctor or whoever he was tried to manipulate the corpse, which was still clothed, and in moving the pilot's arm, which must have already been starting to stiffen, he had to yank it hard and this caused a gush of blood to spurt out on to the floor. It was a terrifying sight, like something from a movie, and the image remained burned in my mind for days and nights afterwards. It gave me nightmares. I never went back to the Aero Club.

☆

As I grew up, Bauru became my city. There was family, there was school, there was football (more of that later), but there was also play. I made friends with lots of the kids from the neighbourhood around my house – black, white, even some Japanese kids. All I wanted to do was play. The yard of our wooden house had vines, a mango tree and some sugar-cane. I was a serious mango-eater. I still love them! My friends would come to the yard and we would invent games, even putting on mini-circuses. The branches of the trees were our trapeze, and the risks we took were terrifying. My mother and my grandmother didn't like these games one bit. I longed for space, and the yard was too small. I moved out on to the street – happy is the child who can play out in the street! – but then the street outside our house wasn't enough, so I began to venture further.

One of the things we used to love was swimming. It could get very hot in Bauru and we'd go down to a river that ran close to the Noroeste (North-west) railway – the company that sponsored the rival club to my father's. The best bit about swimming there was a little waterfall. We'd spend whole afternoons just mucking about: skipping class in order to enjoy the delights of the river and swim, that was normal in those days. But one day it would cost me dearly. I was swimming with some friends, and a big kid called Zinho tried to pull me across the river. I had to kick my legs, while he did the arm-strokes. Halfway across the river we got tangled up as I was holding on to his legs – it was enough for us to begin sinking, and exhausted as we were, we swallowed a lot of water. We almost drowned. The other boys on the bank couldn't do anything, and shouted until a man came along and held out a stick to pull us up. He saved us. Afterwards I remember feeling that God must have been keeping an eye on me, just as he had when I nearly fell from the train.

For a while we didn't swim again, but it was hard to resist. The lesson was learned, though, and from then on we were very careful. We would swim in our school-clothes, then hang them on the trees to dry. We didn't want anyone to see us naked, and my mother couldn't know that we'd been in the river. Even so, sometimes there wasn't time for us to play, dry the clothes and make our way home, and I'd be smacked by Dona Celeste for arriving home with my clothes all wet and filthy. I gave her a lot of trouble – just how much is something you only learn when you become a parent yourself. Don't get me wrong: she was a wonderful mother, a slight woman but very strong, and although she once described me as an 'exemplary son' I know that is far from the truth, at least when I was young.

My mother knew that in order for me to do better at school I'd have to be made to stay at home to study rather than running off to play. This was torture – not only denied the fun of hanging out with friends like Raul and Raquel Lavico, whose grandparents also lived on Rubens Arruda Street, I had to do homework under the watchful eye of Dona Celeste. One time, though, I managed to sneak out to play in a hide-out we'd built in a big hole in the ground alongside a street in Bauru – there were lots of such holes, the roads weren't very good and after a heavy rainfall erosion always made new ones.

This particular hide-out was a really good one, and I was excited to have given my mother the slip and be able to go and play there, even though there had been a lot of rain in the previous few days and it was raining still. Soon, though, she realised what had happened and I had to go back home, tail between my legs. I pleaded with her to let me go out again, but didn't get anywhere. My mother was totally inflexible. I studied a little more, before my mind wandered back to our game, imagining my companions having the best time . . . Annoying maths was keeping me from it. That's when one of the unforgettable events of my childhood happened. One of the boys arrived, running, breathless, hardly able to speak, telling me to come to the place where our hide-out was, because it had slipped or collapsed with one of the gang still in it! I'd have beaten the world speed record, I so wanted to get to my friend and rescue him. There were already a lot of people there when we arrived. It had all happened because of the rain – the earth had become soft and it had all collapsed in on itself. All of our friends and neighbours were working to dig and recover the boy who was trapped inside. It was too late; the boy had earth in his nostrils, his mouth, his eyes – it was a sight I'll never forget. He wasn't one of us; he'd gone in without anyone noticing. Yet again I could have died, I could have been there in his place – but God was keeping an eye on me.

My studies and my mother had prevented a tragedy. I still

remember the dead pilot, the visit to the morgue, and now I had more nightmares to come as I remembered that innocent boy. Because of them I would often awake screaming, both at home and even later, after I'd moved to Santos. I didn't like the dark – it scared me. What had happened meant that I never again thought of digging holes like that. For a while, I retained a child's sense of guilt. It's hard to remember something like that without thinking that I could have been in his place. If that had been the case, I wouldn't have made it more than sixty-five years along the road of life, and of course I wouldn't be here to tell the story either.

✯

My second year at Ernesto Monte was terrible, and probably made worse by the fact that I was missing a lot of lessons. I made friends with boys who were very badly behaved, and I changed from my first year. There were new teachers, too: Dona Lourdes and then Dona Laurinda. Pretty soon I didn't want anything to do with school or studying. Dona Laurinda in particular punished me extremely harshly; I was still a chatterbox so she'd put balls of scrumpled-up paper in my mouth to shut me up. It made my jaw ache. After a while I began to discreetly chew the paper balls to make them smaller so they'd hurt me less. She also used Dona Cida's old trick of making me kneel on a pile of dried beans. Dona Laurinda was strict, but with this punishment, besides being tough and making me face the whole class, I was able to make some good of the situation. They say that when a punishment is repeated again and again, or when it lasts a long time, the person being punished begins improving himself and benefits from it. That's just how it was with me. I transformed the worst into a kind of distraction. Each time Dona Laurinda forgot about me as she carried on with her lesson, I'd remove one of the beans from under my knees, to reduce the pain.

Another of her favourite punishments was to stand me in the corner of the room with my back to my classmates, holding my arms out to the sides like the big statue of Christ the Redeemer in Rio. It was exhausting. As I became more tired and distracted my arms would drop, and immediately I'd get a slap and return to the position she'd put me in. But the moment my energetic teacher looked away, down my arms would come again. I spent a lot of my break-times being punished in that classroom. I didn't stop! Whenever it was break-time I'd try something. I remember one time climbing a mango tree in the yard next to our school to get mangoes for all the boys. When we'd eaten them I made up a game using one of the mangoes; it didn't last long and one of them hit a boy who started crying which attracted everyone's attention – a mango is heavy enough to hurt, after all – and he got his revenge by snitching on the group. We all went to the Head, and I couldn't avoid receiving yet another punishment.

But looking back, there is a kind of innocence to the games we played then, even though we sometimes got into trouble for them. Nowadays there aren't many children who can play on the street, who recognise mango trees and have the privilege of eating a mango just thrown down from the tree, sitting savouring it on the ground, not worrying about the juice running down their arms. Children have almost no responsibility, their minds don't work like they do when we're grown up. A child is content with his own little world. A child has a less extreme idea of poverty. Appeasing your hunger, getting hold of a little toy, being close to your mother, when you're really young all is well. Life is wonderful!

Although I got punished a lot at school, does that mean I was bad? There was a lot of talk of sin, but I don't know if a child can sin. What's a sin to a little boy? I broke into orchards of good mango trees to get fruit to eat. A sin? I don't think so – many mangoes would fall anyway, they wouldn't be collected and they'd go to waste. Trees drop fruit on to the streets too. I've always been a good person to have around, I think – though I wasn't a good student, as I've already said. I would fight to defend my interests. A restless boy, ideas would just spring up in my head. I think that's why I had so many nightmares, and sleepwalking probably has something to do with it. When I was a boy I used to talk a lot in my sleep; I'd even get up – without breaking anything – and then go back to sleep. Later, in Santos, in Dona Georgina and Senhor Raimundo's boarding-house, on trips, even when I was on the national team, people have always said that I talk in my sleep. My teammate Pepe liked to tell the story of how I once got up in the middle of the night, shouted 'Goal!', and then went back to bed. I can't vouch for that . . .

My teacher Dona Laurinda was no angel, but nor was she really the Evil Stepmother I've described. And I was hard work: I fought with my classmates, I had no discipline. I deserved some punishments, but I think the particular punishments I was given were excessive. I know now that that isn't how one ought to treat children, but in those days teachers were very highly respected and even they didn't understand things as they do today. When I was a boy discipline was everything. There wasn't any discussion. Everything operated on the basis of respect – adults were very distant from us, and of course children didn't have the space they have today. Thank goodness things have changed for the better for children in this sense – we see how interesting they are, how much their questions and curiosity can teach us. We know how important each of their discoveries is. We know all about their energy, how their hormones operate, how intelligent they can be – which is why nowadays the child is the most important member of the family. We watch them constantly to see what they need, or what they like, or what they want. We know that a child is a synonym for joy.

And joy, for me, throughout this time and throughout my life, was football. It's time to talk about the beautiful game, and how I fell under its spell.

2

The Beautiful Game

'This is who I told you will be the best in the world'

WALDEMAR DE BRITO

I owe everything I have to football. Towards the end of my career with Santos I even went through a spell when I signed my name 'Edson Arantes do Nascimento *Bola*' (football) – it seemed to be the best way to show gratitude for all that the game has done for me.

I suppose having a footballer as a father was the start of it. Most sons want to be like their fathers and I was no exception. Dondinho scored lots of goals and everyone said he was good. I never thought of playing for Brazil, or of winning the World Cup or anything like that. I just told my friends, 'One day, I'm going to be as good as my dad.' And Dondinho was a good man, too: a marvellous father. And despite the fact that his football never brought in much money, because it was the game that *he* played, I guess I became fascinated by it too. It was in the genes.

And this was Brazil, remember. Football was everywhere when I was growing up. As I played with friends in the yard or the street, there were always games going on around us, usually organised by slightly bigger boys. My friends and I were desperate to take part, but it wasn't easy to get a place in the teams; they said I was too skinny. It's true, I was small and scrawny as a boy. Those were the first times I was barred from a game, and if anything it only made me want it more. The boys we so wanted to join were maybe ten, a few years older than us, and they thought they were kings of the road. This didn't stop us – the young ones – from planning our own revolution. We would hang around outside the pitch and when the ball came out we wouldn't return it, but would start playing with it ourselves. It earned us many slaps and kicks up the backside. My brother Zoca and I wouldn't hang around, though. We were afraid that our mother, Dona Celeste, might show up.

As the appeal of the mini-circuses faded we started to spend more and more time dreaming about football and when we could next get to play. We had no kit, of course – not even a ball, and we had to make do with stuffing paper or rags into a sock or stocking, shaping it as best we could into a sphere and then tying it with string. Every now and then we would come across a new sock or bit of clothing – sometimes, it must be said, from an unattended clothes-line – and the ball would get a little bit bigger, and we'd tie it again. Eventually it came to resemble something close to a proper football.

Which is more than could be said for the pitch – my first matches were held in the prestigious Rubens Arruda Street stadium: 'goal-posts' of old shoes at either end, one where the street finished in a cul-de-sac and the other where it crossed with Sete de Setembro Street (named after Brazil's Independence Day); the touchlines more or less where the houses began on either side. But for me at the time it was like the Maracanã, and the place where I began to develop my skills. As well as the chance to spend time with friends and test myself against them, this was when I first learned the joy of controlling the ball, making it go the way I wanted it to, at the speed I wanted it to – not always easy with a ball made of socks. Playing football soon became more than just a pastime, it became an obsession.

Dona Celeste was quick to notice, naturally, and, ever-vigilant, she was careful to make sure I spent at least some time on my studies. Probably because of her experiences with my father, football to her had until then represented a waste of time, something that had taken him away from home and failed to put food on the table. It must have been hard for her to see her son appearing to rush headlong down the same road, but she must have rationalised that at least I was playing nearby, somewhere she could keep an eye out, and at least I wasn't getting up to something even less desirable. The trade-off for her letting me play was that I had to involve my younger brother Zoca. It was a pain at first as he was too small to be useful and would often run crying into the house when a bigger boy clattered him or ran him off the ball, but I didn't mind. He was my brother, and it meant I got to play.

We'd come in after each session caked in mud. It makes me happy to remember how I'd come in filthy from messing around with the ball, and my mother would order me off to take a bath. I'd wait for her to come and scrub me down and check I was washing properly. I liked watching the dirty water running off my body.

✯

As I have said, I was a restless, creative boy, and soon I decided that what I really wanted was to have a club of our own, for the lads from Sete de Setembro and Rubens Arruda streets. Playing outside the house was great but I yearned to do it properly, to emulate my father and the other players we saw on the Noroeste training pitch which abutted the end of the street. This meant we'd have to buy some proper kit – shirts, shorts, boots, socks, a ball . . . But what about the money? We'd have to get hold of some.

The first meetings took place outside my house. Our priority was to have our own kit. Anyone who wanted to be a part of the team had to sign up (verbally, I mean – there was nothing on paper, of course). The club would meet in the yard of my house, or at one of the members' houses. I had the idea of collecting football stickers, which were all the rage at the time, filling an album or two and then exchanging them for a ball. We'd focus on the big teams from Rio and São Paulo, and that way raise the value of the collection. Everyone thought this was a great idea and it was agreed to start pooling our sticker resources.

'And the kit?' I asked. 'Where will we get the money to buy that?'

'What about collecting old iron, tins, bottles and stuff from around the streets and selling them?' one boy suggested. 'Or kindling?' piped up another. 'We could swipe a little bit from each delivery to our houses and then sell it on.' I knew Dona Celeste would take a very dim view of this so just nodded vaguely. As it turned out, neither of these schemes proved very successful. We gathered up as much as we could – there wasn't a street or a yard that we hadn't searched for material we could sell. So how much did we make? Hardly anything. Not even enough for the socks. It became clear that there were already lots of people in the neighbourhood doing this kind of scrap-dealing and scavenging, and hardly anything of value was left lying around for very long. It was a sign of the times. A further team meeting was convened.

A kid called Zé Porto had the brainwave. He suggested that we sell peanuts at the door to the circus and the cinema. The first problem: where would we get the peanuts? Zé Porto smiled and told us his delinquent idea: 'We'll nick them from the Sorocabana stores.' This was a kind of warehouse down by the railway – there were always workers down there, though, and the plan was risky. I thought of Dona Celeste's frequent admonishments about the sin of stealing being one of the very worst, and I could tell a few of the other boys were nervous. But Zé Porto was convinced, and persuasive. The plan was risky, but it was also audacious. He said there were loads of peanuts in the train-wagons, the wagons would be easier to get into than the warehouse itself, and that it wouldn't hurt anyone if a few kilos went missing.

'Besides,' he went on, 'anyone who doesn't agree is a big shit!'

This conclusive argument settled the matter.

✯

The first assault on the wagons was a real drama. Only two of us could get into the first wagon. Through good or bad luck, I was chosen. I had hoped that my sticker-collecting plan would mean I would be excused peanut-stealing duties, but we had had problems finding the last few stickers of each collection – there were always a couple that were rarer, and were therefore highly prized – and I had to admit my failure to the group. I had made contact with some other kids, not on our fledgling team, who had the precious missing stickers, but they weren't prepared to trade. It was decided – probably by Zé Porto – that my penance would be to go on the Sorocabana mission.

I almost died of fright as I made my way in. We carried old

bowls, sieves, an old bucket to put the peanuts in. We slit some of the sacks, which were huge – the peanuts came spilling out in a flood and we gathered them up as fast as we could, our hearts in our mouths. We filled our pockets too, and put still more in our shirts, and passed them out to the others waiting outside the wagon. And then it was done – we'd got away with it, and ran off laughing at our nerves and our relief.

After our great victory – which had me in a cold sweat throughout – our Sete de Setembro dream was becoming a reality. We toasted the peanuts and went off to sell them. Soon we had money for shirts – well, for vests, there wasn't *that* much money; we bought shorts too. There wasn't enough for socks or boots. Our second attempt to get peanuts was a disaster. We had to run like champions not to get caught, and the matter was closed. But in spite of it all, Sete de Setembro would play its first match. Vests, shorts and no boots (for a while we were known as the 'Shoeless Ones', until we realised there were several other teams in Bauru who shared that nickname, for the same reason we had chosen it).

Tracking down those last few stickers was a nightmare, and demanded great dedication from the whole team. The rarities were all of the great aces of the time: players like Baltazar, Claudio, Mauro, Carbone and many others. We had to trade doubles to get them. But we didn't stop hassling the kids who had them until we'd completed our album. And soon the sticker album was exchanged for a ball. It wasn't an official one – it didn't even have a valve, and sometimes we had to nick one from the wheel of a parked car, often leaving the poor owner with a flat tyre – but that didn't matter. It was a ball, and it wasn't made of socks. Since the sticker plan had been my idea I kept the ball at my house – which made me the boss, the one who owned the ball, and sort of the unofficial captain of the Sete de Setembro team.

✯

The club was coming together. And it had been created from our efforts: a bunch of kids from a poor neighbourhood who just wanted to play football. Our team came to be known in the area quite quickly – we had some talent, didn't lose, and not many people wanted to play against us. There was me and my brother, Zoca; Zé Roberto, known as Toquinho; Vadinho; Ari; Cidão; Dino; a couple of Japanese boys and many others – a squad, really, rather than just a team. Zé Porto, strangely, liked to hang out with us but wasn't that bothered about playing.

One time we approached the employees of the local council, who worked out on the roads pulling up the shrubs that grew up alongside the pavements – tough work. We went over to talk to them, and since there were lots of them and they liked football they agreed to play us. We played on the roads – mainly on my road. Our team would put on our vests and shorts in my yard, and we'd file out, just like proper teams in a proper stadium. Dreaming children always imitate the behaviour of their idols.

We'd play until it got dark. I'd play in goal for half the game, and the other half in midfield or as centre-forward. I was the one who decided on positions – after all, I was the 'Keeper of the Ball', the chief – a bit of a dictator, to be honest. One problem we had was when the ball hit the lighting cables and caused a short circuit, cutting out the power for the whole street. Everyone would curse us and we'd have to bring our game to a close pretty quickly. My mother used to lose her patience – when she got hold of me I really used to get it, and of course Zoca did too as he was always with me. And when my father heard about our mischief he used to punish me too, although I think he was secretly pleased I was enjoying football so much. Uncle Jorge, though, kept quiet. He was always a good friend to me, always calm and supportive.

Sete de Setembro was a rite of passage in my life. In hindsight I can see that it was important that we had to struggle to get the club founded, and I think my father admired our tenacity in pulling it all together. Certainly from around this time we began to spend more time together, and he took more of an active role in my upbringing. I used to love watching him in action when BAC played. I wanted to be a player now – all dreams of aeroplanes and flying were forgotten. The idea horrified my mother, as I have mentioned, but Dondinho was diplomatic, helping me with technique but at the same time keeping her happy. He taught me to kick with my left foot, how to do a good header, he improved my touch with my right foot. When my mother, Dona Celeste, caught us, she'd warn my father and he'd just laugh. 'The boy can't kick with his left foot and I'm just teaching him – that's all!'

Having Dondinho as my first coach maybe gave me the edge with my peer group. There were lots of good kids around, but generally, when choosing teams among ourselves I was always chosen first. For someone so tiny I was pretty strong, could jump high and was fearless – which meant that, like my father, I scored lots of goals with my head.

Dondinho taught me a lot, not just about technique but about how to conduct myself on a football pitch. Some of the tricks and skills that would later help me score so many goals and win medals were established under his watchful eye. He told me about the magic instep, how to pass accurately, and the importance of keeping the ball close. This was something that became a kind of signature to my play – short strides in possession, the head over the ball or as near to it as possible, to ensure close control when dribbling at a defender. I learned quickly how to make use of rapid change of pace, either from fast to slow or the other way round, to fox the opposition. This worked especially well when I was running at a defender with the ball, keeping it close – rather than kicking it on, too far away to control, it meant the defender had to jog back on his heels and could be caught unawares as I flicked the ball past him. The shoulder feint was another trick that could be deployed here, and could be devastating when used alongside a ball that was already moving fast: dipping the shoulder left or right I could leave defenders crumpled on the ground without ever altering the course of the ball.

Dondinho was a classic attacking centre-forward, a number 9. He played in the same position as, say, a Romário or a Ronaldo. As I was developing I realised that I liked to play in a deeper position, a number 10. Even back then I was never the sort of player to stay out in front of the attack. I always liked to come from behind. Often people assume that because I scored so many goals I was an out-and-out striker. But I never was. I was an attacking midfielder, a deep-lying centre-forward.

It was a great education, supplemented by the hours of practice and experience gained with Sete de Setembro. And I loved spending that time with my father, learning football and how to be a man. In fact I had my first big fight at a local derby – Noroeste v. BAC – because of Dondinho. He missed a chance for a goal, right in front of the goalkeeper, and one of the fans nearby shouted, 'Hey! Wooden-leg Dondinho! Go home!' I couldn't listen to that and not react. Although I was very young I retorted immediately, insulting the guy's mother. By the time he'd turned to see who was challenging him I was already brandishing a brick, ready to do battle . . . But he wasn't put off – I was just a kid, after all – and snarled, 'Piss off, darkie, before you get some wallops from me.'

'Go ahead, if you've got the balls!' I replied. At which point a huge black man – who may have been a friend of my father's – appeared next to me; he gave this guy a really ugly look and said, 'You lay one finger on the boy and I'll bash your face in.' And so the fight began – all you could see were kicks on one side, punching and slapping on the other – a real war! The police intervened, hoping to calm everyone down, but they just ended up on the receiving end of a few leftover blows too. I ran away, with my brick and everything. The man who'd started it all got quite a beating and I felt as though I'd been avenged.

My father always gave me wise advice. After that fight he didn't mention it even though he knew full well what had happened. He told me that in football there will always be people who swear at you, and other people who applaud, and that's just something we have to live with. He said that the best response to those who boo is to score a goal against their team. My father should have been luckier at football. He really was good. His explanation was simple, and one he repeated often: 'It's not enough just to know how to play, you also have to follow the right path . . . And you need luck.'

✯

Brazilians like to use nicknames. I should know, since I've had a few. First came Dico. My uncle Jorge thought it up and, for my family, it's the one that has stuck. Dico is still how my mum refers to me now.

At Santos for a while I was called 'Gasolina'. It caught on among the others in the team. I wondered if it would last. Thankfully, it didn't. If Zito, whose idea it was, had thought it up because of the colour of my skin, then more fool him; gasoline comes from petroleum and it's white, or blue or green . . . it's oil that's black. It made no difference to me. Zito was thinking about a Brazilian singer called Gasolina, anyway.

Everyone else, of course, knows me as Pelé. I can remember the name Pelé really bugged me at first. I was really proud that I was named after Thomas Edison and wanted to be called Edson. I thought the name Pelé sounded horrible. It was a rubbish name. Edson sounded so much more serious and important. So when someone said, 'Hey, Pelé,' I would shout back and get angry. On one occasion I punched a classmate because of it and earned a two-day suspension. This, predictably, did not have the desired effect. Other kids realised it annoyed me and so they started calling me Pelé even more. Then I realised that it wasn't up to me what I'm called. Now I love the name – but back then, it wound me up no end.

There have been lots of stories that claim to explain how the name came about. A bit like the legend of Três Corações, you can take your pick from all the different versions. Does it come from the Gaelic for football? A nice story, but unlikely. Was it to do with a Turkish immigrant in Bauru, seeing me handball during a match and mangling the Portuguese for 'The foot, stupid!' Again, it seems far-fetched.

I can never be 100 per cent certain about the origin of 'Pelé', but the most probable version is this. It all started with a teammate of my father's when he played for Vasco de São Lourenço.

The team-mate was a goalkeeper, and was known as 'Bilé', for complicated and very Brazilian reasons.

His real name was José Lino, and he came from a small – really small – town in the south of Minas Gerais called Don Viçoso. At the age of two little José still wasn't speaking, and this worried his mother, a widow called Maria Rosalina, very much. Brazilians are very spiritual people and always believe in the inexplicable, in the supernatural, and Maria Rosalina was no exception. She decided to call a meeting of *benzedeiras*, women who performed a kind of witch-doctor ritual on nights when the moon was full. Even when people don't believe, they still don't dare to question the effects of the ritual, and Maria Rosalina hoped it would help cure José's silent tongue. The *benzedeiras* went about their work, beginning with a shout, 'Bili-bilu-tetéia!' – something like 'Abracadabra!' This didn't happen just once; the story goes that the ritual went on for weeks. And one day, a miracle! The boy shouted out, 'Bilé!' There was general rejoicing – he was cured. And that came to be his nickname – Bilé – a name that stuck when the boy grew up to become the goalie on my father's team.

Some twenty years later Dondinho would take me along to Vasco training sessions – this was before we moved to Bauru, and I must have been three or four. Whenever I could I used to nip into the goal and play around, and whenever I managed to stop a shot I'd shout, 'Good one, Bilé!' or 'Great save, Bilé!' Because I was only young I somehow distorted the nickname and said that when I grew up I wanted to be a goalie like 'Pilé'. When we moved to Bauru, this 'Pilé' became 'Pelé'. Either I changed it myself, or – according to my uncle Jorge – it was because of my thick Minas Gerais accent. I'd speak one way in Bauru and they'd understand me in quite another. And then one boy – I don't remember who – started to tease me by calling me 'Pelé'.

So thanks to that goalie Bilé, and a classmate's little joke, I became Pelé. Now it's known across the world, and I don't mind it so much.

✯

Before 'Pelé' really caught on, I was known as something else: Dondinho's son. At first this made me feel proud – I was the son of the star player at the local club. And it meant that I was getting a reputation for being a good footballer too. Wherever I went it was, 'Look, it's Dondinho's son.' Often youth teams wanted me to play for them in competitions, and sometimes they would even ask my dad for permission. Some teams gave you a sandwich for showing up, other teams couldn't afford even that. I'd usually choose the team based on what my stomach was telling me.

But getting a reputation also had its down-sides. We used to play in the streets a lot. And windows were sometimes smashed. Of course, whenever a window was smashed everyone would scram. The episode would usually end with an angry grown-up knocking at my front door and telling my parents, 'Your son just broke my window.'

Even if mum or dad questioned this assertion, they would be told: 'Your son's the one who plays football, he's the one who's known about round here.'

Often my mum had to pay, which she did by washing and ironing clothes for pennies, even if it wasn't my fault. For a while, every problem in the neighbourhood was blamed on Dondinho's son.

✯

I was nine years old when, in 1950, Brazil hosted the World Cup. On the day of the final, 16 July, my dad decided to have a party at ours. He invited about fifteen friends, including BAC colleagues and their families. Everyone brought something to eat or drink and I remember a table full of cakes, sweets, sandwiches and beer. Brazil were playing Uruguay and the party was for us to celebrate our victory. We were the hosts, the favourites. To reach the final we had trounced Sweden and Spain, 7–1 and 6–1 respectively, and we only needed a draw to take home the trophy.

There was no television in those days, so my understanding of professional football came from the radio and from sticker books. I knew everyone in the Brazilian team. I was especially fond of Ademir, who was the World Cup's top scorer, Zizinho and Barbosa, the goalkeeper. I had stickers of them all.

We had one of those big, square two-button radios. We seemed to get better reception from the Rio stations, rather than the São Paulo ones. It meant that I was more aware of the Rio clubs, and I developed a fondness for Vasco da Gama. Not that this made a difference for international games, of course. There was something magical about listening to football on the radio, it really played to a child's imagination.

I didn't actually listen to all of the final, which was taking place at the newly built Maracanã in Rio. For a start, there were too many adults crammed into my house, all sitting around the radio. And I was a kid, so it seemed just as important to be playing football myself out on the street. We ended up running inside and out, listening to bits of the game and then kicking the ball around between ourselves.

It was the first World Cup since before the war and a strange competition, in many ways: only thirteen teams took part, there was an odd league format for the final stage, and some freak results, the USA famously beating England 1–0. Brazil had never won the World Cup before and a victory would have been a huge boost to our confidence. Apart from a 2–2 wobble against Switzerland, Brazil had won every game and were on course for a great triumph.

And the match started well. Brazil scored first, through Friaça, and everyone went crazy. The house filled with shouting and everyone was jumping up and down. Firecrackers exploded all over Bauru. Shortly afterwards Uruguay equalised, but we remained confident. Then, with about ten minutes to go, Uruguay scored again. I can remember going into the house as the game ended and seeing my father and all his friends absolutely silent. I went to him and asked what had happened. 'Brazil lost,' he replied, like a zombie. 'Brazil lost.'

Just thinking about that afternoon, and remembering the sadness that was everywhere, even today gives me goose-flesh. I told Dondinho not to be sad. But my mum took me away and said, 'Leave your father alone, leave him in peace.' There was silence everywhere. The noise of cheers, and firecrackers and radios turned up to full volume had disappeared into a void of silence. World Cups are so important for Brazil and no one thought we would lose. And especially not in such humiliating circumstances to Uruguay, who together with Argentina are our arch-rivals. People couldn't bear the disappointment. Bauru felt like a ghost town.

It also was the first time I saw my father cry. Many of my father's friends couldn't stop themselves either. It was shocking to me, since I had been brought up thinking that men didn't show their emotions like that. 'One day, I'll win you the World Cup,' I promised my dad, to try to make him feel better. A few days later, when he had recovered, he told me that some people at the Maracanã had actually died from the shock.

Later on that day of the final I went to my father's room, where there was a picture of Jesus on the wall, and I started wailing: 'Why has this happened? Why has it happened to us? We had the better team – how come we lost? Why, Jesus, why are we being punished?' I continued crying, overcome, as I continued my conversation with the picture of Christ: 'You know, if I'd been there I wouldn't have let Brazil lose the Cup. If I'd been there Brazil would have won; or if my dad had been playing, Brazil would have got that goal we needed . . .'

There was no answer. I was a boy who loved football, and the defeat affected me deeply.

✯

Meanwhile the Sete de Setembro side was evolving and growing, and some of us were starting to look further afield. At around this time – the early 1950s – I played for a few other small-town clubs in and around Bauru as well, including São Paulino, in the neighbouring village of Curuçá. In those days I used to play on Saturdays and Sundays, on two or three different teams, which I really enjoyed. When my team-mates came to my house to pick me up, my father used to lean out of the window to ask where the game was, and he always used to say, 'But first he's going to Mass at the Santa Terezinha church!' It never annoyed me – I quickly learned how important faith was in my life. I liked going to church.

I was crazy about football, just couldn't get enough of it.

Playing 'free-for-all' or just having a kickabout – we used to play for hours. We didn't particularly need the right number of players. The pitch we played on a lot was a space near Noroeste's old wooden stadium. I remember one time just after returning home from the 1958 World Cup in Sweden, which we had won, I went past that little pitch and saw some boys having a kickabout. I asked them if they'd let me play too, and they said yes, I could. And of course they were glad to see me, and to see that winning the cup and all those other victories hadn't changed me. So I went home, put on a pair of shorts, took off my shoes, and played barefoot with them. That's how I'd started playing, and I think people should remember their roots – even with all those things I experienced later, it was an intense and beautiful apprenticeship for everything that would come.

A big change in my attitude to the game came when the mayor of Bauru decided to stage a tournament for lots of the small neighbourhood clubs like ours. The lads of Sete de Setembro were desperate to enter and to do well, but couldn't figure out how to get round the rule that all teams had to have proper footwear – we still didn't have any boots. Salvation arrived in the form of Zé Leite, a local salesman who was well known to lots of us and who was father to three of the kids on the team. He promised to get us boots on two conditions: one, that we took our responsibilities to the club even more seriously, and began to do proper training; two, that we change our name from the 'Shoeless Ones', on the grounds that we were no longer shoeless. And so we became Amériquinha.

And we did the training – we worked and worked, with Zé Leite pushing us hard, making us practise all aspects of our play, set-pieces and so on. But it paid off – we did really well in the tournament itself, playing good football despite still getting used to the idea of having shoes on our feet and being so young – many of us weren't even teenagers yet, and were often up against players several years older. We made it to the final, in fact, which was held in the BAC stadium itself – the very place my father played. It was a sell-out, with thousands of spectators, and I remember being nervous before a match for the first time in my life. But our form continued and we won the trophy, and I ended up top scorer. A famous day, one that will always live with me – not just for the victory, or my father's praise after the match, but the memory of the crowd chanting, for the first time, 'Pelé! Pelé!'

Perhaps I could get used to this nickname after all.

✯

In 1954 there was another important event in my life as a football player in Bauru. Lower divisions of the BAC (Bauru Athletic Club) were being set up, including a boys' team to be called Baquinho ('Little BAC'). The man in charge was João Fernandes, from Sanbra, a kind of cotton manufacturers' union. Several of the Amériquinha team, which had carried all before it but which went into decline when Zé Leite and his sons moved to São Paulo, were asked to apply, and I was one of them. I got through the selection process but wasn't sure whether to join or not, but then came the news that former player Waldemar de Brito had been asked to manage this Baquinho team, and had accepted.

At that time I didn't know much about Waldemar de Brito, but my father did, and praised him very highly. 'The Dancer', as he was nicknamed, had retired from a very successful footballing career. He had even played for the national team, and represented them at a World Cup. In 1934 he had sailed to Italy, only for Brazil to be immediately eliminated 3–1 by Spain. Waldemar had won himself a penalty in that game, although he took it and missed. In the 1930s and '40s he was one of Brazil's best players. 'Waldemar was a talented and important centre-forward,' Dondinho told me. He was creative and technically very good. In 1933, playing for São Paulo, he was the Paulista championship's top scorer. He had also played in Argentina, alongside his brother Petronilho, at San Lorenzo. Petronilho was another great player – to many he was the creator of the '*bicicleta*', the bicycle kick, a move sometimes, erroneously, attributed to me.

I may not have invented it, but even as a young boy I found it easy to score goals that way. I scored loads of goals with bicycle kicks. The other kids found it more difficult, and so already it was things like that that set me apart. The propulsion that was crucial for my headers was also helpful in keeping me in the air as I kicked the ball over my head. One of the best pictures anyone took of me is that shot of me doing a bicycle kick – it's the image on my credit card, so I think that is why I am so associated with the move. And it's a very Brazilian move, too, and I'm proud of that.

Encouraged by my father's approval I decided to sign with Baquinho, and received my first proper contract. Incredibly, I was actually being paid to play football. I got 4,500 *réis* in payments – I've no idea what that's worth today, not much probably. But it was a huge change in my fortunes, and came at a very auspicious time as I had just had to repeat my third year at Ernesto Monte primary school (for poor grades and missing classes, mostly), and it looked like I might have to do that in my fourth year too.

(I should add that I had in fact technically received money to play once before. A great football fan called Landão Mandioca, a man with no money at all but who loved football, wanted me to play at Vila Falcão. At the time I didn't want to accept and so I asked him how much he would pay me, thinking this would put him off and it would be a diplomatic way of getting out of it. He said he was going to think it over. He collected some bits of change from his team – really, just odd coins and pennies – and brought the money to me saying, 'That's as much as I was able to get . . .' I felt so sorry for him I agreed to play a few games, so I suppose *that* was my first contract. It's another cherished scene from the film of my childhood, in my memory.)

I think God had his eye on me when he sent Waldemar de Brito to play an important part at that stage in my career. It did seem quite unbelievable that a player of his calibre would come to teach kids – in the middle of nowhere too. Yet he was sincere and committed to the job. He just wanted to teach youngsters. (And when I retired, I understood this feeling entirely.) Although my team-mates and I were young Waldemar spoke to us like adults, and expected us to afford him similar respect. We did – he demanded discipline and he got it. He taught us a lot. We trained hard, and he introduced lots of new techniques, including movement off the ball and how to read the game. Some of us took it in, some of us didn't. I always paid lots of attention. Baquinho were a strong team, and under Waldemar we became even stronger. We were invincible.

There were some great players – Maninho, Paçoca, Edir, Leleco, Osmar Guedes . . . I remember Antoninho too, who was so important to Baquinho. Waldemar used to say that the most important rule for a player to become a great footballer, was that he had to know how to control the ball with both feet, with his head and with his chest; he had to know how to receive a pass too, to touch the ball on to wherever he wants it to go, that the ball is the player's tool – anyone who can't control it will never be a real player, still less a great one. Many of my team-mates were very skilful. They could run well with the ball, tackle well and perform tricks, but not all of them knew how to *receive* the ball. They didn't have this extra vision that I seemed to have. Maybe it's something you can't teach. You either have it or you don't. And this is what I definitely had – an ability to anticipate what was going to happen, slightly before everyone else. Even after I became professional, people would say, 'How did you see that coming?', and I would reply, 'I don't know, I just did.' Lots of kids can be very good but they have a slight delay when they are on the ball. I was just quicker.

Some people have suggested that I was able to see more than other players because my eyes are further apart than normal. That's not true but I did end up doing tests and I do have very good peripheral vision. You know, I cannot remember in three decades of playing football that anyone ever robbed me of the ball by coming at me from behind – not the way I see it happen so often to other players. No one was ever able to do this because I would always notice them coming. I can't explain how, or why – whether I heard them, or whether I saw them, or whether it was a sixth sense. And I've been like that since I was a boy. Maybe I developed it because in those days there would be loads of us playing in very small spaces, so you had to be really quick.

Baquinho was a proper set-up. When I played there I didn't have to worry about shirts, shorts, socks, boots – about anything; everything was there for us, which made it a comfortable experience. When one day Waldemar learned that I'd been turning out for other teams as well, he suspended me. And he was right to do it. I didn't need to complicate things by still turning out for shoeless wonders, and I focused more exclusively on Baquinho from then on. I did, though, still have a part-time job of sorts, selling pies to hungry travellers at the railway station. This worked well unless I was hungry myself, in which case I would have some explaining to do to Dona Filomena, the woman who baked them and to whom I would return with the takings and any unsold pastries. It didn't take her long to work out that the two didn't always add up.

Money would now come to me in mysterious ways. One of my most cherished memories from Baquinho was when we were playing in a tournament at the BAC stadium. In the final game I had scored the winning goal and our supporters invaded the pitch. They then started to throw coins at me. It felt like there were hundreds of them, loads of money, and I scrabbled around picking up all the coins and then took them home to my mum.

My sporting career was going well, even though in its infancy, but things had not improved much for the national team. The 1954 World Cup was in Switzerland, where Brazil were knocked out in a violent match against Hungary. Three players were sent off and there were allegations that Puskas, who was injured and watching from the touchline, had hit our centre-half Pinheiro with a bottle. It was sad and frustrating – and the referee was public enemy number one for a while – but the public reaction was nothing like the defeat of 1950. It was probably because the competition wasn't held in Brazil, and the radio transmissions from Europe weren't that great – we didn't really know exactly what was going on over there.

In 1954 Baquinho were on a roll. The newspaper *Diário de*

Bauru, in association with the *São Paulo Sporting Gazette*, organised the second Youth Championship. It was a triumph – the organisation was perfect. I was player number 997 – I'll never forget it. With me playing striker, we won the championship, scoring 148 goals in 33 games.

✯

I had a couple of great years with Baquinho, and finally managed to finish school during this time as well (only two years late). One particularly memorable game seemed to sum up our dominance and how I was emerging as a player. It was an early championship match away against Flamenguinho, São Paulo's youth champions. As we got off the bus before the match I decided to buy some peanuts. All the rest of the team went inside, but the man at the door blocked my path, threatened me when I protested, dismissing me as just some kid trying it on. I told him I'd come to play in the match, but he wouldn't believe me – he thought I was far too small to possibly be playing in such a big game. The rest of the team then noticed I was missing and came to see what had happened to me, where I'd got to. Finally I got in. The match started and when the doorman saw what I'd done on the field he was amazed at my size and my playing. We won 12–1. I scored seven goals.

But the Baquinho era wasn't to last, and the beginning of the end came when Waldemar de Brito decided to leave to go and coach grown-ups again in São Paulo. Perhaps he felt he had taken us as far as he could, but it was desperately sad to see him go. Everyone was leaving, it seemed – there was none of the happiness we'd become used to about the place, and I began to look around for other opportunities. Noroeste, BAC's great rivals, put up a youth team to play warm-up games before the senior team matches. I played in a couple of friendlies against them, which showed both that my loyalty was to BAC, because of my father, but also that I had nothing against Noroeste, as was sometimes said. I trained with professionals, and was delighted to be able to watch great players showing off their skills. At one event I scored four times in an eight-goal beating we gave to our opponents in Ibitinga. Noroeste tried to sign me, in fact, before Waldemar left, but he put a stop to that. He thought I was destined for greater things, and I think he also had a sneaking loyalty to BAC.

In my mid-teens I also played indoor football, which had just taken off in Bauru, for a team called Radium, and took part in the first *futebol de salão* championship to be held in Bauru. We won. *Futebol de salão* was a new thing and I took to it like a fish to water. It's a lot quicker than football on grass. You have to think really quickly because everyone is close to each other. Learning the game probably helped me think on my feet better. It was through *futebol de salão* that I first got my chance to play with adults. I was about fourteen, and I can remember that there was a tournament for which I was told I was too young to take part. In the end, I was allowed to play. I ended up top scorer, with fourteen or fifteen goals. That gave me a lot of confidence. I knew then not to be afraid of whatever might come.

And soon, opportunities came knocking on my door. First it was a former player called Elba de Pádua Lima, known as Tim, who was coach of the well-known Rio club Bangú. He was on a scouting trip through the interior and came to see Baquinho. He ended up taking three players, and wanted to take me too. Tim had long talks with my father, who thought it would be a good move, but when he raised the issue with my mother she went ballistic.

'No way!' she exclaimed. 'Bangú is in Rio de Janeiro.' Of course she had never been there, but the idea of little me in Brazil's cosmopolitan capital was too daunting for her to contemplate.

'He's going nowhere,' she added. 'He's not going to leave here because look what happened to his dad! He got injured and then what? No, my son is going to study and then work. He is going to be a teacher.'

I was secretly relieved. Going to Rio would have been a great adventure but it was also very intimidating: not just playing against professionals who were much older and bigger than me but also having to fend for myself in a massive city I didn't know. The idea was shelved.

As the months passed, though, I got bigger and stronger, as well as older. My ambitions were changing too. I wanted to be a footballer, to be famous. I didn't think it would make me money, so I knew I would also have to get another job too. That's what my mum had hard-wired into my brain. And I believed her.

As the prospect of a move to a bigger club was becoming more and more likely, again it was Waldemar de Brito who provided the key. One day he turned up in Bauru to see my parents and talked to them about my career. He thought I should go to Santos, a less intimidating city than Rio. It was a little bigger than Bauru and had a good team – they were current state champions. Waldemar thought I could start out in the youth side and progress quickly to the senior eleven. Once again, Dondinho was all for it but my mother was still wary, for much the same reasons as before. But Waldemar was a persistent man and said that he'd fixed everything with the Santos president, that I'd be taken care of personally. Finally my mother gave in, on the condition that Waldemar himself would be there to keep his eye on me.

'You mean I can go?' I said, incredulous.

'You can go,' she said. 'But it's only for a trial.'

I didn't care. My final game in Bauru was for Radium, against Vila Cárdia. The Santos years were about to begin.

3

From Santos to Sweden

'Number 10 at Santos was indisputably mine. Until the arrival of a little black boy with stick-like legs who entered history as Pelé'

VASCONCELOS, EX-SANTOS PLAYER

Leaving Bauru was like a whirlwind – there was so much to do. My mother decided I would look ridiculous on the train sitting there in my short trousers and set about making me two pairs of long pants, in blue cotton – until then I'd only ever worn shorts. For the first fifteen years of my life my clothes had only had to suit the way I'd spent my time, playing football on the streets. I'd never worried about smart clothes, my only real love was the ball. Now, things were starting to change. It was time to go out and face the world, and for that you needed long trousers.

The day of my departure was set for a Sunday. The plan was for Dondinho and me to set off early in the morning for São Paulo, where Waldemar de Brito would be waiting for us at the Estação da Luz, the main railway station. Waldemar would then go with us to Santos to make the necessary introductions at the club. The night before we travelled was taken up with advice and packing, my own suitcase and my father's. I didn't get any sleep.

What would await me in Santos? Would I be good enough? Would I be okay on my own, without my loving parents to look out for me? As my mother pointed out, it was a lot of excitement for a kid. I had so much to think about – my fears, my insecurity – but it was then all on a child's scale; and quite apart from the football, the other thought occupying my mind was that I was going to realise another dream: I was going to see the sea! I knew the players from pictures and stickers, but the idea of seeing the sea seemed like a fantasy – you can't imagine how fascinating it can be for a child living so far away, how grand it all was for me. And at the same time it was all like one big party, a chance to discover life. I started thinking about my responsibilities, and was reminded of many by my family. They were all there that Saturday night, dispensing pearls of wisdom: Uncle Jorge, my grandmother Ambrosina, my brother and sister and, of course, my parents.

My father came to get me so early on the Sunday morning it was still dark. I got up as quietly as I could and put on my new clothes. Ambrosina started crying, and that set off my sister. At the station, waving from the train to my mother and Zoca, I had to fight back the tears myself. I made a promise to my father: 'As soon as I've made some money I'll buy a house for mum.' My father, always realistic, said gently, 'Don't dream just yet, Dico.' I tried to sleep on the train but couldn't – I was too overwhelmed.

Waldemar de Brito was at the Estação da Luz, as had been agreed. We travelled on with him to Santos, on the 'Brazilian Express', a bus company that does the Santos–São Paulo run, and which is still going today. After having some lunch in a restaurant near the station, we carried on, towards my destiny. I was amazed at the skyscrapers in the city, by how beautiful the road from São Paulo to Santos was. São Paulo is on a plateau about 1,000 metres above sea level. When you get to the edge, just before the drop to the coast, there is an eternally breathtaking view of jungle and cliffs . . . It was all just enchanting.

Waldemar talked, while I kept my eyes fixed on the landscape. For a hick like me it was all just too much.

The first lessons Waldemar de Brito taught me on the road to Santos were excellent ones. He told me to play as if I were still in Bauru, just having a kick-around. He told me not to be awed by the stars playing for Santos. It's normal to feel a bit inhibited to begin with, he reassured me, but the people there are great and will help you. He also told me about the press. 'Look here,' he said forcefully, 'something else very important that you will do – you will *not* read the papers and you will *not* listen to the radio.' I was grateful and realised I was lucky to have the guiding voice of someone who had experienced the pressures of the game at the highest level. 'Especially before a game, never read the sports papers or listen to the radio.' And throughout my career, and even afterwards, I hardly ever paid attention to the press. Of course, if I was told that there was a nice piece about me, then I would read it. That was okay. But as a rule, I tried not to be bothered about what people said about me.

Waldemar's words made me feel that he had absolute faith in me, that he wouldn't be staking his name on a boy like me if he didn't. Our conversation really reassured me. And his last words were: 'No smoking, no drinking, no women and no hanging around with a bad crowd.' He was obviously taking his promise to Dona Celeste seriously.

The smoking wasn't a problem. A year or two earlier, I'd been sitting with some friends about fifty yards from home and had accepted a cigarette from one of them. A lot of the kids in my class were addicted, and I was headed that way too. I'd stopped looking out in case anyone came out of my house, when suddenly I saw my father, who walked past us and said

'Hi', smiling as he always did (he was always happy) – and then walked on without reacting at all. I threw my cigarette away, stunned – I knew I could get into real trouble. My friends said not to worry, that he hadn't noticed I was smoking, or trying to smoke. I went home. I thought he hadn't seen anything – I was wrong. Our conversation was simple: 'You were smoking,' and I replied, yes, but I'd only been trying to smoke for a few days. His next question was amazing: 'What does the smoke you're inhaling taste of?' I told him I couldn't tell what it tasted of. I didn't get the slaps and blows that I deserved. My father – who was always my friend, through my whole life – came close to me, looked me in the eye and said, 'You've got a talent for football. You might even get to be a star, but you won't succeed in this profession if you smoke and drink – your body won't be able to take it.' He took his wallet from his pocket, gave me some money and said some words that would teach me another lesson, one I'll never forget: 'If you want to smoke, you should smoke your own cigarettes, don't keep scrounging them from other people.' At that moment I saw again how much he loved me, and I knew that he was right. After that day I never smoked again. I'm absolutely convinced that my father's gesture and his words were what saved me. If I'd been beaten, perhaps I wouldn't have stopped smoking . . . Corporal punishment isn't always the answer. This made me admire my father even more – he was a simple man, but a man of dignity and vision. So Waldemar didn't have to worry on that count.

But women? How could I keep them out of my head? Asking that of a boy nearing sixteen is close to heresy! I was young, I was strong, healthy, and fancied myself as a bit of a ladies' man. And as for my hormones . . . Ever since I'd started playing in Bauru I'd divided my time between chasing the ball and chasing girls. I had even had a few little romances, childish crushes that everyone goes through. There was one, one of the very first, with whom I was very smitten but her father soon put a stop to it – he came to school one day and harangued her for hanging out with me. 'What are you doing with this *negrinho*?' he yelled. It was the first time I had directly experienced racism, I think, and it was completely shocking. My girlfriend was white but it just hadn't occurred to me that someone might have a problem with that, or with me. As her father grabbed her arm and put her across his knee I was so stunned I couldn't move. Everyone was watching and I did nothing. And then I ran home and cried my eyes out. She never spoke to me again.

But there were others: Ivone, Neuzinha, Samira – they all had a special place in my young heart, especially Neuzinha, the sister of a Japanese friend of mine who I admired from afar for ages before we went out together. I used to go to the cinema a lot, watching carefully to see which of the girls was without a boyfriend. My approaches didn't always go to plan but they were fun.

It was Zinho, one of my friends, who persuaded me to go with him to the red-light district for my first sexual experience. I was fourteen. He told me how wonderful it would be but all I could think about was the worry of catching a venereal disease. Thankfully I didn't. It was an experience that caused me more concern than pleasure, but at least it didn't last long.

I should perhaps pause here to help you understand how people behaved in the days when I was a boy. There was much more hierarchy to relationships then than now, and much information that is now handed down routinely that our parents wouldn't dream of passing on. When I say that my first sexual experience was more a worry than a pleasure, it's because in those days absolutely everything was considered a sin. We weren't allowed to swear inside the house, we referred to our parents as Sir and Madam, we never saw our father in the bath, there were certain questions we just couldn't ask – and whatever they said, went. There was no discussion – we'd do what we were told, and fast!

So things were particularly complicated and mysterious where sex was concerned. Neither they nor we dared to mention it, but it would have been much better if we had. Because everything was a sin, we were just supposed to study, to help out at home, to read; we could play too, but sex? No way! They had no idea what hormones were, so we couldn't begin to guess what they meant; all we knew was that we couldn't see a woman without our little eyes gleaming! The girls – poor things – they were no different, but they had to control themselves much more, because if it was a girl who didn't behave, if she was looking at boys, she could quickly get a reputation as a slut. They had this extra burden, whereas we boys didn't – but even we weren't allowed to do anything. People came to know that we were over-excited, and were endlessly on the receiving end of thrashings thanks to our over-abundance of hormones. So we'd have to wait till one fine day when we could pluck up the courage for someone to take us to a house in the red-light district.

You find them in every city, big or small. It was all planned like a military assault, or a crime – we'd discuss it only outside the house in case someone was listening . . . There the so-called 'easy' women would ply their trade in exchange for some paltry amount. And the so-called 'family women' hated these women. When we used to pass the red-light district we often weren't even allowed to turn our heads to look – we'd keep our eyes lowered, and wouldn't say a thing.

Clearly this wasn't good. We felt as though we were doing something wrong, something ugly, and sinful. And our parents wouldn't be the ones to take us – it would be left to a friend, a cousin, an uncle. And as if the sin wasn't enough, there was also the danger that we'd get a disease. How ridiculous! How can anyone be happy like that?

All the mystery that people always create about sex, it's nonsense. And I know that even though we're now at the start of the twenty-first century there are still lots of people who find it hard to deal with this. But parents ought to know that their kids have a lot to deal with at that time of their lives. The hormones are there to give us life, to provoke feelings, and so much more. There's no sin in it if you love someone. But even today those parents who aren't able to talk to their kids about sex should send them off to talk to a friend instead, or a psychologist if they can afford it, but at least someone outside who may be able to deal with this better than the parents. All you need is a bit of common sense, and an understanding that this is all completely natural, that we are all the products of love as demonstrated through sex. I didn't say any of this to Waldemar, of course – I just nodded and agreed that I would be good. The rest of the journey passed in a blur of excitement, with me being bombarded with advice most of which went in one ear and out of the other.

✯

When we finally arrived in Santos, the first thing we did was go and see the sea, and walk along the beach. When I stepped out on to the beach with my father, I reached down to feel the sand in my hands, and I tasted a little of the water. My teacher had always told me that it was salty – and she was right, though I hadn't believed her. That's just how boys are. I was delighted by how vast the Atlantic Ocean was. Since I was a child I'd dreamed of seeing it. After this first impressive sight, we went on to the Vila Belmiro, home of Santos Football Club. From that moment it was as though I'd been picked up by a cyclone and dropped in an enchanted land – like Judy Garland in *The Wizard of Oz*.

Waldemar de Brito had our luggage taken up to the Santos training camp. Because it was a Sunday there was a game going on, Santos v. Comercial in the São Paulo championship, and Waldemar managed to get us some seats. I couldn't take my eyes off the pitch. These men were football stars, playing at the top of the league. That was the moment when I started supporting Santos – and my support has lasted ever since. Until then I'd mostly followed Corinthians, even without ever having seen them play. I liked following their matches on the radio, in the newspapers, through the stickers. I even ended up having a Corinthians 'button' football team – the players represented by little discs that you flicked with your fingers. When I was younger I'd thought about being a goalkeeper, and sometimes when I was playing in goal I'd think about the Corinthians goalie defending against a shot. Just one of those things children do . . .

After the game we went to the team dressing-room; everyone was delighted, as Santos had won and kept its spot at the top of the league. The coach, Luis Alonso, known as Lula, asked with a twinkle in his eye: 'So you're the famous Pelé, eh?' I replied, rather awkwardly, that yes, I was. And straight away I realised that he might take this to mean that I did already think I was famous, which of course was far from the case. But Lula must have recognised my confusion as he just smiled and said he'd been expecting me, and told me to make myself comfortable. The first player I met was Vasconcelos – I liked him. He was a nice man, who grabbed me by the neck, saying to my father, 'We'll take care of the boy!' I was amazed, yet again; here I was, seeing and being introduced to Jaír, Zito, Pepe – all champions. Soon I would be playing with them too. Waldemar de Brito said to me, 'Now you'll see just how good this group is.'

And then it was time for my father and Waldemar to go, back to Bauru and São Paulo respectively. I was dreading being left alone, even though the players seemed friendly and I was reassured to discover that many of them knew of Dondinho as a player, and respected him.

'Don't worry,' my father said. 'You'll be all right.' And after one last hug, off he went.

✯

I spent my first nights in Santos at the Vila Belmiro. Underneath the concrete stands there were several rooms, where most of the single players lived. Even though I was the youngest person there I was made to feel welcome. There were, I think, eight of us in one room, in four sets of bunks. The rooms were very spartan, but there was a good atmosphere. When I visited Santos recently I saw that these rooms are still there, where they are used by youth team players, and they are still as austere as ever. I thought, 'What an embarrassment! Santos has hardly improved its facilities at all.'

Two days later, I had my first training session with the team.

I thought they would try me out with players my own age, but they didn't. They threw me in at the deep end. I was put in with the professionals. And Santos had some team. They had won the São Paulo state championship in 1955 and would win it again in 1956. The Santos team included Jaír da Rosa Pinto, the veteran from the 1950 World Cup, and Helio, Formiga and Pepe, who had also all had call-ups for the national team.

Off the pitch I was a little shy. It had started to rain and I was wearing kit that was too big for me. I was a skinny little thing, less than 60 kilos, and my legs were shaking. Pepe, who would be my friend for my whole life, could tell that I was nervous. He was getting changed next to me, and he said, 'Don't be nervous, the guys are great – you'll see.' On the pitch, however, I became someone else. I was fearless. I had already played with grown-ups in Bauru and I wasn't intimidated by who these players were. Formiga was asked to mark me, and yet I was able to dribble past him twice. I think that's what impressed Lula so much. If it was a test I had definitely passed it. 'I like the way you were playing,' said Lula afterwards. I didn't know what to say. He then continued: 'You're going to have to build up your body, though, if you're going to play in the main team.' I was going to have to spend some time in the junior levels.

Pepe thought I'd trained well, and he said that Urubatão had also been impressed and thought I was going to be a star. Everyone else came up to me to tell me how well I'd done, including the great forward Del Vecchio. But it seemed to Lula that a little mouse like me couldn't play with the big cats. Even though I was allowed to carry on training with the pros, I still had to play with the under-20s and under-18s. And I also trained alone, for hours at a time. I knew I really had to apply myself if I was going to get anywhere. For me I was playing not just for the crowds, but in an attempt to achieve my own ambitions. There was no way I could fail.

I took Lula's advice to heart. I began to eat like a horse, taking full advantage of the excellent food on offer at the club at all hours, in the hope that I would fatten up fast. I couldn't grow up quickly enough.

I was doing well for the under-20s, helping them become champions that year. On one occasion I was chosen to strengthen the under-16s for the final of a local tournament. After all, I was still only fifteen. Even so, it seemed almost like a demotion to have to play with my own age-range. The opposition was Jabaquara, another Santos club. The ref was Romualdo Arppi Filho, who years later would be in charge of the final of the 1986 World Cup. During the match we won a penalty that would settle the result. I took the shot but skied it over the crossbar, and we lost the title. I was devastated. The fans booed. I cried and even wailed, I was so distraught. I felt a mixture of embarrassment and crushing shame, and that evening I decided I could not bear to be in Santos any more.

It was a childish reaction, but a powerful one nonetheless. The following morning I woke up at 6.30 in the morning, fully intending to run back home to Bauru. I quietly packed my suitcase, tiptoed out my room and headed to the door. As I got there I heard a voice.

'Hey, you! Who gave you permission to leave?' It was Sabuzinho, the club's general dogsbody. 'Club rules. All minors need to have written authorisation to leave the building,' he added.

'I know, I know,' I said. 'I've got it, just let me go and I'll bring it to you later.'

'No you won't. You will bring it to me now or you aren't going anywhere.'

And that was that. My plan to leave failed at the first hurdle. Now I realise that it was my good fortune that he stopped me going, even if it was for a typically Brazilian administrative reason. When he realised what I was trying to do, Sabuzinho taught me an important moral lesson. Everyone makes mistakes once in a while, he said: the trick is to learn from them, not give in to them. If I had left, maybe Santos wouldn't have had me back – they were very strict about discipline in those days. I really feel that Sabuzinho saved me, that his being there at that precise time was one of the luckiest things in my life.

✯

The Director of Sports at Santos, Sr Antonio, had told me fairly soon after my arrival that he wanted to offer me a contract. I was thrilled, of course – I hadn't been there for long, and here they were trying to make me stay. But it turned out it wasn't quite the contract I was hoping for – it didn't guarantee first-team play, and because I was still under-age it wasn't strictly legal. It was more an indication of interest, pending a formal contract when I was old enough. But still, it was a step in the right direction and something I couldn't really turn down.

Waldemar de Brito oversaw all the negotiating of the contract, every detail. Six thousand cruzeiros per month, plus food and accommodation. My parents would have to agree to the figures, so we made the trip back to Bauru. It was great to be home, but when I told them that I was going to be staying in Santos everyone cried! I thought they'd be pleased, but my mother and grandmother didn't want to lose the company of their beloved Dico. It turned out my mother had thought I was just going to Santos for a trial, not to live, and she was very upset. So upset, in fact, that it made me upset too, and I decided I couldn't make her so unhappy and would have to say no to the Santos deal and stay in Bauru.

Again, it was Waldemar who stepped in to take charge of the problem – a problem that was rapidly escalating into a full-scale drama. He talked to Dondinho and Dona Celeste about Santos, told them what it was like, what my future would be like, told them that everything would be fine. Eventually he convinced them; and he convinced me too, though I'd been so sure that I wouldn't go back to Vila Belmiro.

I went back to Santos with Waldemar, and the contract was signed. I continued my training with the first team, even though I was playing in the junior teams. I had started as an '*armador*', a supporting midfielder, but now I was being used as an attacking midfielder. My rivals in the first team for this position were Del Vecchio and Vasconcelos. As I watched Del Vecchio and Vasco play, I thought my own chance would be a long time coming. They were the principal goal-scorers and were both excellent players, well established in the side. But God had his eye on me again . . . There was to be a practice game in nearby Cubatão; not all the regular first-team players were going, so I got my chance to pull on a Santos first-team jersey for the first time. We won 6–1, and I scored four times. Because it was only a friendly the result didn't count towards career statistics, so those four goals never appeared in my total, but they were vitally important to me. I could tell that the other players looked at me slightly differently afterwards, as if they were beginning to understand why I'd been let in to the club so young. And it also brought an end to 'Gasolina', the affectionate nickname I'd been given when I arrived – after the Cubatão game I was Pelé again, and that's how I remained. The press also picked up on my performance and this helped increase the pressure on the club to give me a proper try-out in the first XI.

✯

São Paulo is a state best known for its cowboy ranches, its agriculture and its heavy industry. Santos is atypical – it is a beach town, much more similar to Rio de Janeiro than the state's concrete capital, São Paulo. I was very happy that this was the case since it meant that when I wasn't training I could spend as much time as I liked on the beach.

At first, however, I was a little scared of hanging out at the beach. Not because of the sea or anything like that – but because of the women. In Bauru people didn't wear bikinis much – why would they, when the nearest beach was 300 miles away? – and my mum used to tell me that women who wore bikinis – or even jeans, for that matter – weren't proper or decent. She told me to be careful of women who showed too much flesh. Since I was very religious I was really worried about this, since I would get to the beach and the only thing I wanted to do was to stare at the women in their skimpy swimwear. I was terrified that God would punish me, that he would judge that I had sinned. Then I got used to it and realised that for a woman there really wasn't any way to go to the beach other than in a bikini.

I missed my friends and family in Bauru, but gradually began to feel at home with my new footballing family around me. I went to the cinema, we played kickabouts on the beach and we used to spend our days off taking trips on the city's trams. I also really liked to fish. One of my friends had a fishing boat and we used to go out into the sea to fish. I'm not great on the waves, I get seasick easily, but I love fishing and I was pretty good at it too. I had learned to fish in Bauru, in freshwater, and so I already had the knack.

One of the greatest personal tragedies of that time happened during a fishing trip, however. I had gone out to Praia Grande with Claudio, the goalkeeper, and Sabuzinho, the guy who had stopped me quitting Santos that time. Right there in front of me he fell on some rocks and drowned. We couldn't save him in time. I have never forgotten him, his sunny disposition and friendliness.

After a month or so training with the senior team I was finally given a chance to play. I will never forget the date. It was 7 September 1956 – the anniversary of Brazil's independence and also the name of my first shoeless team. It all seemed very appropriate.

The match was against Corinthians – not the main Corinthians, who I had liked as a child, but a smaller team from Santo André. It was a friendly and Lula kept me on the bench for the first half. In the second, he put me on for Del Vecchio. Almost as soon as I came on I scored my first 'official' goal – the first in the tally that ended up at over 1,280. Pepe had taken a shot, the keeper knocked it out and I got it on the rebound. I was ecstatic, and ran around punching the air with delight. It was beyond a dream. I had never expected to be given a chance in a professional team at only fifteen years old.

I ran across the pitch to the coach and hugged him, and then all the other players came and hugged me. And then, all of a sudden, I began to think, 'How am I going to be able to tell my father?' There were no mobile phones in those days. There weren't even any public phones. Even when the game resumed

I had this thing inside my head: 'How will I be able to tell dad?' It was only a friendly, and I knew it wouldn't be on the radio transmissions. It was only the following day that I managed to tell him the news.

At the end of the match the fans applauded – they were all Corinthians fans, because it was at their stadium. I think they had come to watch me out of curiosity, to see if this young boy really was any good. I was already well-known at Santos, because I had played in the junior levels, but I was something new to them. The players too were very kind, they came over at the end to congratulate me.

In retrospect, the Corinthians keeper, Zaluar, was pretty pleased by that day. He later made up a business card that announced him as the 'Goalkeeper who let in Pelé's first goal'. For him to have suffered my first goal seemed almost a greater privilege than for me to have scored it.

✯

Even before I made my debut in a competitive match I was causing a lot of excitement in Santos. In those days you would get crowds of about five or six thousand to watch the training games. But when it was the reserves versus the first team (and I was always in the reserves then) the crowds doubled to about ten thousand, which is half the capacity at Vila Belmiro. And most of the fans seemed to be cheering for us, the reserves. Fans would jump and shout my name. It was like a proper competitive game. And it gave me lots and lots of confidence. I got used to the attention and it helped me when I eventually became a regular in the first team.

You need luck in football, and I was definitely getting it –

even though it might have been at someone else's expense. In this case, the victim was my friend Vasconcelos.

Santos were playing São Paulo in a championship match at a packed Vila Belmiro, and the game started badly for the home side and then just got worse. Santos were 3–1 down in the second half when Vasco had an awful collision with Mauro Ramos de Oliveira (who would later play for, and coach, Santos himself). Vasconcelos fell, and began writhing about – you might have thought he was playing it up, but unfortunately that wasn't the case. It was serious: his leg was broken.

I thought about the advice that had been given to me by my father and Waldemar, about how fickle a game football was and how it can surprise you at any time. I understood that I ought to save some of the money I was being paid, and send most of my income to my father, who would look after it and maybe invest some in a house in Bauru, so they could get out of the rented one. It was a lesson in humility: Vasconcelos came back after his leg healed, but he was never the same player again and soon moved on to another club. Although he was my friend and my first thoughts were for his welfare, after it became clear he would be out for a while I realised it would give me a chance to break into the first team.

My official debut came in the New Year. It was 12 January and Santos were playing the Swedish team AIK, who were here to take part in a competition with Brazilian clubs. I felt that it was my first big test, especially because they were a foreign team. But I was confident nevertheless. I didn't score – that role fell to Feijó, the left back, from a free kick – but I think I did well because everyone came to hug me afterwards.

From then on, with Vasco sidelined, it became the norm for Del Vecchio, or Deo as we called him, and me to alternate. Lula did it to keep us both on our toes and it is a testament to his man-management skills that it caused no ill-feeling between Deo and me. There was no resentment, just respect. We trained hard and played hard together, for Santos, and if the coach decided that one or other of us was going to play that day, that's just the way it was. The other sat on the bench and cheered the team on.

In early 1957 it came to the attention of the Santos directors that the contract I had with them, such as it was, no longer held much water now I was sixteen. Waldemar and Dondinho came down to thrash out the terms – I'd been hoping for a better deal, since I was playing so well, but the club argued that I was still young and on the small side, and therefore liable to get injured at any time. (All the more reason to pay me more, I reckoned.) Anyway they negotiated another 1,000 cruzeiros a month and the deal was done on 8 April 1957, a contract that would tie me to the club for eighteen months.

It was also at that time that I moved out of the Vila Belmiro. The Santos masseur, Raimundo, was a retired basketball player married to a woman called Dona Georgina. My mum had visited once and got to know her, since she was around giving the players and their wives manicures, and she offered to put me up at her place. There were a handful of young footballers there – including Dorval and Coutinho and a keeper called Lalá. Dona Georgina's place became my home for several years, and I have wonderful memories of the friendships I forged there.

In the first half of 1957 I was getting regular games and was scoring a few goals. I was well-known, however, only at a local level. It was only in June that I really got the chance to announce myself to the rest of the country. There was to be a tournament in Rio de Janeiro between four European clubs and four Brazilian clubs. One of the Brazilian sides was to be made up of players from both Santos and Rio's Vasco da Gama. I was picked to play centre-forward in the team.

The trip was the first time I had been to Rio, which is a 300-mile drive up the coast from Santos. I didn't really know what to expect. I knew the city was Brazil's capital, and was a bit bigger than Santos. I wasn't a tourist, however, and our coach took us straight to São Januário, the Vasco stadium, where we slept in dorms and trained during the day.

It was also the first opportunity I had to play in the Maracanã. I knew all about the Maracanã from the 1950 World Cup. It was built for the competition and was still the largest stadium in the world. We had one training session there and when I saw it, it really felt like a dream. I thought, 'Something of this size is out of this world!' The place was absolutely enormous. When I walked on to the pitch for the first time I realised that the pitch was pretty big too. It made the Vila Belmiro look minuscule. I was completely taken aback with it. When we were training sometimes I just stared and stared at the stands.

Even though I played at Santos all my career in Brazil, the Maracanã has a very special place in my heart. I know that it was the scene of the tragic defeat in 1950, but for me I played many of my most important games there (more about those later). The first game, for the Santos/Vasco all-stars against Belenenses of Portugal, was possibly a sign of how lucky the Maracanã would be for me. The stadium was full, there were firecrackers as we ran on to the pitch. The atmosphere was fantastic. And I got a hat-trick. For the first goal I received the ball surrounded by three defenders in the box, and whacked it into the net. For the second I dribbled past the defence and tapped it over the diving keeper. And the last was a thunderbolt from outside the box. Three very different goals, and I think I showed everyone there what I was capable of.

We played two more games in that tournament, against Flamengo and São Paulo, and I made the scoresheet in both. I must have impressed, since immediately afterwards I got a call-up for the national team. The game was the first leg of the following month's Copa Roca, a traditional challenge against Argentina. I was still just sixteen. Again, the match was at the Maracanã, against Argentina. I came on in the second half (again, for my club colleague Del Vecchio), wearing the number 13 shirt. Brazil were 1–0 down, and a few moments later I scored. Argentina won that game 2–1, and so it was all to play for in the second leg.

The match was at the Pacaembu in São Paulo and, for the first time, I was included in the starting line-up. I played well from the start and after 18 minutes ran into the box and opened the scoring. Mazzola scored the second, the game finished 2–0, meaning that Brazil had won the Copa Roca. It was my first international title; I did not realise it would be the first of many . . .

In my first full season at Santos I made the number 10 shirt my own. I was the highest scorer in the São Paulo state championship, which was the main league we played in, with seventeen goals. My training and eating was also changing my body. After six months I had put on more muscle, I was stronger. Actually, my legs put on so much bulk that each of my thighs had the same circumference as my waist. It amazed me how my body was looking different.

I trained hard. I've always been a perfectionist – I still am. I worked most on my left foot, since it wasn't as powerful as the right foot. I also practised headers. Back in those days there was a contraption that had a ball hanging from it, that you would jump up to practise heading. You don't get them any more, but they were very important. Santos also had a gym and for a year I learned karate, which was very useful in learning how to fall and how to jump. I learned judo after that. They really helped in increasing balance and agility. When I dribbled past players I hardly ever fell.

I was the youngest player in the league and I looked up to the veterans, especially Zizinho, who played at São Paulo. He had been Brazil's most exciting player for the 1950 World Cup. I was thrilled to be able to now play against him. I remember a match in November 1957 when São Paulo got the better of us. They beat us 6–2 and Zizinho gave a masterclass. He was astonishing. His passes, his shots, his positioning – it was all very beautiful. He helped São Paulo win the state championship that year.

Zizinho was the player I most idolised. He was certainly good enough to be called up to play in the 1958 World Cup, but he ruled himself out. He sensed that his time had come to an end. It's a pity, and he is remembered as perhaps the best Brazilian never to have won a World Cup. He wasn't lucky enough to live through the age of television and video – if he was he would be remembered much more than he is.

Despite the 6–2 thrashing he gave us that day, Zizinho later said that when he first saw me he was impressed. 'He fought like a real warrior for the whole match! I liked his technical qualities tremendously, and those that go beyond sport too. I thought he'd go far. And I wasn't wrong.' When, many years later, I said how much I looked up to him, I received the following message: 'Dear Athlete of the Century, great King Pelé, if I was a useful mirror for you at the start of your career, you can be sure that fills me with pride.'

✯

When 1958 came around, there was an added excitement to the club games. It was a World Cup year, and so we all played with that little bit extra to impress the national team selectors. Dondinho heard first that I had got the call-up, but he wasn't sure. He spoke to me on the phone from Bauru and said that he was listening on the radio and they had mentioned either Telê, who played for Fluminense, or Pelé. 'I *think* you are in the team, son,' he said. So I went and asked around at Santos. It was Modesto Roma, the chairman at the time, who told me: 'Hey kiddo, you've made the *Seleção*.'

The man tasked with taking us to Sweden was Vicente Feola. First he had to make the terrible final selection of players who would go. The system at the time was such that many more of us had got the initial call than would actually get on a plane to the World Cup, and it was a nerve-wracking experience. We were all called together by the head of the Brazilian delegation, Dr Paulo Machado de Carvalho, and it fell to him to read out the list of the damned. All of us were sick with nerves, it was such a big moment. When Dr Paulo finished, and my name still had not been mentioned, I thought at first that he must be reading the list of people who were going – he had read the name of Luizinho, for example, who was a star player for Corinthians and a shoo-in for a place on the aeroplane. But no, Luizinho was not selected. And I was.

The coach's decision was final, but such was the outcry at the omission of Luizinho that a practice match against

Corinthians was set up in Pacaembu, presumably as a way for him to impress and show the error of the selectors' ways. The stadium was packed, and the Corinthians' fans were booing us. It was as though Corinthians were the national squad and we were some team from abroad. Orlando had to mark Luizinho and seemed really nervous. But Luizinho did not play very well. We were the ones who dominated in defence and midfield, scoring goals in attack too. When it was 3–1 to the national side I received the ball in the Corinthians' midfield, and was headed for the penalty area when Ari Clemente appeared from nowhere, lunging in the tackle. I tried to dribble past him, but as he tried to get the ball off me he struck my right knee. I went down. I wondered if I'd be able to carry on – yes, I could, I told myself – but my knee gave way the first time I tried to put pressure on it.

I was taken off, and remember looking anxiously at Dr Hilton Gosling, the team doctor, and Mario Américo, our physio. It seemed they were holding my entire future in their hands. Dr Gosling wanted to keep my spirits up and told me nothing was wrong. They put some ice on the place that had received the force of the impact, and Mario Américo, who stammered a little, said, 'Listen, Crioulo, I'm going to make sure you're just fine.' The word *crioulo* means creole, or black man, and was another nickname that I had in those days. In fact, many black players are called Crioulo. Mario Américo was a much-loved and unforgettable character in Brazilian football, and he too was black; so when he called me 'Crioulo' it was only with affection. He and I got along really well – there was a special bond between us. That night I began to worry whether I'd be able to make it to Sweden. I spoke to Dr Paulo Machado de Carvalho, the 'Victory Marshal' (as he was dubbed at the

Pacaembu stadium), a man of great faith, and I told him I didn't want to be a dead weight on the team. He believed that I'd recover. But later I discovered that I had in fact come very close to being dropped. They thought about it long and hard.

Apparently Dr Gosling had told some friends that he thought there was no way I'd be able to play in the national team's practice matches, and that I was doubtful for the World Cup itself. He'd seen me up and about, knew I wasn't comfortable, was running with a limp and not hitting the ball firmly. Later I discovered they looked at Almir, a midfielder for Vasco da Gama, as a possible replacement. But Dr Gosling hoped for more than any of us dared to: I was kept on, and much to my surprise found myself on the plane to Italy, where we were due to play some warm-up games before the biggest tournament in the world.

✯

As a child I had wanted to be a pilot. On 24 May 1958 I finally walked up the steps into my first plane. It was a DC7-C, belonging to Panair do Brasil, and it was taking the national team to Europe. Everything was amazing and new for me, and I kept my eyes wide open. When we reached Recife to refuel, it began to sink in exactly what the national team meant to Brazilians. There were thousands of people at the airport and we left the plane to attend a huge reception of local dignitaries.

After a twelve-hour flight we landed in Lisbon. The team dentist, Dr Mario Trigo, ensured that the trip was always lively, doing everything he could to take our minds off the travelling (I only ever saw Dr Mario playing the clown – fortunately, I've always had excellent teeth, and he even said mine were the best in the squad). He even made up a quiz, with Mazzola acting as his assistant. He called his game 'The sky's the limit', the name of a Brazilian TV programme. I was the butt of the jokes but I always laughed – we were all so happy to be together, to be on our way to represent our country. One time he asked, 'What's the capital of Italy?' I replied that it was Aracaju, which is the capital of the state of Sergipe; and he went on, 'What's the biggest city in the world?'; and I answered that it was Raiz da Serra, where Garrincha was born. Everybody laughed, everyone had a great time, and the trip passed happily. It was especially good for me, there like a sailor on his first voyage, and took my mind off my knee.

Three hours' more flying took us to Rome, the city of the Pope, the centre of the Catholic world. We stayed at the Universo hotel where we slept, recovered our strength, and then we took a bus tour around the 'eternal city'. That morning, 26 May 1958, I remembered just how important it was being there, in the cradle of civilisation and at the birthplace of some amazing history. It was a Monday. We went to the Vatican, and though we weren't able to see the Pope we did attend Mass. The driver did the usual route: the Coliseum, the Trevi Fountain, the Olympic Stadium, the Via Veneto and other historic sites. And all we really wanted to do was make the most of the amazing Italian food. We all started shouting, 'Lunch! Lunch!' and off we went to eat – something else to remember Rome by.

The national team bosses had arranged two practice friendlies against Italian clubs as part of our World Cup preparations. The first was against Fiorentina, in Florence. I was examined again and ruled out of this game – I didn't know it at the time, but Dr Gosling was still worried I might be out for a month or more. I saw Dr Paulo, and once more ventured my concerns that I might be taking up a place on the squad. To his credit he deferred the decision to Dr Gosling, on purely medical grounds, but he knew that José de Almeida, one of the directors of the national team, was in fact already making noises about sending me home. I was told nothing of this, but instead was given a stark ultimatum by the doctor: if I wanted to have any chance of playing in Sweden, I'd have to undergo a very intensive and painful series of treatments on my knee. Of course, there was no choice at all, and I began the treatment. He was right, it was tough: mostly involving boiling-hot towels.

The second game was in Milan, against Internazionale. I was still on the bench. We then flew over the Swiss Alps – a beautiful view – across Germany to Copenhagen, in Denmark. We had a snack at the airport and took a 'Convair' plane, just like the ones that Varig and others used to fly in Brazil. After a final forty-five-minute flight through clear blue skies we landed uneventfully in the airport at Gothenburg. It was 2 June, and the first match was only six days away. We'd been drawn in Group 4, against Austria, England and the USSR, and would play them in that order.

Our base for the World Cup was Hindas, a short bus-ride from Gothenburg. The hotel we stayed in was very comfortable – luxurious, in fact, with juices, croissants, yoghurts and much more all on tap. Dr Gosling had spent a lot of time researching venues for our base camp and he came up trumps. I grew to like Sweden as a country very quickly – it has beautiful scenery, with lots of lakes and trees and clear, pure air. Everything was well organised, and the Swedes were lovely, considerate and charming hosts.

Most dishes in the hotel were based on fish, but we also ate real Portuguese sardines too, and of course meat. We were missing rice, but once the organisers had managed to secure a bag of this precious commodity for us we found out that Mario Américo and Castilho were excellent cooks! From then on we had rice with our dinner, and nobody could complain about our food, which was varied and good quality. Unless we were travelling, that is – Dr Gosling had a thing about food-poisoning and insisted we ate only sandwiches when we were travelling to or from a game.

There was a good feeling in the team. We bonded, and everyone had a nickname as well as their 'player' name. There were some weird ones – none of us could avoid it. In Sweden Gilmar was 'Giraffe', perhaps because of his long neck; Castilho, now sadly dead, but a great character, was 'Buris', though I wasn't sure whether this was due to some resemblance to the movie actor Boris Karloff or because he'd said 'buris' when asking once for a *bule*, a coffee-pot. De Sordi was 'Cabeça' or 'Head'; Djalma Santos had various nicknames, but 'Rato' ('Rat') was the one most people liked to use. Bellini, who had been 'Captain' at Vasco, was now 'Boi' – 'Ox'. Dino Sani was 'Joelho', 'Knee', because he was bald and without hair his head looked like a knee. I can't tell you the names we had for Zito and Orlando – they wouldn't forgive me, even now. Didi was 'Black Heron'; Mazzola was 'Cara de Pedra' – 'Stony Face'. Pepe was 'Macaroni' – I have no idea why. Zagallo was the 'Crybaby'; and I, being black, was called Alemão, 'The German' – again, I have no idea why.

They were just silly jokes, little things, but they helped unite us and forged a spirit that would take us all the way. We already knew we were a strong team, and we'd had good preparation: as well as Feola and Dr Gosling we had Paulo Amaral to help us, a pioneer in physical training. He worked us very hard, there was no let-up, and no complaints were tolerated. My only criticism at the time – not that I expressed it to him, of course! – was that he made everyone do the same exercises, regardless of their condition, age or body type. As well as being injured I was only seventeen, remember, so I felt the effects of this regime. But in those days, the mere presence of a trainer with any sort of strategy was progress. And in truth the intensity was good, especially for such a short campaign as the World Cup, with only a maximum of six games to play.

Another bonding exercise apart from the nicknames and the workouts was to go on little team trips together, too – to the Liseberg park in Gothenburg, for example, where I had great fun shooting darts at targets. We also went along to a dance-hall where you could hear bands play or watch a show, and where there were always lots of girls. The Swedish girls loved us. Especially the black players. I guess we were something new. I remember that all the fourteen- and fifteen-year-old girls were after me. Usually, the guys who got most attention were the tall, handsome ones, like Mauro, or Gilmar the goalkeeper, or Nilton Santos. But no – these girls just wanted the little Crioulos; me, Didi, Moacir. They said we were beautiful! It was a wonderful time. I even had a little fling, in fact, with a gorgeous Swedish girl called Ilena, who was as fascinated by my black skin as I was by her blue eyes and blonde hair. At Hindas we also had the opportunity to go fishing, which I loved. It was calm and quiet, and my thoughts could soar . . . Dreaming of a knee that was better, dreaming of playing.

★

It hadn't got better in time for our opening game in Udevalla, against Austria. So I watched from the touchline. We made a good start. Mazzola put us in front before Nilton Santos waltzed through to make it 2–0, with Mazzola adding a third in the last minute. We were all delighted with the win.

Three days later we played England at Gothenburg, and again Dr Gosling said it was too early to test the knee, despite all the treatment. This match proved harder than the first and we could only draw 0–0 – the English had done their homework and devised a tight back four, including Billy Wright of Wolves and Don Howe of West Bromwich Albion. They kept Didi quiet, although Vavá hit the bar and Mazzola had two shots saved brilliantly by the England keeper, Colin McDonald.

And so the third match loomed, against the USSR, the last of the group stage. The result was crucial, and we were worried since we didn't feel that we had been playing as well as we could. Also, the USSR were a very well-fancied side. There was a Cold War fear of them, and they had also won the Olympic gold in the 1952 Helsinki Games. Like us, the USSR had beaten Austria and drawn with England, meaning that the winner would take the group. By that time I was bouncing off the walls with frustration. In the practice matches between the main team and the reserves, Garrincha and I (for the reserves) were wiping the floor with the first choicers. We made them go wild. When Paulo Amaral refereed these practice games he had to give dodgy decisions in their favour, there was no other way to beat us.

I knew that I would play the day before the game. Zito, my midfield team-mate at Santos, came to speak to me and said, 'I think the moment has come for us.' I replied, 'What, for this game, the most difficult one?' He said that Mazzola wasn't feeling too good, and he thought we'd both be given a chance. And then one of the heads of the delegation, Nascimento, asked me: 'Are you ready? Feola is going to put you on.'

Garrincha and I played with the main team in the final training session. It was scheduled for the afternoon, but Feola got wind that there was a journalist passing information to the Soviets so he switched the session to the morning at the last minute. No sooner had we finished breakfast than we made the short journey to the training ground. I knew everyone would be watching me very closely, so I was careful, but desperate to impress. I played in goal for a bit, and then as inside-left; it was when I moved up-field that I began to feel confident in my knee, and my running and jumping were strong. I felt good.

Dr Paulo later wrote that Feola turned to him at this moment and said, 'Thank God, Dr Paulo; it looks as though the kid is back to a hundred per cent.' Paulo asked if he would play me, and Feola replied, 'Of course! I've wanted to put him in for ages.' Dr Gosling agreed with this diagnosis. It looked like I was home and dry.

There was, however, another obstacle. As part of our preparations the team psychologist, Dr João Carvalhaes, had conducted tests on all the players. We had to draw sketches of people and answer questions – which would help Dr João make assessments about whether we should be picked or not. It was either ahead of its time for football or just odd, or maybe both. About me he concluded that I should not be selected: 'Pelé is obviously infantile. He lacks the necessary fighting spirit.' He also advised against Garrincha, who was not seen as responsible enough. Fortunately for me and for Garrincha, Feola was always guided by his instincts rather than experts and he just nodded gravely at the psychologist, saying, 'You may be right.

The thing is, you don't know anything about football. If Pelé's knee is ready, he plays!'

Once my name went up on the team-sheet there was a lot of curiosity. I was seventeen, the youngest player in the tournament, and the press started to prick up their ears. Until then all the focus had been on the Soviet side – they were among the tournament favourites and had some world-class players, including the man-mountain goalkeeper, Yashin; and the striker Simonian.

When on 15 June I ran out into Gothenburg's Nya Ullevi stadium, there must have been a fair few of the 50,000 spectators who were taken aback to see a little black kid with the teams. And they must have been astonished when I stripped off my tracksuit to reveal a Brazil shirt with a big number 10 on the back. I imagine there were some who assumed I was a kind of mascot, especially when compared with the physique of the Russians, who were all huge. I remember looking at them and thinking, 'They're big . . . but big trees can be felled too.' I wasn't there just for good luck. Just moments before, Mario Américo had finished a final massage on my knee and packed me off with the words: 'You're going on now, kid.' The words have stayed with me ever since.

We lined up for the national anthems, and I felt a surge of emotion course through my veins: this was what it was all about. This was what all the training had been for, all the pain of the treatment. To represent one's country, a football-mad country, in the biggest competition of them all. It was simultaneously awe-inspiring and yet distracting: I knew I had to focus on the challenge of the match.

As soon as the whistle went we were playing a different sort of football than in the first two games. Garrincha was immediately effective, dribbling menacingly up the right wing and exposing weaknesses in the Russian lines. I thought we had got off to a flyer when he sped past a defender and thumped the ball towards Yashin's goal. The big man misjudged it but the ball hit the post and rebounded to safety; just moments later I got the ball and – bang! I hit the woodwork too. For a second time the cry 'Goal!' died in my mouth. Didi shouted at me, 'Relax, kid, the goal will come, take it easy.'

In the opening minutes of the game our pace was mesmerising. Soon we were able to let rip, as Didi put through Vavá with a lovely, unexpected ball and Vavá smashed it into the net. We all went berserk, jumping on Vavá and screaming with joy. Only three minutes were gone, and we were one up.

After that the game settled down and I started to feel my knee more and more, although I tried hard to hide it. I was playing quite well but felt anxious, wanting to preserve our lead and for the game to end *now*. Always a mistake, often fatal. I missed two attempts at goal that I would surely have buried had I been more relaxed. The Russians came at us strongly in the second half but our defence was impregnable, and then finally the tension was lifted when we caught them flat at the back as they pushed forward and Vavá again beat Yashin. This time the relief was intense, and the celebration went a bit too far – Vavá was mobbed to the point that he actually got injured and had to leave the field for a few minutes. But the job was done. We were through to the quarter-finals of the Cup, and suddenly favourites to win it.

✯

That night, after our celebration dinner, I went back to my room and replayed in my mind every move, every kick. I wasn't too pleased with my performance – I could have played better. I'd tried to chip Yashin at one point and realised that was just pure cheek on my part – in those days he was considered one of the best goalkeepers in the world. That was something I'd have to work on. The adrenaline was still pumping through my body and it was impossible to sleep – it made me think of the night before leaving Bauru.

That evening we'd learned that our next opponents would be Wales, who had brilliantly beaten Hungary 2–1 in their play-off to finish second in their group. Some were surprised that they'd come this far, but they had some decent players – including the great John Charles, who unfortunately for them was injured for our match – and worked as a real unit.

The Wales game took place only two days after my first. Jack Kelsey, the Welsh goalie, was in great form and his team were forceful in defence. The first half ended 0–0 and Feola gave us a rousing locker-room talk. In the second half I received the ball from Didi with my back to the goal, chested it on to my right foot, turned past the defender and scored. It was my first goal in a World Cup – and it was the winning goal of that match.

The USSR game had been tough and it was important for Brazil because we qualified as top of the group. But on a personal level, I consider the game against Wales my most important of the tournament. I knew that if we lost we would be knocked out of the competition. And the goal was, perhaps, the most unforgettable of my career. It boosted my confidence completely. The world now knew about Pelé. I was on a roll.

For the semis we travelled for the first time to Stockholm. Our opponents were France, who had thrashed Northern Ireland 4–0 in their quarter-final. The game was a seven-goal thriller. Almost as soon as it began we were one up, thanks to Vavá. Just Fontaine (who scored thirteen goals in the tournament, still a World Cup record) equalised – the first goal we had conceded. I picked the ball out of the net and walked with it to the centre circle. I think it showed just how much I had grown in strength and confidence since the Wales game. Near the end of the first half Didi put us ahead again with a stunning long drive.

In the second half, in the 52nd minute, the 64th minute and the 75th, I was the Pelé I wanted to be, scoring three goals and playing with considerable boldness for a seventeen-year-old boy, chipping the ball over opponents' heads and everything . . . I was on song, and the game was made safe despite a late second goal for France by Roger Piantoni. We'd won 5–2 and were in the final.

By the end of the France game, I think everyone in the world had become a Brazil supporter. European teams defend well. That's because generally they tend to have more defenders than attackers. It makes them hard to score against. But we were playing this exciting, irreverent, attacking football and the crowds went wild. Although most teams in the tournament played a 4–4–2 formation, we were often more like 4–2–4: once we had control of the ball and were attacking, there would be four of us up front working in tandem. Garrincha was key to this. His dribbles up the right wing drove defenders crazy – and he made the crowds erupt in cheers and laughter; they had never seen anything like it. Once he had the ball, the other side could not get it off him. They did not know which way he would turn. This always gave time for our players who had been moving back to advance into attacking positions.

Although sometimes he drove us crazy too. We didn't know

what he would do either. I, for one, would sometimes get exasperated with him. When he got the ball I knew he would dribble past at least one person, and I would then expect him to cross. But he would as often bring the ball back himself, which would put me offside so I had to go back too. We often argued with him about this. Yet despite these small frustrations, of course, we had wonderful synchronicity. Neither me nor Garrincha knew it at the time, but that World Cup was the beginning of a historic partnership in the national team: whenever we played together, Brazil never ever lost a game. (This statistical truth is something that neither Garrincha nor I realised during our careers together. We never, for example, joked about it before going on – we were actually quite separate, socially, since outside the *Seleção* he lived and played in Rio and I was in São Paulo.)

I should also mention Didi, especially since at the end of the tournament he was voted best player. I think he deserved it. Me and Garrincha were young and a bit naïve. Didi was very smart. He was our maestro, he would always belt out to us, 'Pay attention to where you are going to kick the ball!' He was too smart at times. He would pretend that he was going to cross the ball to one side of the pitch, and then cross it to the other. It sometimes confused us instead. He would shout, 'No, you idiots, I'm trying to confuse the other team!'

By this stage I had also made another observation about the World Cup. All the other teams had only white people. I thought it was really weird. I can remember asking my teammates, 'Is it only in Brazil that there are blacks?'

The 29th of June 1958 dawned to grey skies, as a storm broke over Stockholm that morning. Everyone said this would be to the advantage of the Swedes. But it rains in Brazil too, and we were used to playing on muddy pitches. Because Sweden also have yellow shirts, for this match we would have to change our strip and play in blue. A few thought this was a bad omen but Dr Paulo, the head of the delegation, turned it round cleverly. He said blue would be lucky, it was the colour of Brazil's patron saint, Nossa Senhora de Aparecida, and it had served previous teams well – including the opponents the last time Brazil had got to a World Cup Final, in 1950. So we played in blue.

The only change to our line-up was that Djalma Santos was brought in to replace De Sordi. Many people have speculated that Feola was trying to honour Djalma Santos in doing so: De Sordi had played well in all of the five preceding matches and no one would have made a change like that without good reason. But the truth was much more prosaic – De Sordi wasn't fit. He hadn't slept well before the Final and had been feeling pains in one of his legs. He had told Dr Gosling who had naturally passed on the information to the Technical Commission – they were the ones who left him out. So Djalma Santos got his chance.

There were 49,737 people inside the stadium that day, most of them supporting the home country, of course, but they were fair and applauded good play on both sides. As the anthems began I had a sudden vision of Dondinho at home, my father hunched over the radio, at once nervous and proud. I was determined to justify his faith in me, and make good on my promise of 1950.

The Swedes began very well, though, taking us by surprise, and within four minutes their centre-forward, Liedholm, had scored. There was a huge roar in the stadium, and hats and papers and all sorts went flying. It was the first time in the whole competition that we had been behind, and I was worried we would panic. I implored my team-mates not to worry, as did Didi and Vavá. We resumed, businesslike, focused, knowing that our blend of teamwork and individual flair should be enough to see us to victory. With some great play from Garrincha on the right, the Swedish keeper was pulled out of position and Vavá equalised. Not long after I found Garrincha and, in an almost identical move, he passed to Vavá again to score. Garrincha also had a great shot come back off the post. We still held the lead at half-time.

In the second half we showed our true class, sweeping Sweden aside. I made it 3–1 eleven minutes into the second half, after shouting to Nilton Santos to cross a long centre to me. As it came in I caught it first on my chest, then let it drop as the defender Gustavsson came at me. Flipping the ball over his head I ran round him and volleyed home the shot. Though I say so myself, it was a nice goal – and a goal in a World Cup Final! It is one of my all-time favourite goals – because I was so young, but also because no one had seen a goal like that before. Ten minutes later Zagallo scored our fourth, after Sweden failed to clear his corner. I was beginning to feel that the title was within reach, even after Simonsson scored for Sweden with eleven minutes to go. We just knocked it about, keeping possession, revelling in the chant from our fans: '*Samba! Samba!*'

The final play was a high cross: I outjumped two Swedish defenders, touched the ball with my head and – as if in slow motion – watched it loop into the corner of the net, Brazil's fifth goal and my second of the match. The game was assured. *We were going to be World Champions!* Then, all of a sudden, I passed out in front of the goal. Garrincha came over and picked up my legs to circulate the blood to my head. When I came to the game was already over. I was overcome with emotion. My first thoughts were about my family in Bauru. Did they know that we were champions? I wanted to speak to my parents, but there were no telephones, and so I kept on saying, 'I've got to tell my dad, I've got to tell my dad.' (I only managed to speak to him in the following days, using an international radio. I can remember saying things like: 'Did you see me with the Swedish king? Over,' and 'I shook the king's hand. Over.' Things have come a long way since then. Now you can pick up a mobile and say: 'Mum, I just scored a goal!')

As the fact that we were World Champions sank in, the tears came. All of us were crying, I wept on Gilmar's shoulder and then within seconds it seemed we were all weeping with joy and relief. Meanwhile Mario Américo was after his own prize – he pinched the ball from the referee and danced off to the dressing-room, much to the fury of the ref.

We did a lap of honour around the stadium, carrying a huge Swedish flag, and then King Gustav came down on to the pitch to congratulate us, amazingly generous in his praise despite the fact that his own country had just lost – a sentiment reflected in the comment later by Sigge Parling, the defender who had marked me: 'After the fifth goal,' he said, 'even I wanted to cheer for him.' Later on there was a tremendous celebration meal at our hotel, where we all ate more than our fill and people drank champagne from the Jules Rimet trophy. There was a party at the Brazilian Embassy, but I went to bed early. I was just thinking about how to speak to my parents. The Embassy do was like a formal reception. It's funny to compare it with how celebrations are nowadays, when inevitably everyone ends up in a nightclub.

At last, after the bitter disappointments of 1950 and 1954, we were World Champions for the first time. It was an indescribable feeling, and one I wanted to experience again. And again.

4

Joy and Pain

'When I saw Pelé play, I just wanted to hang up my boots'

JUST FONTAINE, TOP SCORER IN THE 1958 WORLD CUP

The 1958 World Cup was my launching-pad. I was on the front pages of newspapers and magazines all over the world. *Paris Match* ran a cover story immediately after the victory, saying that there was a new king on the block. The name stuck, and very soon I started to be called King Pelé. Or, more simply, the King. My friends used to tell me that I was a real king, because I had been chosen by the people.

The return trip to Brazil after the highs of Stockholm couldn't pass quickly enough. The whole team was emotionally drained as well as physically exhausted, and we all just wanted to get home as soon as possible. Our first taste of the scale of our achievement came when we touched down on Brazilian soil in Recife, on the eastern tip of the country, and a great roar went up as the plane's doors opened – it was mayhem, despite the pouring rain. Every player ended up being hoisted high on shoulders as we acknowledged the jubilant crowd. But that was nothing compared to arriving in Rio later that day.

There were fans thronging the streets in every direction, and after a parade on fire engines we had a lovely surprise: Senator Assis Chateaubriand, who owned an important magazine in Brazil in those days called *Cruzeiro*, as well as radio stations, TV channels and other media interests, used his clout to arrange for the whole Brazilian delegation to go to the *Cruzeiro* offices. And there, waiting for us, were all our families. My father Dondinho, choked with emotion, and other relatives; and my mother Celeste, who kissed me with tears in her eyes, and tried unsuccessfully to remain strong as she said – with a lump in her throat – 'Congratulations, Dico . . .' Through her tears she told me she had missed me, and about the party in Bauru after our win, and how all our neighbours had forgotten my annoying antics playing football in the street and bringing down the power lines now I had brought the World Cup to Brazil for the first time. It was a wonderful moment for me, and for us all – she didn't say as much, but it was clear that my mother had finally understood that this game could be a power for good in our family, and perhaps my father was seeing some of the disappointment in his own frustrated career swept away by my success. I could tell he was proud of his son, and that meant so much to me. All of the players were very grateful for this surprise: it was the first time we had seen our families for weeks in what was, for many of us, the first time we had been abroad. And it was a moment of rest, of stopping for a bit, of being at ease.

The party resumed, however, when we moved on to São Paulo the next day – if anything, it became even crazier. All Brazil wanted to pay tribute to her heroes. People everywhere, cheering, waving and chanting, confetti raining down on us from every window during another parade, everyone wanting to embrace us and shake our hands – if we had had any doubts about what winning the World Cup would mean to the people of Brazil, they were quickly dispelled in those first few days of madness and euphoria. It was a unique experience, and very touching – we would bring home the trophy again, and there would be more ecstatic celebrations, but there can only be one first time.

The next few days were a blur of congratulations and back-slapping, as the team did the rounds of dinners and lunches and parties of all descriptions, many of which the players found themselves ushered in and out of without really knowing what they were for or who was hosting them. But that was fine – everyone was so happy and we felt honoured to have created such happiness, even if it also meant a very steep learning curve for us: no one had given us any lessons in how to be celebrities. The press attention and questioning were never-ending and it was an effort to come up with different or interesting answers; pretty soon we gave up trying.

The sweetest moment for me, after a quick trip to Santos with my triumphant team-mates Zito and Pepe – during which we threatened not to speak to one more reporter until someone brought us a sandwich, so starving were we – came when all the official functions were over and we were at last allowed to go home and be with our families. Having left Bauru only two years earlier as an unknown teenager fearfully making his way towards what he hoped would be a career in football, here I was on the verge of returning, and with a World Cup winner's medal in my hand. It seemed literally incredible, too preposterous to be true. I was nervous about the reception I would get, although people were saying the whole town would be turning out, which seemed ludicrous. But as the plane touched down after the short flight – suddenly it seemed I was flying everywhere – those whispers looked true. Hordes and hordes of people, pressed up against the fences on the side of the runway, waving and cheering as I came down the steps to a phalanx of photographers. And among them my family: as well as my parents, Jorge was there, and my sister Maria Lúcia and brother Zoca. And friends too: as I was whisked on to a flat-bed truck for a victory parade through town, which looked as though it had been newly painted for the purpose, all sorts of familiar faces from my past popped up on either side to grab a quick handshake or kiss of congratulation.

The mayor of Bauru, Nicola Avalone Jr, had put up a stand in the main square in my honour, and eventually the parade wound its way there through the crowds. I was greeted by the mayor on behalf of the people – I've never seen so many people out on the streets in Bauru. I was given trophies, medals, gifts . . . One of the medals was presented to me by my mother. She was meant to speak, but couldn't, so she just kissed me, her eyes filled with tears. Once the tributes were over, there was a further surprise, and the biggest gift of all – on a smaller stand, next to ours, was a large object covered by a sheet of tarpaulin. I knew it was going to be a car. I looked at the crowds, a band was playing, it was a big party – and, buoyed up by the grandeur of the occasion, I imagined the kind of car it would be. A convertible perhaps, something glamorous in which I could cruise up and down the beachfront at Santos? (When I got my licence, of course!) Then the tarpaulin was whisked off and my jaw dropped – out of disappointment. It was a little Romisetta, a tiny three-wheeled banger very popular at that time. Could I drive it in Santos? It wouldn't even get there on the motorway. Still, I was grateful to have been paid tribute in this way. And a car is a car, even if it only has three wheels.

When I woke up the following morning the Romisetta was parked outside our house, delivered by someone at the mayor's office. I got in. It was mine, even though I wasn't even old enough for a licence. But there was time for all that. I tried moving the steering wheel, like the kid I was, playing with my surprising new toy. But I had already decided what I should do with it. I called my father over.

'It's yours,' I said to him.

'What are you talking about?' he said. 'It's not mine, it's yours.'

'But it's my gift to you,' I replied. 'I want you to have it.'

Typically, Dondinho balked at this. 'But you were given it as a gift, you shouldn't give it to anyone else . . .'

I told him I wouldn't be able to take it to Santos, but my father said someone could drive it there for me. Don't bother, I said, I'll sell it. My father was outraged – 'Sell it? Have you gone crazy? You don't sell something you've been given as a present!' So I offered my parting shot: '*You* keep it, then.' Once my mother had talked about the dangers I'd face with a car in Santos, my father finally agreed to accept this compromise. This was his deal: 'I'll keep the car, but it's yours and you'll take it to Santos whenever you can.'

✯

The World Cup victory seemed to transform my parents' life even more than it did mine. In Bauru, they were invited to parties and events that they would never have been privy to before. It was a bit embarrassing since my mum didn't have a smart dress and my dad didn't have a suit to wear. The change happened so suddenly it was actually quite difficult for them to cope.

In Santos, however, my life stayed more or less the same. I was still living with my team-mates, and even though people were more curious about me than before, life wasn't really that much different. I think I was lucky to have started at Santos at the age of fifteen and to have been playing since I was sixteen – I didn't know anything else but being a footballer. My personality had been formed by this experience. Nowadays young kids just want to be famous, and when they get there their personalities change. I think one of the gifts God gave me was that my personality did not change once I became a World Cup champion. I was still me, just me, living in Santos with my friends and doing what I loved to do – playing football.

I was not allowed to get big-headed. Because of the way my contract had been drafted, I wasn't even the best-paid member of the team. I used to find ways of making my money back. When the team was together in the evening, the older players used to play cards for money. I never did. They used to shout over to me, 'Hey, Pelé, get us some coffee! Pelé, get us some fags!' And they would pay me with their poker chips to go across the road and fetch them drinks and snacks. I made a tidy sum that way.

Back from international duty my thoughts turned to more pressing football challenges. First up was the São Paulo state championship – the title Santos had won in 1956 but lost to Palmeiras the year after. There was no national league at that time in Brazil because the size of the country would have made it impossible. The big teams in Rio had their own league – the 'Carioca' – and we had the 'Paulista', which was a tough league and included teams such as Corinthians and São Paulo FC. Santos were on fire, racking up outrageous scorelines like 10–0, 9–1, 7–1 and 8–1. In thirty-eight games I scored fifty-eight goals, conveniently for 1958 – this was a championship record and Santos won the title. Del Vecchio had left to go and play in Europe so I was now always in the starting line-up.

There were limited opportunities to play against the big Rio clubs – Botafogo, where Garrincha was, or Vasco, Flamengo and Fluminense. At the beginning of the year, however, there was a small tournament, the annual 'Rio–São Paulo', which brought us all together. In 1959, Santos won this title for the first time. Later that year, we failed to recapture the Paulista – but we did win it three times in a row after that. I was always top scorer.

The Santos of that era was on a different level. In the forward line-up we had Pepe, who had been in the national squad with me; Pagão and Coutinho. Pepe was very quick and had a very powerful foot. He ranks as Santos' second highest all-time goalscorer, after me, even though he is hardly known internationally. Pagão was technically very accomplished, although I think Coutinho was probably a better centre-forward. He certainly helped me a lot. We became known for our *tabelinhas*, or one–twos – quick-fire passes which confused the opposition players marking us. We practised them a lot together and they were quite something. Playing the 'Garrincha role' was Dorval, who I used to call the George Best of the right wing. In midfield, Zito was always majestic. He held things together, he was a very intelligent player. We had Mauro in central defence, who went on to captain Brazil in 1962, and in goal we had the World Cup veteran Gilmar. Santos were a goal machine – we won something like 85 per cent of the games we played in those years.

A few months after the World Cup we had a big game against Corinthians. For matches like this we would have to stay at the Vila Belmiro the night before. In Brazil a training camp is called *concentração*, and the reason for it is to keep the players together and stop them from getting sidelined by non-footballing distractions. Such as meeting girls – but that is easier said than done, especially where Brazilian footballers are concerned. We were kicking our heels a bit so I suggested we go down to the gym where a women's basketball match was being played. It was the healthiest thing I could think of for us to do. Five of us went. Atlético Santista, a Santos team, were playing Corinthians from São Paulo. A few of the girls came over to talk to us, apart from one who was sitting on the reserves bench. I glanced over at her and she caught my eye. I was surprised – and by the time I noticed what was going on she was right beside me.

'Hi – you're Pelé, right?' she said.

'That's right,' I replied, pleased as punch that she had recognised me.

'Don't beat Corinthians too badly tomorrow.'

And with that, off she went, back to the reserves bench where she'd been sitting. I kept watching her, looking at her lovely brown hair, thinking what a beautiful girl she was . . . even my team-mates noticed that I'd been smitten, and they took the mickey a bit because she was only about fourteen years old (although I was only three years older myself). She'd really made quite an impression on me, and after she'd gone off to the changing-rooms and we'd returned to the training camp I couldn't stop thinking about her.

During the game the next day I convinced myself that she would have come to watch, and as a result spent more time searching the stands than watching the ball – it's a wonder I wasn't taken off. But she wasn't there, and it was some time later before our paths crossed again. I bumped into some of the other girls from the basketball match one day in the street, purely by chance, and was surprised to see them in Santos – I'd assumed they were from the São Paulo team. When it turned out they were themselves from Santos I quickly found out the brown-haired girl's name – Rosemeri – and where she worked, a record shop not far away. I rushed round there as nonchalantly as I could.

'Hello again,' I said after nervously making my approach.

'Hi.'

'Tell me, why did you want Corinthians to win if you're from Santos?' I asked.

'Because I support Corinthians,' she replied. 'Except I don't really like football.'

From this inauspicious start I managed to get her to agree to see me again – although she said she was far too young to be going out with boys and that if I wanted to talk to her I should go round to her house one Saturday. Like the good boy I was, I did just as I was told – and there I was, one Saturday, in my best clothes, shoes shined, my nails cut and cleaned, my face glowing! Rose's parents were friendly when they received me; I was the first young man to come calling on their daughter, and – of course – the first visitor who was black. Her mother, Dona Idalina, prepared some biscuits. Rosemeri's father, Guilherme Cholbi, worked at the Santos docks and was a real football fan. I was happy, I was made to feel comfortable in their house, and I spent a Saturday that I'll remember for ever. I felt that sense of family again, like with my own parents.

There would be many other visits over the coming months and years – our courtship was a very long and drawn-out affair. No one in Rose's family wanted the press to hear about our relationship, so when we went to see a movie, there would always be an aunt of hers with us. They'd go in first, and only then, once the lights had gone down, could I go in too and sit beside her. But what an amazing feeling to be near her! Despite the very restricted nature of our relationship I knew how I felt, and I started to think about the day when we could get married.

I wanted her to be my wife, I knew that. But for all my passion, for all my desire to be married to her, I worried that she was so young, that she didn't like football, and wondered if it was really me she liked, or Pelé the famous footballer. I thought about it a lot, and thinking about it brought up memories of Bauru. When I was with Neuzinha's family there – the Japanese girl I'd liked a lot – I never felt that they saw me as a footballer, I was just a boy. I felt they liked Edson just for being Edson. And even Ilena, the girl I met in Gothenburg during the 1958 World Cup – I really don't think she was that bothered by the fact that I was in the Brazilian national squad. We were just two young people who liked each other and each other's differences. All these thoughts went through my head and I struggled with them, before coming to my decision – I would marry Rose.

✯

But first I had another big institution to contend with: the Brazilian army. They say that football is sometimes like war – especially in a World Cup – and I definitely felt that in Sweden I had served my country and won them a great victory. A few months after I returned to Brazil I had my eighteenth birthday, and with it the prospect of a year's compulsory military service. I wasn't very keen on the idea, so I approached two of Santos' directors, who were army men. 'I've already fought for my country,' I argued. 'Surely I don't need to go to the army to do so again. I've already done my bit.' They looked at me and laughed. The only way to get exemption was by claiming some kind of medical excuse. 'Are you mad?' they replied. 'How can we say you have a dodgy pair of lungs, or a gammy leg? You've just won the World Cup. The whole country knows you are a shining example of health. If you weren't so high-profile, then there might be a way. But not you. If there is any eighteen-year-old Brazilian who *has* to do military service, then it's you.'

I was a recruit in the 6 GAC – the Sixth Group of the Motorised Coast Artillery in Santos. It was under the command of a Colonel Osman, who was a great guy and a real football fan, but very demanding. I was still playing for Santos, and Brazil too when internationals came up, and now I was expected to turn out for the barracks team as well as the Army. It was one day on, one day off.

Fortunately there wasn't that much asked of me in the barracks where I was serving. After all, I was an athlete and I had certain advantages, certain privileges – that's how it is for anyone who plays football or basketball and is doing military service. But not all the officers felt the same – some of them didn't want anything to do with 'making things easy' for upstart prima donnas. I'd grab a hoe to cut the grass in the barracks yard, then sweep it all up; I'd wash clothes and shine shoes, just so everyone could see that the new recruit wasn't getting any molly-coddling – I was Pelé, a World Champion, but also a soldier like any other. I was able to understand how things were, and it didn't bother me. As a soldier, I obeyed orders. There was a Captain Aurino, the head of my battery, who was particularly tough; and Sergeant Carlos, who didn't give me a break at all, and often gave me extra duties. But the sergeants and lieutenants weren't really bad people, they were just doing their job.

The barracks football team was 'managed' by Lieutenant

Falcão. He took this task very seriously indeed, and sometimes behaved as if he were coaching a major national or even international side. If the team played badly in training we'd be punished by being made to stay in the yard, doing chores and even sleeping there. But he was fair, and wanted us to be the best, and we subsequently became good friends.

He had some good material to work with, too. Apart from me there were several other professional footballers in the barracks, including Lorico, who played for Portuguesa de Desportos and Vasco da Gama; Célio, from Jabaquara; and Lara, who would eventually die of a heart attack at Vila Belmiro in the middle of a game. So we were a serious team, and we won the competition that pitted teams from different garrisons in Santos against each other, and another championship that included São Paulo barracks too.

In November 1959 I was picked to play for the Army XI in the South American Military Championships. In the finals against the Argentinians, in the General Severiano stadium in Rio, the Botafogo ground, I was sent off for the first time in my career. There was one Argentine player who decided to go for me, kicking and grabbing at me whenever he could – when I had had enough and hit back, aiming a kick at his shins, a proper fight broke out. That's always how it is when you play Argentina – there's such rivalry. (We still won the match 2–1, I'm pleased to say.)

The day after our game against Argentina in Rio, I had to be in Porto Alegre to play for Santos against Grêmio. It was always like that while I was in the army: a match here for the barracks on one day; a match there for Santos the next. It was exhausting.

But despite the relentlessness and the hard physical work I learned some valuable lessons during my career as Private Pelé.

When I was sent off in the Argentina match Colonel Osman said, 'You have to be able to control your temper. I know the Argentinian kept kicking you, but it's best to beat your opponent with technique.' In the army I learned the importance of discipline, and of appreciating how much my country means to me.

✯

The World Cup victory helped me financially. I was able to renew my contract with Santos for more money, which helped me buy the family home in Bauru outright. My parents could stop worrying about paying the rent. The World Cup also helped the club financially, since now everyone wanted to play us. Brazil had an international reputation for its amazing way of playing football and Santos were seen as its finest proponents. We were in demand – and the suits were very keen to cash in. It meant that we started to tour regularly, usually every six months – to the Americas at the beginning of the year and to Europe in the middle of the year.

The first year of this rollercoaster, 1959, was madness. With all my commitments at club, national and military level I played 103 matches, for five teams: Santos, Brazil, an all-star São Paulo side, the barracks team and the Army team. On nine occasions I played two games within twenty-four hours, and on one occasion I played three in forty-eight hours! A professional player nowadays would never accept a schedule like this. On our first Europe trip we played twenty-two games in only six weeks. It was ridiculous – there was no time to relax; there was barely enough to travel from stadium to stadium.

Still, on that trip we won thirteen matches, drew five and

lost only four. One of our defeats was against Real Madrid, who were considered the best team in Europe at the time. (They won the first five European Cups, from 1956 to 1960.) The match was pitched as a duel to see who could claim the moral title of best team in the world – but it was an unfair challenge. It was our fourteenth game of the tour (in almost as many countries) and we were bruised and drained.

Our second European trip was more enjoyable, mostly because there were fewer fixtures on the schedule and therefore more time to see the sights and recuperate between games, especially on the first leg when I was playing for Brazil. We also visited Egypt, and did touristy things like see the Pyramids and ride on camels. On our way there, though, on a stopover in Beirut, an enormous crowd stormed the airport and threatened to kidnap me unless we agreed to play a match against a Lebanon team. Fortunately the police dealt with it firmly and we flew on to Egypt. Another strange thing happened when we got off the plane at Cairo – the people who were there to meet us did so by kissing us on the lips! I was right behind Djalma Santos and noticed that after receiving his kiss he managed to remain quite composed. I steeled myself and received the kisses totally naturally. Every country has its customs, after all.

Another memory from that trip is when I joined up with Santos for the second leg, and we visited Paris, where I met an actress-model called Kiki. We were never lovers but she showed me all the sights of that beautiful city and we ended up spending a few days together, getting photographed a lot in the process. It shows my naivety then that I thought nothing of it – after all, I knew there was nothing going on between us – but of course the photos were all over the papers back home in Brazil and I heard a lot about it from Rosemeri when we got back. It was another valuable lesson for the future.

One Brazil game I particularly remember from this period after the World Cup was a match against England in May 1959, at the Maracanã. Although it was a friendly, both sides were taking it very seriously – we were up against a strong team we'd been unable to beat in Sweden, and there was a massive crowd in the stadium, many of whom had come specifically to see Garrincha. He wasn't in a good state physically, however, and coach Feola decided to select Julinho instead. When Julinho's name was announced instead of Garrincha's there was a huge boo from the crowd. But I thought to myself, 'Only real star players get booed,' and within ten minutes Julinho had slipped his marker, scoring not only the first goal but setting up the play for the second, which was completed by Flamengo's Henrique Frade. The fans had started to cheer him by now. They had forgotten about Garrincha. With Brazil at this time, we would usually win whatever the opposition.

It was also during this period that I got my one chance to act as referee in a football match. I was invited to preside over a game between Santos and São Paulo referees, at Vila Belmiro, and sent off Olten Ayres de Abreu, who in those days was one of the best-known São Paulo refs – only days earlier, in the Santos–Juventus match, he had shown *me* the red card. It was sweet revenge, and that was a party night for me.

My success for Santos and Brazil would have a mixed effect on my younger brother, Zoca, however. He was a good footballer too, and once I had left home he started playing in midfield for Baquinho's Bauru rivals, Noroeste. Word got about and Santos started to ask me about him. I said he played well, so he did a trial and was given a contract. He moved to Dona

Georgina's and lived with me and the others there. He played for a few years in the reserves, and even got some games for the first team – although never when I was playing too. With a potential career ahead of him, however, he hung up his boots. I can remember asking him why. 'Wherever I play for the reserves I'm always mobbed by reporters – and all they want to know about is you. I'm going to stop now and study to become a lawyer.' Which is exactly what he did.

Playing so many games occasionally took its toll, and in February 1961 I suffered probably the most serious injury of my career so far. We were playing Necaxa in Mexico City. We'd come from a long tour and were all tired and struggling with the altitude. We were losing 2–0, but then we scored. We started to play better, and thought we were in with a chance of nicking the game. There was a high cross to the penalty area – the goalie and I both jumped for it, and I was hit in the face and knocked on the shoulder by the Argentine defender Dalacho. I fell in a faint. When I was brought round by Macedo and Dr Lauro I could tell there was something wrong with my vision. But I wanted to keep playing, so I got to my feet – and promptly fell over again, completely dizzy. We ended up losing a tense game 4–3.

That night I couldn't sleep for the headaches and the pain in my shoulders and across my face. The whole left side of my face was numb. In the morning I was taken to the hospital in Mexico City, where eight X-rays were taken of my face and shoulder. Nothing was broken, thank God. A lot of people from the Mexican press said that I just didn't want to play the other games, that I just wanted to play for Santos in Europe where I could make more money. But I'm someone who has always fulfilled my obligations, I've always wanted to play, just as keenly, with Santos, the national team, in Europe or anywhere in the world.

The injury kept me off the national team for the games against Paraguay and Chile, and I didn't play football for nearly three weeks, one of the longest breaks I would have for years. When I returned, though, I played my part in dramatic victories over Guadalajara, América and Atlas. By March I had made a full recovery. It was then, during a match against Fluminense, that I scored what many consider to be my most spectacular goal. Again, the stage was the Maracanã. I picked up the ball outside our own penalty area and started running with it towards the Fluminense goal. One player came at me to tackle, then another, then a third, a fourth, a fifth, a sixth . . . I just danced around them all before beating the goalkeeper as well. The São Paulo paper *O Esporte* heralded it as the 'most beautiful goal' ever scored in the Maracanã. Because the game wasn't televised, it exists only in the memory of those who saw it. As a way of remembering it, however, the paper had a bronze plaque cast which was mounted at the entrance to the stadium. The goal is known as the '*gol de placa*' – the goal of the plaque – and whenever people in Brazil describe goals now as a '*gol de placa*' they are comparing them to the perfection that I attained that day.

In June of that year I was still getting pains in my shoulder and had to delay travelling out to Europe for another Santos tour because of a medical check-up. When I finally arrived for a game in Basel, Switzerland, the posters announcing the game had a strip added across them, saying, 'Pelé has arrived, and he's playing!' I did play, and what a game it was. We won 8–2. I scored five goals, and Coutinho the other three. What was odd was that after the game the Swiss fans got a bit carried away and stormed the pitch, intending to carry our players aloft, me and Coutinho especially. We ran to the dressing-rooms, and the fans got us confused with two other black players on the team and carried them around instead of us. When they realised their mistake, they put our team-mates down and started shouting in French that it wasn't me – *'Pas Pelé! Pas Pelé!'* Later on in the dressing-room the French journalist François Tebaud said to me, 'Pelé, this is crazy! I've never seen anything like it.' It really was crazy – you can see what the Europeans made of Brazilian football.

I couldn't stop scoring. In one three-week period in September 1961 I scored twenty-three goals in six matches, a statistic that seems unreal even to me. I bagged five against Olympico when we thrashed them 8–0; four against São Paulo four days later; another five against Juventus (of São Paulo, not Turin) in a 10–1 win three days after that; one against Botafogo and then had two four-goal hauls in three days the following week.

On another occasion not long afterwards I was even awarded a goal that wasn't really a goal. It came during a São Paulo championship match against Guarani, of Campinas. At one point I had lobbed two defenders before beating a third and then fired a powerful shot at goal. The ball thundered against the crossbar and then hit the ground before bouncing out. The referee, João Etzel Filho, awarded the goal despite the protests of the Guarani players and fans, who said that it hadn't gone in. Etzel said, 'You know something? It was such a lovely piece of play I'm going to give the goal, whether it went in or not. It's a goal to Pelé, and that's final!'

I was really becoming a national celebrity. Two books came out about my life and I starred in a biopic called *Eu Sou Pelé* ('I Am Pelé'). I was in constant demand – not just in Brazil, but there were also interesting approaches from Europe. One of the directors of Inter Milan sought me out to see whether I'd agree a transfer there. They'd pay 40 million cruzeiros, he said – a real fortune. I didn't accept, and nor were Santos prepared to trade me (the story goes that around this time the Brazilian Congress had me officially declared a 'non-exportable national treasure'). And in Turin, when Santos were playing in the 'Italia '61' championship (which we would eventually win), I was invited to have lunch with Umberto Agnelli, the owner of Fiat and Juventus, the team we were about to play. Also invited was Dr Athiê Jorge Coury, the President of Santos, and a couple of others. At the appointed time we all arrived. Agnelli was elegantly dressed and treated us well, and it wasn't until late in the meal that he casually turned to Dr Athiê and asked, 'Would you be interested in negotiating Pelé's transfer to Juventus?' Athiê nearly choked, and I was stunned! When Athiê had recovered, he replied, 'We don't negotiate for Pelé. He'd be much too expensive—' Agnelli interrupted him, and suggested, 'So how about we start with one million dollars?' You can't imagine what this meant in those days, what a significant sum that was. And as if that wasn't enough, Agnelli then continued, in a very classy way, 'Oh, it's such a lovely day, the sky is blue – let's not spoil it by talking about money . . .' Agnelli's offer didn't stop there; he ended up offering a lot for me to transfer – the equivalent of tens of millions of dollars today – but it never happened (to give you an idea of what his proposal meant, in those days Santos would play abroad for five thousand dollars). But I was keen to stay in Brazil at the time: I was still trying to persuade Rosemeri to marry me – she was still too young, she said, and she probably was – and had also decided to diversify my interests with a view to the future, and make a few investments.

I was earning decent money by now, certainly by Brazilian standards, and my profile had risen to the point where I was able to make extra cash by lending my name to various product endorsements. Others clearly assumed I was raking it in: one day I got a letter from someone in Recife, which read: 'Dear Pelé, I'd like you to buy me a car – brand-new, nothing on the clock – latest model. I'm a taxi-driver, and need to trade my car in.' Can requests like this be for real? It was one of the first, but it would by no means be the last.

Although it was nice to see the money adding up and to be able to help out my parents, I was mindful of the experience of my old team-mate Vasconcelos and his career-shortening injury, and I realised I should start to make the money work a bit harder. I asked a few people at Santos I was close to and decided to put some money into a business venture with Zito and a Spaniard called José Gonzáles, known as 'Pepe Gordo' (Fat Pepe), who was involved in a company called Sanitária Santista, which supplied building materials. I liked him immediately, and even gave him power of attorney over my financial affairs. Rashly, as it turned out – but it would be another couple of years before that particular chicken returned home to roost.

✯

In the more immediate future there was the 1962 World Cup in Chile. Brazil would start the tournament not only as holders but as favourites to retain the trophy. In the run-up to the finals we followed much the same strategy as in 1958. Feola had fallen ill so we had a new coach in Aymoré Moreira, but the back-room staff and much of the team were the same. Gilmar, Djalma Santos, Nilton Santos, Didi, Garrincha, Zito, Zagallo, Vavá and

I were all still there. My Santos team-mates Mauro, at centre-half, and Coutinho were also in the squad.

The head of the delegation, Dr Paulo Machado de Carvalho, wanted our preparation for 1962 to mirror that of 1958 as much as possible in the hope of replicating our victory. He took this to some interesting extremes, even arranging for the pilot of the Panair do Brazil aeroplane that had flown us to Sweden, Captain Bugner, to take us to Santiago. And although the Captain was now working for Varig, which had taken over Panair's routes when that airline had folded, one of the turbine engines on our plane in 1962 carried the Panair logo. How did the turbine get there? Dr Paulo wanted *everything* to be just like 1958. He was a truly superstitious man, and since the 1958 win had worn only brown suits, for luck. The only thing he wasn't able to guarantee about the flight was good weather, and as we were crossing the Andes there was a lot of turbulence. Most of the players were freaking out. But turbulence has never bothered me. I believe in God – if we are going to die, then so be it. What's the point of getting scared? I just pray and switch off. The others were going crazy, saying that I was crazy. 'Don't you have family?' they shrieked. 'What do you want me to do?' I replied, staying calm in my seat. The turbulence didn't last long. It had happened as we were about to eat and soon we were all joking about how our steaks had moved to other people's plates.

The most significant moment of 1962 for me, however, was the groin strain that was caused by the excessive number of games I played. Although I was young, I started feeling twinges in the adductor muscle, and was in some discomfort after a friendly against Portugal. I talked to Dr Hilton Gosling, the team doctor, and Mario Américo about the 'tiny little bit of pain' I was feeling, but they thought nothing of it – I'd have to keep playing. And on top of that there was the tough physical training, from which nobody was excused. Our trainer, Paulo Amaral, always used to say, 'Everyone has to take part in training.' If anyone from the Technical Commission tried to interfere in his programme, Paulo would just say, 'I know what I'm doing. I don't want anyone else to meddle in my work – which is why I don't meddle in theirs!' Paulo's relationship to the players became quite complicated; on one occasion Nilton Santos refused to jump a hurdle, and when he was reprimanded he replied, 'I'm not in Chile for an athletics championship . . .' As in 1958, it looked like an injury might dictate how many games I played. But for now I kept my anxieties to myself.

We had been drawn in Group 3, alongside Mexico, Czechoslovakia and Spain, and would play our matches in the small but pretty new Sausalito stadium by the sea at Viña del Mar. We were expected to qualify easily from this group, but actually our first match, on 30 May 1962, was surprisingly tough. Mexico were brave and organised, and we had to revert from 4–2–4 to 4–3–3. It worked, though, and in the second half we played better and put two past them, first a header by Zagallo from my cross, and then I scored myself. It was a goal I really enjoyed, taking the ball past four defenders before beating the great Mexican keeper, Carbajal, with a powerful shot.

The first game may have been safely negotiated but I was in trouble. I walked off the pitch feeling unusually tired, really weary in my bones, and I knew I had to go and see Dr Gosling. He made me promise I'd keep him informed about how it felt, and I did, but in truth I was terrified he'd put me on the bench and so I kept the real extent of my worries to myself.

A few days later, on 2 June, we played Czechoslovakia. I was desperate to get through the ninety minutes and to play well – it was a game we had to win or draw to have any chance of progressing to the knock-out stages. We knew they marked well, so we were told to try to shoot from middle distance. I started off well enough, ignoring the pain in my groin, but disaster struck after only twenty-five minutes. I took a pass from Garrincha and set off downfield, dribbling past several defenders before giving the ball a real hammering towards goal. It hit the post and rebounded at real pace; I was ready for it, though, and tried to hit it again. But this time something went – I felt something shift deep within me, the kind of internal movement you know shouldn't really be happening, and I crumpled to the ground pulling my leg up to my chest to ease the pain.

Mario Américo rushed on to the pitch, concern in his eyes. The score was 0–0, we were only a quarter of the way through the match, and we would be in trouble if I had to go off – there were no substitutes allowed in those days. I gritted my teeth and told him I was okay to continue, feeling anything but. I knew I was in real danger of missing the rest of the World Cup, and yet I still had to hobble through the rest of this match – probably getting clattered at every turn by what was a very tough and physical Czech side.

But then something remarkable happened – I didn't have a miraculous recovery or anything like that, but I felt as though I was handed a lifeline by the generosity and spirit of the Czech players, three of them in particular. They could see I was suffering, but rather than exploiting that weakness and potentially going in for 'the kill' – seeing me off the pitch certainly for the rest of the game, perhaps even permanently – they chose just to gently neutralise me. When Masopust and Popluhar saw me with the ball they'd let me finish my play, as long as it didn't put them under any threat: they didn't put pressure on me, didn't try to take it off me. The right-back, Lala, was the same – when I started just making up the numbers on the left side, he made it easier for me to move. That's the definition of fair play, as far as I am concerned – after all, the Czechs were fighting for the title too, they also needed to win – but they put the longer-term prospects of an injured opponent first. That experience with the Czech players was really moving, and one of the revelations of the 1962 Cup that I'm most grateful for.

The match ended in a goalless draw. By the time we reached the training camp just outside the centre of Viña del Mar after the game, I could hardly walk. I still hoped I'd get better within the week and would be able to get back on the team. It was the first severe muscle-strain of my career, and this – coupled with the fact that I was still young – would make Dr Gosling's work easier, although after examining me, he said darkly, 'I don't think there's any way you'll be playing a further part in this World Cup.' But being young, I was sure I could defy his diagnosis, just as I had in 1958.

Garrincha stayed with me the whole time I was hurt, and he used to say, 'You're not going to abandon me, are you? You'll get over this and you'll be playing again soon . . .' A good friend and companion, Garrincha was very upset at my injury, and tried to influence the treatment I was receiving, saying he was going to suggest to the medics that they send me to Pau Grande – his home town – to see a faith-healer, a woman in whom he had great confidence and who – he always claimed – performed genuine 'miracles'. There was also a rumour going round about Garrincha and me concerning Elza Soares, a famous and very beautiful Brazilian samba singer. She had been introduced to me in Chile by one of the directors of the delegation, since she was in the country to perform. After that she started seeing Garrincha. People joked that he had stolen her from me, but that was never the case, it was just idle gossip.

The next match, the last of the group stages, was against Spain, just four days after the Czech game. The day before the match I found Dr Gosling and begged him: 'Doctor, give me an anaesthetic – I really want to play!' He replied instantly, without hesitation: 'No, I would never do that.' I kept insisting, and he always gave the same reply.

'You have to get treatment – that's the right thing to do. I won't give you an anaesthetic – it could ruin your life! I know this is a World Cup, I know you're a great player – but I'm really not going to do it.'

At the training camp my team-mates tried to cheer me up. 'It's nothing, it'll pass, don't worry . . .' The doctor wasn't optimistic, though, and he was the one who knew best. The treatment was not very sophisticated. I spent five days lying down, with Mario Américo applying his hot towels. I watched our 2–1 win over Spain on television. Amarildo replaced me, and did very well – no sign of any nerves at all. When I thought I was getting better I tried to get up, and found I couldn't even move my legs. I thought that having spent so long lying down had had a detrimental effect on my condition. But three days later I was back on my feet, my leg didn't hurt so much, and my hope of playing in the Cup had returned. Still in the training camp I started practising with a ball; I went slowly, my optimism gradually increasing . . . The days went on, the treatment continued, and the Cup did too.

On the 10th we played England in the quarter-final, and won 3–1. Garrincha was outstanding, he took them apart, even though in Moore, Greaves and Charlton they had the makings of a team that would lift the trophy four years later. And then, three days after that, the semi-final against the hosts, Chile. I watched this one from the stands, confident that at least I was making some progress with the treatment and if we won, I was adamant I would play in the final.

Again it was Garrincha's game. He was in a different league. He demonstrated his great talent, giving everything to the team, he was the leader, he scored goals, and his dribbling was amazing. Garrincha owned that 1962 World Cup. It was a pity that, after bossing the match and scoring two terrific goals, he got tired of being hacked down by the Chilean players and retaliated to one onslaught, getting sent off for his trouble. Worse, as he walked off around the touchline, some thug chucked a bottle at him, hitting him on the head and causing a cut that needed stitches. But we'd won – Vavá added two goals of his own and we were through to our second successive World Cup Final.

Our opponents would be Czechoslovakia, the team we'd been playing when I had the injury. They'd beaten Yugoslavia 3–1 in their own semi-final, against the form-book. I went to do one final trial, with a ball and in my boots, with my team-mates. I hardly felt any pain. I said I was fine, and could do the session. I so wanted to play in the final . . .

I went to take a corner – Paulo Amaral was right beside me – but as I went to take the kick I felt that familiar lightning-flash of pain through my groin. Never have I felt such pain . . . And I knew then that there was no way I would play. It was hard even to walk.

It's difficult now to describe the devastation I felt, the disillusionment. I cried so much, and not just because I was in agony. It seemed so unfair, after turning up to games day in, day out for my club, army and country, here I was sidelined before the second biggest game of my life.

I was inconsolable, and asked the team management to let me go home to lick my wounds. But they made me see that I was more use to the morale of the team in Chile than I would be in Brazil. Dr Paulo said to me, 'If we keep talking about the possibility that you might be able to play in the final, this will be one more thing for our opponents to worry about. They'll have to change their strategies at the eleventh hour, as they won't know our line-up till we're in the stadium at the last possible moment . . .' I could see that he and the rest of the management team were right.

I couldn't refuse. Even though I didn't play I was always involved, I took part in all the team talks and made my voice heard. I tried to encourage the team as they prepared to win the World Cup for a second time. It wasn't easy watching it all from the stands, watching from a seat like just any other spectator, while my team-mates were out there fighting for the title that was mine too. I suffered a lot, going crazy just watching without being able to do anything. In the final, the Czechs were, again, very sporting players. The Brazilian team for the final was made up of Gilmar, Djalma Santos, Mauro, Zózimo and Nilton Santos, Zito and Didi, Garrincha, Vavá, Amarildo and Zagallo. Though four years older, they played with the same passion, the same desire to win as they had in 1958, to keep the Jules Rimet for ourselves. Brazil won 3–1, with Amarildo – my replacement – equalising after an early Czech goal. Was this the new Pelé? Despite my delight at the team's win, I couldn't help being plagued with doubts about my place in the side, my future as a player.

Once we had won we all piled into the changing rooms to celebrate. And Elza Soares was there too – I think it was the first time that a woman had ever been to a place like that. At that time there were hardly any women around football. She was there for Garrincha – there was no more gossip about us after that.

✯

At the age of twenty-one I was already a personality known across the globe. But I never forgot my origins and everything I'd learned at home, rules which have remained very useful to me. I should be polite and kind to everybody. I should be honest and responsible. I should always be humble, and I should work hard, totally devoted to what I was doing. I'm grateful for the discipline my family gave me. For all the prizes, receptions, the honours and the glory I've received, I'd like to think my basic character hasn't changed, and it was this that helped me get over the problems I faced in the 1962 World Cup.

The experience in Chile allowed me to reflect on my life. My family, my friends and team-mates from Santos would be important in helping me in my recovery. Everyone was very supportive in Chile, and when I got home the Brazilian people didn't let me down either. Shortly afterwards, once I had recovered, Santos made the final of the Libertadores Cup. The competition is the South American equivalent of the European Cup. It was founded in 1960 and the first two titles were won by Peñarol, from Uruguay. They were also our opposition in 1962. I wasn't able to play in the first two legs but I was back for the play-off, which took place in Buenos Aires. I scored two goals in our 3–0 victory. I remember that the Argentinian fans invaded the pitch after the final whistle and ripped off all my clothes – including my shorts! It was a great moment, since the victory meant that we were the first Brazilian club to win the trophy.

It also qualified us to play against Benfica, the European champions, in the Intercontinental Club Cup. The Portuguese team had the great Eusébio, who was playing at the peak of his powers. Santos chose to have the home leg at the Maracanã, rather than at the Vila Belmiro, because on a bigger pitch the game would flow better and we knew we could rely on the cheers of the Rio crowds. Again, the Maracanã was a stage for a great personal performance. I opened the scoring with an opportunistic goalmouth tap-in off a defender. Coutinho got a second and I got a third, but Benfica were tenacious and the game ended 3–2. It was enough to give them hope for the return game.

When we arrived in Lisbon, we realised that Benfica were so confident of beating us they were already talking about selling tickets for a play-off game. They had banners done up saying 'Benfica: World Champions'. This really wound us up and helped us put in one of the best Santos performances ever. The match was the best game of my career.

Not long after the start Pepe crossed the ball to me from the left and I knocked it in. My next goal was a delight. I dribbled past five players and shot cleanly into the top right of the net. Even the Benfica fans were cheering. In the second half I again dribbled past three players and passed precisely to Coutinho for our third. It really felt like a gala performance – no one could stop me. I scored another two, to put us 5–0 up, and even though Benfica got two late consolation goals Santos were world club champions. It was an amazing performance, a piece of footballing art I'll never forget.

After the disappointment of Chile, it was like starting a new life.

5

Target Man

'I sometimes feel that the game of football was invented for this magical player'

BOBBY CHARLTON

Footballers returning from World Cups nowadays return home to lives of privilege and luxury that were unthinkable to us back then. It's funny to think that, going back to Santos after Chile in 1962, I was still living at Dona Georgina's place with Zoca and a bunch of team-mates. On a day-to-day level, life was pretty much as it had always been.

On the pitch, however, there was a change in how I was regarded. Instead of the young upstart, an intriguing novelty, as a world champion for club and country I was now the man to beat. In 1963 I played more than fifty matches abroad for Santos. The flurry of invitations didn't come about just because coaches wanted the chance to admire our style, our rhythm, our creativity. They also wanted to know how to hold us back, whether we had any weaknesses and if so, where they were; they wanted to know how to target individual players to make them less effective, to use fouls if necessary, even a certain amount of violence. Many coaches told their players to play 'forcefully' against us, and the art of football was certainly harmed by this. Defenders were ordered to man-mark me wherever I was – and this got to absurd levels. I can remember moments when I had to go off the pitch to tie my laces or something, and there by my side would be the defender, hands on hips, supervising me as I crouched down.

At home, our opponents gave no quarter, either. As well as the physical challenge there was the psychological one, too – players always tried to wind each other up to get a reaction, or put you off your game. Yet I was no shrinking violet. I'll never forget a match against Vasco da Gama at the Maracanã in February 1963. Vasco were winning 2–0, with very little time left on the clock, and Fontana and Brito started jeering at me. 'Where's the so-called King?' Fontana mocked. Brito chipped in too, calling out, 'Where's the Santos striker? Have they got one?' It got worse and worse. I scored a goal, but still they didn't stop the taunting – they were so sure their victory was guaranteed. But in the closing moments of the game I scored the goal that gave us the draw. I retrieved the ball from the back of the net, jogged over to Fontana and handed it to him, saying, 'Here – take this back to your mother. It's a present from the King.'

Each country has its own playing style, its own footballing character – we certainly had ours, although of course it was developing and evolving all the time. Brazilians generally based their playing on ball-control, on delicate touches, with passes driving the team up-field, creating an attacking style of play that was both extremely effective and attractive to watch. The Argentinians had some similar characteristics but were more physical. They are our eternal rivals so matches against them were always difficult. One of the toughest games of that era was Santos' second consecutive Libertadores Cup final, in 1963. The game was against Boca Juniors at their home ground, La Bonbonera, in Buenos Aires. It's an intimidating and claustrophobic stadium for visitors because the spectators are so close

The start of it all: one of the balls I made out of socks for my boyhood kickabouts in Bauru.

1

2

A family meal with my mother and father, Dona Celeste and João Ramos do Nascimento (known as Dondinho), and sister Maria Lúcia, in the mid-1950s.

3

My first proper kit for my first proper team, Baquinho, in about 1954. Our coach, Waldemar de Brito, who was responsible for taking me to Santos and so much else besides, is on the extreme right and I am sitting on the floor.

Learning the ropes at Santos. The player I am tussling with is Mario Zagallo, then of Botafogo, who I would play alongside in the World Cups of 1958 and 1962, and who would coach Brazil to victory in 1970.

4

Having been selected to represent Brazil in the 1958 World Cup I then had to endure the agony of not being able to play in the opening matches because of an injury. Here my old friend Mario Américo works his magic with the hot towels.

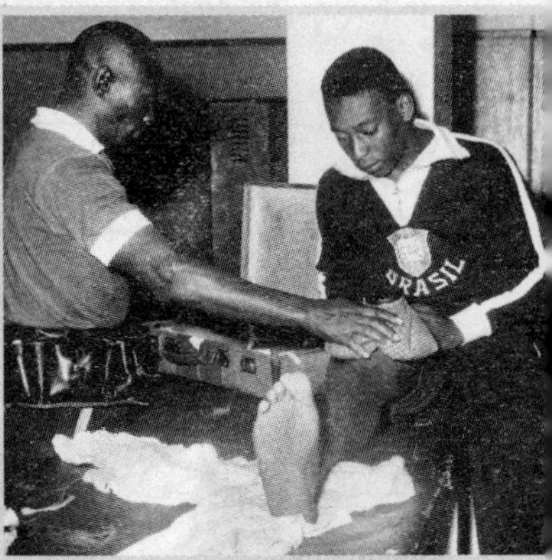

6

At last – my chance to help the cause, and **my first goal in World Cup football**. We played Wales on 19 June 1958 in Gothenburg, and I scored the only goal in our 1–0 win.

7

Airborne: jumping against Svensson, the Swedish goalkeeper, during the 1958 World Cup Final in Stockholm. I scored twice as we ran out 5–2 winners.

8

And here's what it means: crying with joy and relief on Gilmar's shoulder after the final whistle.

A rest from training at Santos, 1960.

Feeling the challenge of Czechoslovakia's Ladislav Novak during our second match of the 1962 World Cup. Despite the Czechs' sportsmanship in not taking unfair advantage of my injury, I would watch the rest of Brazil's campaign from the touchline. 10

I was just as delighted when we won, though – celebrating here with coach Aymoré Moreira. 11

12

The title that salved some of the frustrations of Chile: the Santos captain, Zito, with the Intercontinental Club Cup we won after beating Benfica 5–2 in Lisbon on 11 October 1962. I am on the right, exhausted but jubilant after my hat-trick.

Training in goal: I've always loved playing goalie, and was for many years Santos' reserve keeper.

13

With Garrincha, the 'Little Bird', in his Botafogo kit, August 1963. Although rivals at club level, Brazil never lost a game when we played together in the national side.

 15

The 1966 World Cup was an experience best forgotten, unless you are English! Over-confidence and poor preparation meant that we struggled to qualify for the second round, and had to beat Eusébio's Portugal when we played them at Goodison Park on 19 July 1966.

 16

But we were outplayed, losing 3–1. And I was the target man again, here trudging off injured after being hacked and kicked all afternoon. It was the end of my – and Brazil's – World Cup.

17

Rosemeri and I getting married, 1966 . . .

18

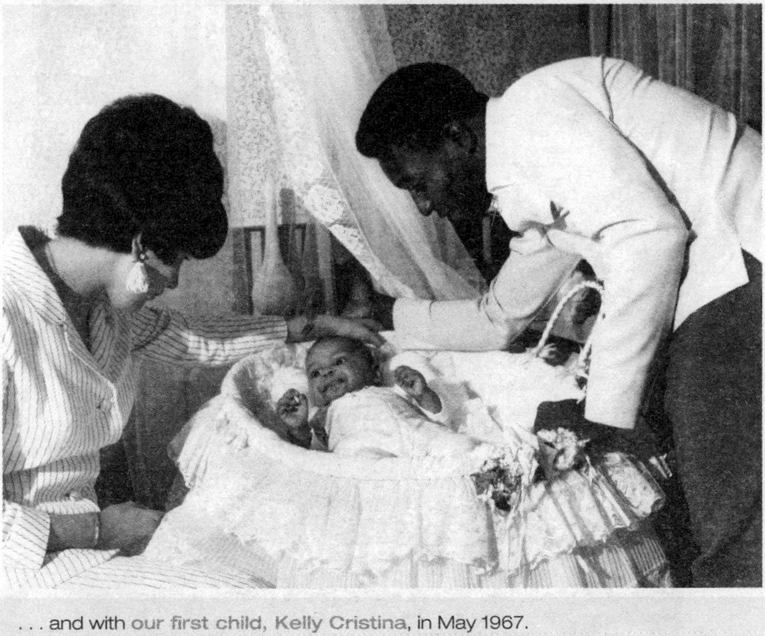

. . . and with our first child, Kelly Cristina, in May 1967.

19

20

21

The much-anticipated 1,000th goal, celebrated at Santos v. Vasco da Gama, Maracanã, 19 November 1969. The Vasco keeper, Andrada, failed to stop my penalty and the burden was lifted.

22

Scoring for Brazil against Czechoslovakia in the 1970 World Cup in Mexico. It was in this match that I tried to chip the goalkeeper from the halfway line.

During the game against England in Guadalajara thieves stole all my team shirts from our training camp, and before the next match against Romania I thought I'd have to ask Bobby Moore for my shirt back, so I would have something to wear.

23

Olé! Celebrating with Jairzinho my opening goal in the 1970 World Cup Final against Italy.

Elation: a hug for Ado, our reserve goalkeeper, after beating Italy 4–1 to become World Champions for the third time. 25

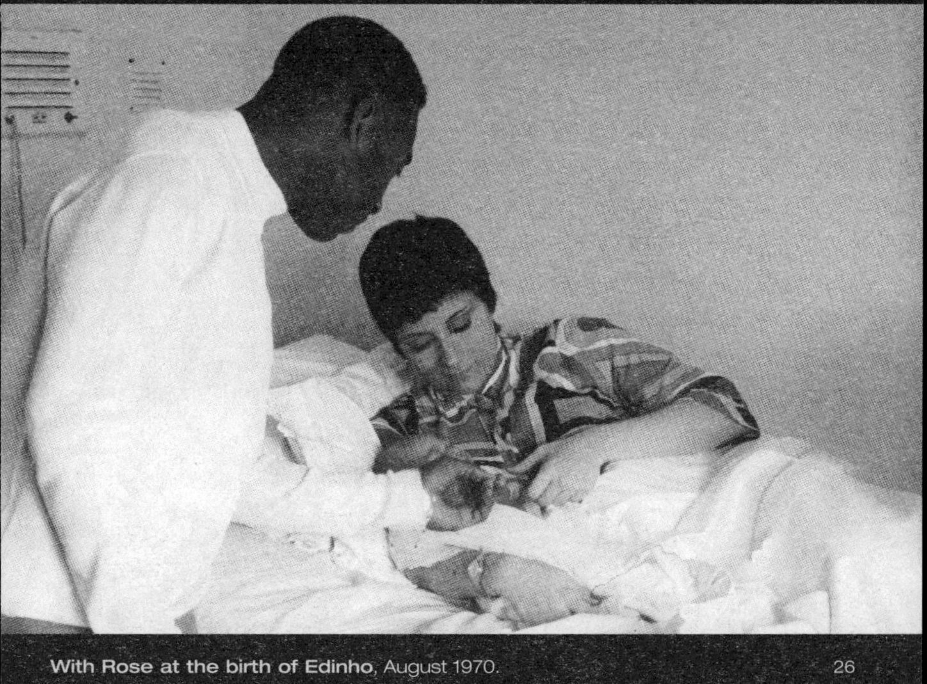

With Rose at the birth of Edinho, August 1970. 26

In full

flight for Santos, 1971.

The first farewell: my final game for Brazil, against Yugoslavia at the Maracanã, 18 July 1971.

to the pitch. And the Boca fans are famously loud and passionate. They chanted *'Macaquitos de Brasil'* at us (Brazilian monkeys) – it got our adrenaline going, but I was never really that bothered by this sort of racist chanting. It happened all the time. We would swear back, and when the whistle blew for full time it always stopped.

In that game, the Argentinians were marking me really hard. There was lots of body contact between the players. I was pushed and shoved and knocked about. In one collision, an Argentinian lunged from behind and ripped my shorts. If that had happened nowadays he would have got a red card, but they didn't exist then. And what was I to do with a ripped pair of shorts? The masseur ran on with a spare pair, and I had to lie down in the middle of the pitch (surrounded by some team-mates to give me a little privacy) and change into them.

The stadium erupted in a roar as Boca went one up, but then I set up Coutinho with a tidy pass to my right and he equalised. The atmosphere was like a war. With only eight minutes to go I scored the winner, receiving a Coutinho pass, dribbling a defender, and then shooting past two others into the left corner of the net. The joy and release of scoring felt like nothing I'd experienced before. I was euphoric. Santos were South American champions again.

This time our European opponents in the Intercontinental club competition were AC Milan. The first game was in Milan, and even though I scored twice we lost 4–2 and I was injured. The final, again, was in the Maracanã. I couldn't play, and neither could Zito, but it showed that Santos were not solely reliant on us. We won 4–2 and in the play-off we won 1–0. Just as Brazil were double World Champions, so too were Santos.

In order to say thank-you to the Rio crowds, who had been

so supportive whenever Santos played international matches at the Maracanã, we decided to have a friendly match against Fluminense. Each Santos player wore the shirt of a different Rio club. I did not wear the shirt of any of the big clubs, since I didn't want to show favouritism; instead I put on the colours of Olaria, a small team from Rio's northern suburbs.

✯

I enjoyed playing abroad. We were always well received and warmly applauded by thousands of fans. It was also an education. We learned more about the European style of play. The English liked their traditional long passes, with lethal crosses aimed at a big centre-forward and ending up with well-placed long or short headers. The style of the Eastern European teams, the Czechs, the Poles and Russians, was closer to the South Americans' – especially the Hungarians, who played beautiful football. Italy always relied on a strong defence, which many people called 'anti-play', but which could produce devastating results in counter-attack. The clubs from Scandinavia, Belgium and Holland demonstrated good collective movement and fine strategy.

As time went on the European sides became much harder to beat. They were physically better prepared, using one-on-one marking as their main form of defence, really overdoing the heavy play. Their coaches had done their homework well. They had spent hours analysing our technique, and devised increasingly brutal strategies to stop us playing our natural game. I remember one time, when I was being marked very closely and roughly, I said to the player marking me: 'Are you going to play cleanly without kicking me, or not? I know how to kick too, you know . . .' Sometimes that worked. It was a way of avoiding getting injured. The Latin players never liked being under pressure from the men marking them, they never liked games of physical domination, which would eventually come to be the prevailing style. Were the coaches to blame? Had they told their players how to contain our skill and technique, with skill and technique of their own? I don't know. I blame the referees, who started to slacken in their interpretation of the rules of the game, allowing rough play to go unpunished.

In the meantime we had to keep abreast of changes in the game too, and in 1964 there was an important development in this area, and one that would prove significant to me personally. Santos hired Professor Julio Mazzei as technical instructor, with a brief to take care of all aspects of the team's physical preparation. It was a coup for Santos to get him – he'd enjoyed three years of success with Palmeiras, in São Paulo, helping them to the Paulista title on one occasion and on two others contesting it with Santos itself. He had studied in the United States and was a cultured, worldly individual, a supremely civilised man. Mazzei's arrival was a revelation for my teammates, for me and for the members of the technical team. Slowly but surely we established a great relationship: player–coach, and friends. Today, nearly forty-five years on, we're like brothers. Mazzei's style changed the way each of us trained. He was a natural teacher, and he also became our adviser for any problems we were experiencing either individually or collectively: he'd sit down, listen, and engage with the issue until a solution was found. He opened our eyes to how we ought to be behaving in hotels, in airports, and during our stays in the many cities we visited.

On one such trip I felt I was able to lay to rest some of the ghosts of 1962. We went back to Chile, to Santiago, in January 1965 and it was there that I played in one of the most exciting games of my career. Our opponents were the Czech national team, the team from the 1962 World Cup – the only difference, it seemed, to the match three years earlier was the fact that I was turning out for Santos rather than Brazil. I remembered how I hadn't been able to play in the World Cup Final against those same Czech players, but now I had the chance to meet them again, and show them what I could do. The National Stadium was packed, and I scored a hat-trick in an action-packed game we won 6–4. The next day the Chilean papers reported that it had been 'the game of their dreams'.

Professor Mazzei helped me with all sorts of things in those first few months after his arrival, not least in recognising that I was no longer a boy, I was now a senior member of both the Santos and Brazil teams and had responsibilities to the game as well as to my family. It was an indication of his influence, either directly or indirectly, that I came to the conclusion that it was time I put my relationship with Rosemeri on a more formal basis. By 1965 we'd been going out together for seven years, and for the last few of those years each time I had raised the subject of marriage she had said it was too soon, she was too young. One day we sat down and had a serious talk – again she said we should wait a bit longer, but this time I was adamant. I was due to see her father the following weekend to go fishing, and I told Rose I was going to ask permission to marry her.

I was pretty confident he would give us his blessing – after all, I had shown my love for her in my patient wooing over the years, and he knew I was making a good living and could provide for her. I was no longer living at Dona Georgina's. After a while living with Pepe Gordo, I was now in my own home –

a big house not far from the beach, a condition of my new contract with Santos. I had in fact just recently moved all my family there. Everyone came – the house was plenty big enough to accommodate us all, and we could have fitted the little house in Bauru into it several times over. With Dona Celeste, Dondinho, uncle Jorge and grandma Ambrosina around me, as well as my brother Zoca and sister Maria Lúcia, it felt right to bring in Rose too, as my wife.

So Rosemeri's father, Guilherme, and I went off in our little fishing boat and I told him I intended to marry his daughter. But instead of beaming with joy and giving me a big hug he just nodded and said, 'We'll see. Let's discuss it with my wife when we get back.' The rest of the day seemed interminable, but eventually we got back to their house and gave Dona Idalina the news. She, at least, seemed happy with the idea, and said she couldn't understand why we had taken so long to get round to it. But we had, eventually, and at last we were engaged.

And one beautiful day a few months later, during Carnival week in 1966, Rose and I got married. It was a simple ceremony, with just a few friends – my family and Rose's, our wedding godparents. She took my name – Nascimento – after her own, Cholbi.

There had been a lot of speculation in the press in the run-up to the wedding, almost all of it nonsense. One report had it that we were going to be married by the Pope himself (although we did meet him on our honeymoon), another that we had invited so many people that we'd had to hire the Pacaembu stadium as the venue for the ceremony. (I actually said to Rose that if we *had* invited all the people who'd wanted to come, we'd have needed the Maracanã . . .). It was understandable that there was a lot of interest, but some of the attention went too far, and I was deeply offended by some articles expressing disapproval that I, a black man, was marrying a white woman. Race had never been an issue for Rose and me – we were just two people in love – and it shocked me to think that there were journalists out there making a living by commenting on it.

Crowds of people turned up when word got out that we were holding the ceremony at home, but eventually things calmed down enough for Rose and I to escape and start our honeymoon. This was to be a trip to Europe courtesy of a wealthy German businessman called Roland Endler, who was a big fan of Santos, and of mine, and followed the team whenever he could – later, he would even be elected Emeritus member of the club. He insisted I allow him to pay for our holiday and is a hard man to deny, so Rose and I duly headed off to Europe, staying first with Roland in Germany for a few days. The generosity we experienced there was boundless – in all the shops we went in to, whenever I was about to pay for whatever it was we wanted to buy, the interpreter would say there was no need to pay, that I should consider it a wedding present. It got to the point where we didn't go into any shops in case they thought we were trying to take advantage of them. There were all sorts of things I wasn't able to bring back to Brazil – even a car. It wasn't until I spent time there that I realised how emotional Germans can be, and how much they like Brazil.

We then moved on to France and Switzerland, and then to Austria, where we were afforded the honour of a second wedding ceremony conducted by the mayor of Vienna. And then we had a trip to Italy, during which we had the great thrill of being received at the Vatican by Pope Paul VI, something Rose had always dreamed of doing.

We returned to Santos exhausted but happy. It felt like all the pieces of my life were in place – Rose and I had our own smart apartment; my parents were safely ensconced in the big house nearby; I was playing well, both for club and country. The only blemish on this rosy picture was represented by the enigmatic figure of Pepe Gordo, the businessman with whom I had invested a few years earlier. He had been a controversial presence at our wedding, where he had acted as my 'godfather', akin to a best man, a service I had asked him to perform not long after I had got to know him and entrusted him with my power-of-attorney. At that time he seemed just the sort of man you would have as a wedding godfather, but things had changed. And how.

It all came to light a few months before the wedding, when Pepe Gordo came and asked me for money. Since I had handed over most of my business affairs to him, I didn't really understand why he was coming to me for money, and told him to just go to the bank. It turned out that some of the investments he'd been making with my money, and in particular the building materials business, Sanitária Santista, had turned out badly. I had had such faith in him that I had taken my eye off the ball, to be honest, so it was a complete shock when, after a bit more digging and prodding, Pepe Gordo confessed that the Pelé coffers were more or less empty. All that hard-earned money, the gradually increasing contracts, the win bonuses, the endorsement fees – all of it had been frittered away. And not only had several hundred thousand dollars of my capital gone, it transpired I owed a load of money as well – and the creditors were now knocking on the door.

I had been really stupid. Not least because there had been warning signs – Rose had never trusted him, she had repeatedly said the business wasn't doing as well as it should, but I had ignored her. And even Zito, the team-mate I'd gone into business with in the first place, had long since pulled out, citing differences of opinion with Pepe Gordo. I had been blinded by the trust I had put in him – another example of naïvety, I suppose, a trait I was having to learn how to shed pretty quickly. That's always been my problem: I trust people too much. A further audit of my accounts and various interests – property and so on – revealed that even if I got rid of all my assets I would still owe money. Filing for bankruptcy was suggested, but I was appalled by this idea. Not just out of pride – I knew that it would look bad. Everyone assumed I was very rich – and I should have been – so to claim bankruptcy would just look very odd, and there were those who might assume I had some nefarious motive. No, I vowed, I would never claim to be bankrupt.

The only option, it seemed, was to borrow money to pay off my immediate debts, and then to work as hard as I could to restore my assets. I put my case before the board of directors at Santos FC, and they offered to put up the cash if I signed a new contract on very favourable terms to the club. I had no choice but to accept. I had been at Santos nearly a decade, I was their most famous player, and yet I was not even the highest-paid member of the squad. At least it kept a lid on the severe embarrassment of Pepe Gordo's spectacular mishandling of my affairs. I cancelled the power-of-attorney immediately, of course, and swore never to assign it to anyone else. There was no evidence of any criminal activity on his part, and although I was furious with him I felt I had to follow through on my earlier request for him to act as my wedding godfather. Rose couldn't believe it, and asked me to withdraw the invitation, but I didn't. Perhaps

I should have, but anyway, there he was at the wedding, the ghost at the feast.

*

In the run-up to the 1966 World Cup in England everyone was still obsessing about our victories in 1958 and '62. *Everyone* – supporters, journalists, managers, players even – was still talking about the titles Brazil had won in Sweden and Chile. We were thinking about the possibilities of being *thrice* champions now, and of winning the Jules Rimet trophy for good. The whole country was buzzing with the possibility. There wasn't a soul who was not touched by this exaggerated optimism. As far as the directors were concerned, we were just going over there to fetch the cup, take it around to show the other countries, and then bring it home. Everyone thought we'd win with ease. But our preparations were not planned with the same humility as in 1958 or 1962. We were already starting to lose the title before we even set foot in England.

Since 1958 a number of good new players had emerged in Brazil. But you don't just replace players like Didi and Garrincha, Gilmar and Mauro or Nilton Santos without thinking about it long and hard. The selection process ended up being a fudge, with too many players making the cut to begin training – there were more than forty names on the list, half of whom wouldn't end up making the trip to Europe. And this time being overseas was no obstacle: Amarildo and Jaír da Costa, who'd been among the 1962 champions but were now playing in Italy, ended up coming along. I have a lot of respect for them, I thought they were great players, but we should remember that back in 1962 we hadn't called Orlando over from Argentina, or

Sormani, Altafini and Dino from Italy, great though they all were. (As it turned out, neither took part in the Finals: Jaír da Costa turned up, but clearly wasn't fit enough and didn't play; Amarildo was injured in a pre-tournament friendly in Sweden.) I think that this large number of players and the division of the squad into four teams, and the general over-confidence, all ultimately proved fatal to our chances.

Another complication was that there was no one place set for our training, so we ended up all over the country – Três Rios, Belo Horizonte, Caxambu, São Paulo, Niterói, Rio and other places too. It's not easy putting together a team, looking after them, preparing them well; harder still to prepare *four* teams with so many players. And that's what happened: we left Brazil with no main team; there was nothing holding the group together. There was even a certain amount of animosity, for which some of the directors were responsible. Vicente Feola had returned to the management of the team but seemed a shadow of his former self, with little of the authority of 1958; and Dr Paulo Machado de Carvalho had stepped down as head of the delegation. His replacement, Carlos Nascimento, didn't see eye to eye with Feola on team selection, or anything else for that matter. He would even come to the senior players to ask us to mediate, which put us in a very awkward position.

We had a new trainer, too, in Bruno Hermany, although Paulo Amaral was still around as a member of the management team and could not resist sticking his oar in. Paulo wasn't a great collaborator, it must be said, and instead of advising Bruno Hermany it seemed to me he was undermining him. He should have told young Bruno how you prepare a team, what training is required – but as it turned out the training was all wrong and the team wasn't as prepared as it should have been.

So there were lots of misunderstandings, a lot of friction and uncertainty, and even when a good team of eleven players was picked for the pre-tournament friendlies it wouldn't necessarily be kept on for the subsequent match. The management would ring the changes for no apparent reason and throw different players into the mix seemingly for the hell of it. The same team never played together twice, and after they dropped Carlos Alberto, a new team-mate at Santos, and Djalma Dias, things just got worse. They were players who were in excellent shape, and could have been really useful to us. We'd all assumed that once we left Brazil the Technical Commission would confirm the final number of players, but even that never happened. Several players came with us just so their observation could continue! The whole thing was really unsettling.

One friendly we had before the tournament began summed up our predicament. We played Scotland at Hampden Park at the end of June with a forward line consisting of me, Gerson, Jairzinho and Servílio. I thought it was a really good front four, and we played well although we drew the match 1–1. The Brazil goal was scored by Servílio, who was technically very good and with whom Gerson and I got on very well. But after the match Servílio was dropped without warning or explanation and sent home. The same thing happened to Valdir, the goalkeeper. It was baffling.

By now the players had no faith in the squad, still less in the Technical Commission. All they thought about was getting an easy win, they never thought about the team itself. When we were all together you could tell that the directors were ill at ease – even more than the players. There were so many mistakes in the lead-up to the Cup, we could easily not have won any matches at all . . . All that coming and going, the training sessions, the matches, the change of climate and food, the lack of adequate preparation, the directors' over-confidence – all this led to what happened in England – total, shameful failure.

✯

There was something else not quite right when we landed in England. The cars were driving on the wrong side of the road. We all thought this was terribly odd. We used to laugh about it a lot. In fact, whenever the Brazilian team was together, in all the World Cups, we had a lot of fun on a personal level. In 1966 we messed about the whole time – maybe to cover up the more serious problems. Gerson was a real wag, and Jairzinho too. I couldn't speak English properly and would joke about just replying 'Yes, yes, yes, I know, thank you' to whatever anyone said to me.

All our games were at Goodison Park, in Liverpool. Once again Dr Gosling had scouted a good base for us, in Lymm near Warrington. But the facilities couldn't disguise the fact that our preparation was sadly lacking, and the team management incapable of pulling the situation out of the fire. The decision-making generally was poor and impossible to make sense of. There was also a clash of cultures. Our delegation, as ever, had imposed strict rules about what we could and couldn't do. It was a World Cup, and that's what we were there for. We had to stay in the hotel, we had to do as we were told. But the 1960s in England was a time of long hair and youthful rebellion. Before the tournament started a journalist told me that the Beatles loved football and they wanted to perform a tribute show for us. I thought it seemed like a good idea, it would be a good way to relax, so I went to speak to Feola and Carlos Nascimento. I'd heard of the Beatles by name, of course, but I hadn't met them. Nascimento, who was of an older generation, was not impressed. He didn't really have a clue who they were. 'What, those hairy kids?' he exclaimed. 'Look, you guys are here to play football, not to play rock'n'roll. I will not allow it.' I was furious.

It wasn't until ten years later that I got to meet John Lennon. I was living in New York, playing for the Cosmos, and I was going for English lessons at the Berlitz school near Central Park. Lennon was studying Japanese at the same school. I would chat with him in the corridor between lessons, we would have lunch together, and once Yoko even came to pick him up. He asked me then if I knew that the Beatles were going to play for the Brazil team in 1966, but it didn't work out. 'I absolutely know!' I said. 'I even asked for permission!' He said that he loved football, that he admired Brazil.

Our first match was against Bulgaria on 12 July. We fielded a good line-up, but one that had never started a match together before – an incredible proposition, when you think about it. Apart from me there were four other 1958 veterans in the team: Gilmar in goal, Djalma Santos and Bellini in defence, and Garrincha. Bellini was back as captain, after only being in the reserves in 1962. Some people wonder why I was never captain of the national team. I may have been an obvious candidate, since – even though I was only twenty-five – I was very experienced and it was my third World Cup. Yet I have always refused this role. I was never captain – not for Santos, not for the Cosmos, not for Brazil. I always used to explain to the Technical Commissions of these teams that as Pelé, I already had the respect of the players, the public and the attention of the referee. If I was captain, then that would mean that one less player would also have influence on the pitch. With another person as captain, there would be two people with authority on the team.

We won 2–0, with the first goal coming from me and the second from Garrincha, one in each half, and both from free kicks. The English press made a big deal of my effort, which they described as a 'banana shot'. Garrincha was not at his very best, though. He had been injured in a motor accident relatively recently, and according to Dr Gosling was still recovering. Still, his swerving shot was superb. The game was actually the last that Garrincha and I ever played together (and by coincidence, the first time we played on the same Brazil side, back in 1958, the opposition had also been Bulgaria). The victory only increased the confidence of our directors. They felt vindicated; they thought this was proof that the brilliance of individuals could decide the outcome of a game. And we did have good players, but we lacked unity, something fundamental in football. The Bulgarians were pretty rough, and during our match against them my leg ached a bit – partly from tiredness, because we hadn't been properly prepared for the match. But partly because I kept getting tripped up and kicked to pieces, especially by Zhechev, who seemed to mistake my ankles for the ball. He didn't stop kicking me, and the referee did nothing to protect me or my team-mates from these rough-house tactics.

In their wisdom the selectors decided I should be protected from similar treatment in the next match, against Hungary, and I was rested. I thought this was a mistake. I didn't say anything, though – after all, I was only a player, but the others agreed with me; it was important to beat Hungary, even if that meant making my injury worse. If we beat them we'd have qualified already, and it wouldn't matter if I played Portugal in the final group match or not. But they thought it would be easy to beat Hungary (I don't know where they got that idea). So in came Tostão for me; and there were other changes as well – Gerson coming in for Denilson, for example, even though they played in different positions.

We ended the first half 1–1; when Tostão scored his equalising goal I thought we'd be able to hold them to a draw. I don't know if that's what the players were told to do; I don't think so. But the Hungarians were playing well, Florian Albert in particular, and took the score up to 3–1, with a great goal from Farkas and then a penalty, as the disorganisation in our defence was exposed. All we'd needed was a draw, and now we had a defeat. With Portugal and Hungary on four points each and Brazil on two, only God could help us qualify now. We'd need a substantial victory against Portugal for it to be at all possible. The Portuguese team, managed by the Brazilian Otto Glória, was strong, with a lot of Benfica players, and their morale was good. The lead-up to the Brazil–Portugal match was very strange, with no one having any idea who was going to play, and the whole team being constantly shuffled around until the very last minute. The selectors were in a complete panic.

I was back on the line-up, even though I wasn't fully fit, helping our desperate attempt to qualify. Gilmar couldn't play, and was replaced in goal by Manga, who was a bag of nerves at the burden of responsibility being placed on him, repeatedly crossing himself as we came out on to the pitch. Djalma Santos, Bellini and Garrincha were all out too, but the veteran Orlando, who hadn't played a World Cup match since 1958, was in.

Manga's nerves got the better of him after just fourteen minutes as he flailed at a cross, weakly punching it straight to Simoes, who headed in. Ten minutes later we were 2–0 down after another header, this time from the great Eusébio. Although Rildo pulled one back for us in the second half Portugal were never really in trouble, and they got their third when Eusébio scored again. We lost, 3–1, and were out of the Cup.

We'd played like novices, and all because we had been badly prepared. We did as much as we were able to do. All the players faced that match with character and dedication. I hurt my knee in the first half, but there were still no substitutions allowed so I had to stay on, and I received some pretty rough treatment even when the match was dead, especially at the hands (or rather feet) of Morais, who kicked and sniped at me relentlessly. He put me out of the match, in fact, with a vicious double-foul which went inexplicably unpunished by the referee, George McCabe. Either of his two assaults should have earned him a red card, but he stayed on. By the end of the match I was limping and just there to make up the numbers.

But the physical nature of the match doesn't explain our defeat. We just failed.

I was annoyed by everything that happened in 1966. I let my disappointment show and said I wasn't going to play in another World Cup; from then on I'd only play for Santos, and occasionally friendlies with the national squad. And I was devastated not to get the chance to play at Wembley – I never played there, even in a friendly. England went on to lift the trophy, the first time the hosts had done so since 1934, beating West Germany in the final 4–2 after extra time. It was widely regarded as the best World Cup Final for years, in fact, marked by Geoff Hurst's hat-trick and the famous judgement by the Russian linesman, Bakhramov, but we were all too disappointed to pay much attention.

And so we returned, empty-handed. Pride goeth before a fall, it says in the book of Proverbs, and that was never more true than with Brazil in the 1966 World Cup. When we left to fly home our Varig plane was grounded for some time at the airport in London – for technical reasons, we were told, but it turned out that the delay was really to ensure that we'd arrive in Brazil in the middle of the night, in case there was a hostile reception awaiting us. There wasn't. And once we were on the runway at Galeão airport in Rio, the players from São Paulo (myself included) were rushed straight on to another plane. It was like a military campaign, though hardly necessary. But when 1970 came, we'd be able to forget the sadness of 1966.

6

Glory

'I told myself, "He's flesh and blood, just like me." I was wrong'

TARCISIO BURGNICH, ITALIAN DEFENDER, 1970 WORLD CUP FINAL

It took a while to recover from the strains of 1966, both physically and mentally. My legs had taken a battering from the likes of Zhechev and Morais, and I had found the violence and lack of sportsmanship as dispiriting as the weak refereeing that allowed it to go unchecked for so long. My outburst about never playing another World Cup match may have been a reaction to the heat of the moment, but it was genuine enough *in* that moment. The whole competition had lost some of its allure for me.

It ended up being an unsatisfactory year all round, from a football point of view. I scored fewer goals than ever before – although I played fewer games too, because of the injury. But there were some highlights: in particular I remember Santos toured the United States for the first time. Two champion European teams were taking part also, Benfica and Internazionale of Milan. On 21 August 1966 we played Benfica, the backbone of the Portuguese national team, at Randall's Island in New York, where I would later play for the Cosmos. It was a chance to atone for the terrible defeat to Portugal at Goodison Park almost exactly a month earlier, when I'd been injured but had had to stay on the pitch to make up the numbers. We were desperate to show them what we could do, and the crowd was one of the most excited and engaged that I can remember. We won 4–0, with one of the goals from me. Every time we scored there was a huge celebration among the fans, and at one point they stormed the pitch and the police had to restore order before play could resume. It was a thrilling victory.

The final was held in the Yankee Stadium, the 'temple of baseball' which was hosting a football match for the first time. We beat Internazionale 4–1, in front of a then-record football crowd of 44,000 – most of New York's 'Little Italy', it seemed, had turned up. Santos, as ever, was doing its bit to revive the image of Brazilian football.

I also took the opportunity to consolidate some of my finances after the Pepe Gordo business, and set up an office to manage my affairs. In 1966 my friend Pepito – José Fornos Rodrigues – took charge of everything, alongside nine other staff, five lawyers, two economists, a publicist and a secretary. Most of the previous interests had been folded to cut losses, but we had kept a business called Pelé Physiotherapy going, in partnership with Lima, a Santos player who was married to Rose's sister Vera. We also kept Fiolax, a limited company based in Santo André which made rubber parts for car manufacturers, and in which I had a 6 per cent share. It had been Nestor Pacheco from the Banco do Brasil – and a director of Santos – who'd persuaded me to get involved with them. He told me that Fiolax might allow me to recover the money I'd lost in the Sanitária Santista débâcle. My brother Zoca represented me at Fiolax, but that too was destined for trouble. I've earned a lot of money in my lifetime, but the truth is that I never learned how to make my money work for me the way some people do. I was good at football; not so good at business.

But there was cause for great celebration at this time too,

with the birth of our first child in January 1967. All through Rosemeri's pregnancy I had convinced myself that we were going to have a boy – not really because I had a strong preference, or even a hunch. I think my focus on a male child had more to do with my anxiety about what he would do when he grew up, and the fact that he would be so much more likely to be compared to me than a daughter. I had no reason to worry on that score, though (at least, not yet!), as Rose safely delivered a beautiful baby girl we called Kelly Cristina.

Fatherhood was a revelation to me, and did so much to cure my disaffection with football and with the constant pressures of touring and playing. Even after the most desultory game or humiliating defeat it was such a tonic to return home and play with my baby daughter, whose sunny smile at her father knew nothing of the pressures and frustrations of the adult world. It was impossible not to shrug off those pressures when I was around her, and it really helped me rediscover my love of the game.

Another event that caused me to consider my own sense of identity and place in the world came a few months later, when I travelled to sub-Saharan Africa for the first time. Santos still went on as many foreign trips as possible, and had started to go further and further afield. In May we flew off to play Senegal, Gabon, Congo and the Ivory Coast. It was an experience that changed not just my view of the world, but of how the world viewed me. The interest in the team and in me was extraordinary – tens of thousands of people at matches, and at the airports when we arrived, and lining the streets wherever we went. Often the country we were visiting had to deploy soldiers just to keep the crowds under control – everyone in Africa, it seemed, wanted to see us, touch us, almost as if they wanted to make sure we were real.

As a black man who grew up in Brazil, I am the descendant of Africans brought over as slaves. Slavery is not too far in the past – I am only the third generation in my family that was born free. My grandmother Ambrosina, who died aged ninety-seven in 1976, was the first generation – her parents were slaves. In Brazil slavery was only abolished in 1888, the last country in the Americas to ban this evil practice.

Journalists have tried to trace my genealogy. There are two versions – one that my ancestors came from Angola, the other that they came from Nigeria. Apparently Nascimento was the name of the owner of the plantation where the first of my ancestors to come to Brazil worked.

The experience of being black in Brazil is sometimes hard to explain. All the races are mixed together – everyone has some black, or indigenous Indian or European or whatever. In Brazil there were many, many slaves, but after abolition there was never anything like apartheid or segregation, so we have no fault-line between races like in South Africa or the US. I've experienced very little prejudice because of the colour of my skin, and I have never judged anyone because of it. My first girlfriend was Japanese, then there was the Swedish girl, and my children are mixed-race. Of course racism exists in Brazil, but I was fortunate to become both famous and wealthy at a young age, and people treat you differently when you have money and celebrity. It is almost like a race apart – not black or white, but famous.

Being in Africa was a simultaneously humbling and gratifying experience for me. I could sense the hope the Africans derived from seeing a black man who had been so successful in the world. I could also sense their pride in my own pride that this was the land of my forefathers. It was a realisation for me that I had become famous on several different levels – I was now known as a footballer even by people who didn't really follow football. And here in Africa, as well as that, I was a world-famous *black man*, and that meant something different still.

Ironically it was in Africa that I did experience the strange blindness of racial prejudice. We were checking into a hotel in Dakar in Senegal, and there was the by-now customary crowd of people straining to get a glimpse of me through the lobby door. The woman behind reception, who was white, took one look at the mêlée and imperiously instructed a black policeman who was accompanying us to move the 'savages' away from her hotel. To his enormous credit, rather than obeying this order the policeman promptly arrested *her*. Because I was famous I must have come to inhabit a different area of classification in her head, but I identified with the people she had insulted, and refused to intervene when her boss asked me to help get her out of jail.

In the game against Senegal, I scored a goal. Nothing unusual about that! But there was something that sticks in my mind. When I put the ball past the keeper he started to cry. He blubbed and blubbed and blubbed. In fact, he was such an emotional wreck that his coach had to take him off. I know that I was the bane of goalkeepers worldwide, but his reaction still seemed over the top. In the changing room after the match I went to see him to explain that it was just a game of football. He wasn't interested to hear any of my words, though. Later I heard that he was so upset because he had made a wager with his friends: 'That Pelé, huh, he thinks he is so good! I bet you he will not score against me. Any other Santos player, no problem . . . but not him.' I understood then that there would be no cheering him up.

Senegal was a fascinating country, as were all the other places we visited in Africa. The trip had been a fantastic education, and I would always be happy to get the opportunity to return.

On our way back from Africa we stopped to play in Germany and Italy. In Munich we were put up in flats – very nice flats, incidentally – belonging to a Physical Education School, with a football pitch and loads of other facilities, all of us really well looked after. And Santos really did need to stay in a place like that, to let us recover from the five games we'd played in Africa and all the travelling we'd done.

We went into training to prepare for the first match, and recovered well. In one of our last group sessions, however, with many German television reporters and cameras present, Carlos Alberto tackled me roughly, and Zito gave the big defender a dressing-down in pretty forceful language. He thought that the TV cameras were only capturing pictures, but he was wrong – it turned out the sound was being recorded too. That night we went for dinner at the house of the Brazilian consul, and just after we arrived one of the consul's daughters said, 'You were pretty worked up in your training session – it's just as well the Germans don't speak our language!' We didn't know how to react, and were saved by the consul, who said, 'Don't worry about it. You had no way of knowing that the session was being recorded with full sound, and that your quarrels would be broadcast in all their glory all over the German news . . .' We learned our lesson.

✯

As the memory of the disappointments of 1966 receded and I started to enjoy family life more and more, Santos too entered a new golden period. I think 1968 was probably the club's most important year since I had joined. We won all five major competitions we entered, picking up titles in Chile, Argentina, the South American Inter-Club in Brazil, and more. We played in six countries, with a win-to-game ratio that was second to none. The 'footballing machine' was better than ever. Journalists from Brazil and abroad acknowledged that Santos was the greatest team in the world. The players were truly excellent, and the classic Santos strip was respected across the globe. We'd walk out on to the pitch and acknowledge the crowd by bowing to them respectfully. Everything we did was copied, and this was good for the spectacle of football.

It also meant that our value, as what would now be known as a 'brand', was worth more than ever, mine in particular. The fees we got paid to play overseas went up and up, and I was able to take advantage of my growing fame financially. I could now insist that whatever fee Santos received, I would get half, and, finally, I became the best-paid player in the team. I also met a man called Marby Ramundini, who had fingers in lots of pies including television and personality representation, and he said he could help me. Through this connection I did a lot more commercials and endorsement work, and even landed a role in a television soap opera called *Os Estranhos*, which I really enjoyed doing although Rose thought it was crazy to add to my already long list of commitments. And it was Ramundini who had a true understanding of the power the name 'Pelé' now commanded. Soon I had earned enough to bring to an end my obligations to Santos for covering my debts.

Santos were a successful team, for sure, but now also a marked one. We won a lot of games that year but it seemed there were a lot of controversies too. Of all the many footballing tales told about me, often the most ludicrous are the ones that are true. One of my favourite stories happened as we were flying back from the US tour and landed in Bogotá for a game against the Colombian Olympic team. In this game something happened which I'm sure has never happened at any other time in football history.

During the match the referee, Guillermo 'Chato' Velazquez, let a goal stand that blatantly should have been disallowed. It might have been a friendly game, but we still took all our engagements seriously and would get furious if we thought we were being treated unfairly. Lima, my team-mate, went to protest at Chato's decision. The ref was a bit of a fiery character and started to intimidate him physically – and then he sent Lima off. It was an absolute outrage. I was fuming. I didn't hold back – I went up to Chato and continued where Lima had left off. Chato then sent *me* off.

I'm not sure who was more shocked – me or the crowd. He could have sent off anyone, but not the man everyone had come to see. The stadium went crazy. Fans started to throw cushions, papers and other rubbish. There was chaos around the dugouts. Dozens of officials and police with batons came on to the pitch, to protect Chato. The stadium was baying for his blood.

The chants started: 'Pelé! Pelé!' They had paid to see me, and weren't going to let a referee spoil their day. The only solution was the unprecedented decision to send Chato *himself* off. And with the referee sent off, I could be 'un-sent off'. I was readmitted into the game, and everyone was happy. Everyone, apart from Chato, of course.

In the changing-rooms after the match, however, getting ready to go to the airport and go home, we were all in good spirits when some policemen and the local chief of police came in. It seemed Chato had made a complaint, and some of our players – Pepe, Oberdã, Laércio and others – were arrested. It was by now very early in the morning. We talked to the referee, came to an agreement, and headed off to find a hotel. The plane had already left without us, of course – it had other passengers to take.

The next day we were about to board another flight, but now there was some local tax problem that prevented us. Back to the city we went – to a third hotel. Very early the next morning an APSA flight, from the now-defunct Peruvian airline, finally brought us back home to Brazil, where everyone was bemused by the delay. No one was sure what exactly had been going on. But that's what happened. We had been arrested, and released; one more drama in the story of Santos, a team that travelled a lot and didn't want to miss any chance to play.

It was also in this year that another frustration of 1966 was laid to rest. Before that World Cup in England I had had fond imaginings of going up to receive the trophy from the Queen at Wembley – alas, it was to be the great Bobby Moore who had that honour. But in November 1968 I did finally get to meet Elizabeth II, when she was visiting Brazil and came to see an exhibition match at the Maracanã in Rio that had been set up in her honour. They used to call me the King in those days, but I was a king without a crown, and was now facing a *real* queen, which really stretched my imagination! Before this great event, in which I was to play for a São Paulo invitation side, some flunky from the Brazilian foreign ministry came round to make sure I didn't commit any gaffes or breach the etiquette of meeting royalty. He gave a little lecture about the importance of waiting for her to speak, of standing still, of showing deference – basically, the importance of draining any humanity from the simple act of two people meeting each other.

His fussy entreaties made me even more nervous about the presentation to Her Majesty, and when I was waiting for her to come in to the room at the stadium where we would meet before the match, I couldn't remember any of the instructions I'd been given. But I needn't have worried – as soon as she entered, she came straight over with a big smile and just started chatting, saying how pleased she was to meet me, and that her husband Prince Philip was a great admirer of mine. We talked about football and England, and I shared my disappointment at Brazil's poor showing there. She was completely charming. It felt like I had known her for ages, in fact, and I remember concluding that the obsession over protocol said more about the flunkeys who enforced it than it did about the people it was supposed to protect.

✯

In early 1969 we went over to Africa again. It was another extraordinary tour. We first flew into Brazzaville, in Congo, and I remember there were tanks and guns in the street. While we were there I remember the possibility arose of a quick hop to play a match in Nigeria. Yet there was a worrying issue: Nigeria was involved in a civil war with Biafra, an area in the south-east of the country. 'Don't worry,' said our business manager. 'They'll stop the war. It won't be a problem.' I told him he was crazy! All I know is that we went to Nigeria, played a game which we drew 2–2, and then flew out again. It is said that there really was a forty-eight-hour ceasefire in the war, made just for us, and my team-mates remember seeing white flags and posters saying there would be peace just to see Pelé play. Well, I'm not sure that is completely true, but the Nigerians certainly made sure the Biafrans wouldn't invade Lagos when we were there. There was a huge military presence on the streets and we were well protected by the army and police.

That spring and summer, back home in Brazil, I was playing better than ever before, despite the accelerating merry-go-round of life with Santos and Brazil. Nine games in March, six in April and six in May – the pattern was not unusual. In June, although I played only five matches in the month, they were all really tough fixtures: Santos faced Corinthians, winning 3–1, then I played for Brazil against England, the World Champions, and we won 2–1. We faced Palmeiras, São Paulo FC, and on the 24th I was with Santos in Milan playing the powerful Inter for the Cup-Winners' Cup. We won 1–0, but it wasn't easy. Playing so much in just a few days was what my life had become.

In the late summer and autumn of 1969 all the attention started to focus on me reaching a thousand goals, a feat which had never been achieved before (and still hasn't been equalled). It became *the* story of the year. The press – locally and internationally – seemed to talk about nothing else. At each Santos game there were hordes of reporters. By October, I had scored 989, according to the stats of the time. Then I scored four in a game against Portuguesa. I was over the 990 barrier, psychologically within kicking distance of the milestone. At each game the pressure grew, as well as the excitement of the fans and of the journalists in tow.

Two more came a week later against Coritiba, in Curitiba, and the momentum felt that the thousandth goal was only a few matches away. Maybe even in the next match, since I'd scored five in a game a few times before. However, my rate slowed a little. The next game was a nil–nil draw. A week later against Flamengo, I made the scoresheet again with a single goal. Four to go.

The media circus then moved to the north-east of Brazil. In November Santos flew to Recife to play Santa Cruz. I chalked up a brace. With now only two goals to go until the magic number, newspapers moved into a hyped-up state of delirium. It was said that scoring a thousand goals would make me immortal. Nonsense, of course, but I did feel the pressure.

When we flew into João Pessoa, the capital of the small state of Paraiba, where we were due to play the local side Botafogo (no relation to the Rio club), the scenes were incredible. The airport was packed with thousands and thousands of people. They were cheering as if the celebration party had begun already, as if I had already achieved the result. The local politicians made a real song and dance about me. I was given the title Citizen of João Pessoa. They were obviously keen that I score the thousandth goal right there.

Once the match started Santos made it 2–0 quite comfortably. The game was pretty easy and as I was wondering if this was deliberate, the referee awarded us a penalty. The crowd erupted in euphoria and started chanting, 'Pelé! Pelé!' But I was not the team's regular penalty-taker. I have taken a few penalties, evidently, in my career, but neither in the national team nor at Santos was I the first choice. I always say that if I had been, I would have got to a thousand goals much quicker!

In normal circumstances, Carlos Alberto would have taken the kick. But this time he refused. The pressure on me to take it was enormous. My team-mates told me that if I didn't, the crowd would never let us get out the stadium! So I caved in and put the ball on the spot. Whack. My 999th goal. One to go.

The Paraiba fans were ecstatic. It really looked like they

would see what they had been hoping for, when something very bizarre happened. Our goalkeeper, Jair Estevão, collapsed on the floor. He was writhing about in pain, his arms flailing in the air to catch the attention of the ref. He was taken off ill. In those days there were no substitutions. I was always Santos' reserve keeper – so I had to do my duty and I spent the rest of the match in the goal. I kept a clean sheet – although I didn't score again and the local fans did not get what they wanted. (Even though I am not very tall, I was always a good goalkeeper because of my propulsion. For Santos and the national team I was always the reserve keeper. I played four times in goal for Santos and only once, in a friendly, for Brazil. But frequently I used to train with the goalkeepers for both teams.)

I have no recollection of this, but my team-mates now say that before the game the coach had told us, 'If the game gets really easy, the keeper will get injured and Pelé is going in goal.' I don't know if it is true or not, but look what happened. The keeper did get injured. And very theatrically so, I might add! Lots of people speculated that it was deliberate, so I could score my final goal in either Rio or São Paulo – but I did not have that wish. I just wanted to get it over with as soon as possible.

We had one more match in our tour of the Brazilian northeast: against Bahia in Salvador. You cannot imagine the scenes there. There were parades in the streets, it was like it was carnival. Rumour had it that a special Thanksgiving Mass had been arranged, so confident were locals that the goal would be scored here. The stadium was rammed, with a Cup final atmosphere. There were flags and banners and drummers and a huge, contagious excitement.

The weight of expectation was crippling. I couldn't wait to score this damn goal! I had two chances. I hit the woodwork in one. In the second I got the ball near the penalty spot, turned and passed a player and ran to the right of the goal. I shot past the keeper and – from nowhere – a defender lunged and, on the goal line, kicked the ball away. But instead of his fans cheering, the entire stadium started to boo. It was surreal. I don't think that has ever happened before or since – supporters of a team booing one of their own players because he has performed a brilliant save.

The following game was only three days later, against Vasco at the Maracanã. And the stakes were raised once more. The biggest stadium in the world was full to bursting point. The date was 19 November, which is Brazil's National Flag Day. The teams came on holding the flag between them, there was a military band on the pitch and balloons were released into the sky. It was a good day for commemorations.

The majority of the fans in the Maracanã might have wanted to see the goal, but the Vasco players were set on frustrating all of us. They teased me, tapping my head and joking: 'Not today, Crioulo.' They did all they could to stop me scoring. Vasco's keeper, Andrada, an Argentinian, was on formidable form. And then, a cross came to me in a perfect position to head the ball. It looked like it could all be over when Renê, a Vasco player, got there first and headed the ball into his own net. Even that seemed preferable to them than giving me the luxury of scoring.

Something had to give. And it did. I was tripped up as I made a run into the box and the referee awarded a penalty. Despite Vasco's protests the decision stood. This penalty I was going to take.

For the first time in my career I felt nervous. I had never felt a responsibility like this before. I was shaking. I was on my own now. My team-mates left me alone and stood along the centre line of the pitch.

I ran to the spot, seemingly in slow-motion, struck the ball . . .

Before we get there, a slight diversion about the way I took penalties. The art of taking a good penalty is to place the ball exactly where the goalkeeper is not. Goalkeepers try to predict where the penalty-taker will put it, and penalty-takers correspondingly try to outwit them by aiming in the other direction. In 1959, I can remember a training session with the national team where I saw Didi invent a new trick. He ran up to the ball, but just before he kicked it he stopped and instantly looked up to see which way the keeper was moving. In that split second he judged where to kick the ball and, of course, beat the keeper. I thought this was a brilliant idea – slightly on the edge of the rules, because you are supposed to kick the ball before the keeper moves. In reality, the keeper starts to move just before you kick the ball – so by looking up just before you kick it you are already in an advantageous position.

So, even though I credit Didi with the idea, he never used it in an official game. I did. It became known in Brazil as the '*paradinha*', the little stop, because I would always run up to the ball and then stop slightly as I looked up, and then kick. Goalkeepers started complaining that it wasn't fair and in the 1970s FIFA banned the *paradinha*. Now referees are less strict and I've seen players get away with it again.

Back to Santos v. Vasco on 19 November 1969. I ran to the spot, made a *paradinha*, and struck the ball.

Gooooooooal!

I ran straight to the back of the net and picked up the ball and kissed it. The stadium was erupting with firecrackers and cheers. All of a sudden I was surrounded by a huge crowd of journalists and reporters. They put their microphones in my face and I dedicated the goal to the children of Brazil. I said we needed to look after the *criancinhas*, the little children. Then I cried, I was put on someone's shoulders and I held the ball up high. Play stopped for twenty minutes as I did a lap of the pitch. Some Vasco supporters ran up to me and gave me a Vasco shirt with the number 1,000 on it. I thought it was odd, but I had no choice but to put it on there and then.

Why did I mention the *criancinhas*? It was my mum's birthday that day, and so maybe I should have dedicated the goal to her. I don't know why I didn't think of that. But I instantly thought of children. What happened was that I remembered an incident that had taken place in Santos a few months before. I had left training a little early and seen some kids trying to steal a car that was parked near mine. They were small kids, who usually you would pay a few pennies to wash your car. I challenged them as to what they were doing, and they replied that I shouldn't worry, because they were only going to steal cars with São Paulo plates. I said that they weren't going to steal cars from anywhere and told them to scram. I then remember chatting afterwards to a team-mate about these kids, about the problems of growing up in Brazil. I was already worried about kids' education, and that was the first thing that came into my head when I scored the goal.

I think lots of people didn't understand what I was trying to say. I was criticised a bit, people accused me of being a demagogue. Or they thought I was being insincere. But I wasn't bothered by that. I think it is important for people like me to put across messages about education. There will be no future if you don't educate young children. And nowadays, when you look around Brazil and see the inner-city problems we have with the homeless and gangs, they are made up of the kids from back then. Now people say Pelé was right. I am not afraid to speak from my heart.

✯

After the disappointment of 1966, I had retired from the national team. However, when thoughts turned to the 1970 World Cup in Mexico I had a change of heart and – after a two-year gap – decided to play for my country again. There were a number of factors for this volte-face. Santos were playing well and I was maintaining my role as their leading scorer, and this filled me with confidence. More importantly, I decided that I was not going to end my career as a loser. After everything I had achieved, after the buzz of scoring a thousand goals, I was not going to take my leave from the international game under a cloud. I was going to go out on top.

I may have competed in three World Cups already, but in none of them did I take part in every game in the tournament. I was desperate to play a complete tournament. That gave me a lot of focus. I had something to prove. There was also the important motivation of national pride. If we could win Brazil a third championship, then the Jules Rimet trophy would be ours for good.

It helped that there had been important changes to the administration of the national team. The Confederação Brasileira de Desportos (CBD), or Brazilian Sports Confederation, football's governing body in our country, was still run by Dr João Havelange, but the lessons of 1966 had been learned and he was changing the whole Technical Commission. The press, too, seemed to understand what was required this time round, and the general atmosphere in the preparatory period was much more focused, more understanding of the challenge ahead rather than just considering it a foregone conclusion.

Another factor was the venue itself: I had a lot of respect for Mexican football crowds, who'd always treated me and Santos well. Neither the altitude of many of the cities where the games would be played, nor the heat, was a problem to me, although many countries were very critical of the choice of Mexico as hosts.

Despite the new seriousness of purpose, though, there were still things that took us by surprise. In early 1969, for example, with the tournament a year away but still at an important stage of the road to Mexico, João Saldanha replaced Aymoré Moreira as coach. Saldanha was a unique character. He had started out as a journalist who loved football, in particular Botafogo, and he had ended up coaching the club. He was smart and sharp-tongued and he brought a new directness to the job of national coach. At first, his appointment seemed to make sense. The call-ups had been a little bit all over the place and he was very decisive. Straight away he called everyone together and said, 'Santos and Botafogo are the best teams in Brazil. So, the base of the national team will be Santos and Botafogo. That's that, you can say what you like but I'm not changing my mind.'

Saldanha was very entertaining. He was always being funny. He had a lung condition, pulmonary emphysema I think, which meant he could only use one lung. He was a very good swimmer and during training he was always chastising us, saying that he smoked, he drank and he only had one lung, but he was much fitter than any of us. Often he came up to me to give me advice. He had been a journalist and he gave us impromptu media training. He would say, 'Pelé, you have got to learn how to speak. Look, when we go somewhere like Porto Alegre to train, you have got to find out beforehand who the best-known baker is and the name of the local tailor. Then when you give interviews you say you have known the baker since you were a small child and that the tailor makes your dad's suits.' I thought this was funny, but he was absolutely right. Often you get caught by surprise by journalists and you have to say something, you have to invent something there and then.

Saldanha's plain-speaking, hard-man approach, however, started to be a problem. He couldn't take criticism and the relationship between him and his former colleagues in the press deteriorated. He liked a drink and started to behave erratically during call-ups. There was also a story that he had even threatened the Flamengo coach with a gun. One fight he did have, and was bound to lose, was with João Havelange. When he was removed from the job as coach, he told the press that the team was in trouble. He said Gerson had psychological problems, that Leão, the reserve keeper, had short arms, and that I would be kept out of the side because I was short-sighted.

Now, Gerson did not have mental problems – he was the way he was, it was just his personality. Leão sometimes trained badly but of course he didn't have short arms. And what about me? It was ridiculous. In tests it had been shown that I was a tiny bit myopic. But lots of players are a tiny bit myopic, and for me at least it was never a problem. Now I joke that if I wasn't short-sighted I would have scored two thousand goals. The press had a field day, of course, and comments about my eyesight carried on all through the World Cup campaign.

Havelange gave the coach's job to Mario Zagallo, my old

team-mate from the 1958 and 1962 World Cups. The side was more or less chosen, but there were a few changes to be made. Saldanha had said that the base would be Santos and Botafogo, but what about good players from other clubs, like Tostão at Cruzeiro? Zagallo gave Tostão a chance – and then the press started to say that Tostão and Pelé were too similar to play in the same team. They complained that Rivelino and Gerson played in the same position, so should not both be first choices. But Zagallo had his own point of view: 'What this team needs are great players, players who are intelligent. Let's go with that and see where it takes us.'

I had a very good relationship with Zagallo. 'You must understand that I don't insist on playing,' I told him. 'If there's another player who would do better in my position, don't worry about it, just do what you think is right. But I ask one thing of you: be honest with me.' I needn't have worried: Zagallo was a serious, honest, hard-working man who never took part in conspiracies. We were an experienced side, and didn't need to have our wrists slapped or be ranted and raved at. The more senior players, like me, Gerson and Carlos Alberto, were able to go to him and make suggestions about selection, and he would listen, but the theory that the three of us actually chose the team is nonsense – it was all done in an atmosphere of mutual respect and cordiality. 'Any self-respecting boss should never stop listening to his subordinates,' Zagallo would say.

Qualification was straightforward. We played six matches and won them all. I scored six goals, including the goal in the 1–0 victory against Paraguay that assured our trip to Mexico. Our strength was that the core of Saldanha's team had stayed. We had spent about a year and a half playing together and we understood each other perfectly. These days national teams maybe get to be together for a maximum of two months before a World Cup. But we had been playing alongside each other for a long time. I think that is what gave us a great advantage, and what made the 1970 team the best national team that there has ever been.

The preparation was very professional. Zagallo brought technical staff in like Claudio Coutinho and Carlos Alberto Parreira (who later became coach himself, and won the World Cup in 1994). We spent three weeks in Mexico before the tournament started, to acclimatise to the heat. It was brutal, but easier for us than for the Europeans, and we did get used to it more quickly than the management thought we would. Security was tight, though – the Mexican police had had reports that I was a target for kidnapping, and even arrested someone they said was the plot's ringleader, a Venezuelan. From then on the police took more care with the training camps of Brazil and the other teams in our Guadalajara group, England, Czechoslovakia and Romania.

We took advantage of technological developments. Our team shirts were re-designed to prevent the collars accumulating sweat, and each player's kit was made to measure. The research was second to none – so sophisticated, in fact, in its detailed analysis of players' physiology that we were mocked in some quarters, presumably for taking things too seriously. But it *was* serious – over 90 million people back home were counting on us to bring the trophy home. After the disaster of 1966 we would only lose this one by being beaten by a better team, not for lack of preparation or consideration of our tactics.

We had regular team meetings, and I remember speaking in one of the very early ones about our duty, partly as a way of reminding the younger players they were here to do a job, not to lark about. Zagallo, as ever, was very supportive.

Another central factor in our campaign turned out to be prayer. We prayed almost daily throughout the tournament, usually after dinner. It wasn't compulsory, though – we weren't even all Catholics. It all began when I was on the phone to Brazil, and Rose told me that every day the family were getting together to pray for us. I thought it was a wonderful idea, and the idea of getting the group together to pray made me cry. I explained my idea to the players. I first spoke to Rogério and Carlos Alberto. They agreed at once. We talked to Antonio do Passo from the management of the national squad, and he signed up as well. It started with the four of us. Then Tostão and Piazza joined in, and Mario Américo. There were about forty people in the delegation in all, and as the tournament went on almost everyone got together. We found something to pray for every day – the sick, the war in Vietnam, the health of someone who needed our prayers, all sorts of things. We never prayed to win the World Cup title. We asked only that no one get seriously injured, and that we get a little bit of luck. I believe this work was an important factor in uniting us as a team. People's spirits lightened. We lived as a real family, we cultivated mutual respect, abandoned any bitter words. We all got along. With all this, how could we fail?

I've always been religious. I come from a Catholic family, full of faith and always looking for God along my paths through life. When I was a child I wasn't allowed out to play with the other boys unless I went to Mass at the Santa Terezinha church. I had to keep the customs my parents kept; as a child I became religious through these customs. Love for my family and respect for all people gave my life structure and great spiritual strength. God has given me a talent, and I have always felt an obligation to develop it for good things. In Chile in the 1962

World Cup I realised with total clarity that I was just a simple mortal, passing across this earth with a sort of mission. I felt that since we all die we ought to have respect for life, we ought to be useful, and to behave towards others as we'd like them to behave towards us. Everything I am and everything I've done, I owe to God. My faith has helped me along my path. I have respect for all religions who believe in God. I don't mind what their origins are because I believe that all paths lead to God. We must respect our neighbours, their faith and their religion, as long as they don't cause trouble for anyone else.

✯

Our opening game was on 3 June 1970, against Czechoslovakia, in the baking heat of the Jalisco stadium in front of 53,000 people. The first line-up was Félix in goal; our captain, Carlos Alberto; Brito, Piazza, Everaldo; Clodoaldo and Gerson; Jairzinho, Tostão, Rivelino and me: the core eleven of the squad. A lot of people were worried when the part-timer Petras made it 1–0 to Czechoslovakia. For many commentators it merely underlined all the pre-tournament hype about us being a team of attackers with no defence. But I knew our team was good enough to turn the game around, these were not the Czechs of 1962, and I was far from the 'spent force' their coach had claimed I was.

Ten minutes later Rivelino equalised from a low, hard free kick after I had been fouled on the edge of the area, and it was soon after this goal that I nearly, so nearly, added to the score with a long-range effort that has since been shown time and time again on television – a little piece of audacity which would have been all the more beautiful if the damn ball had just gone in the net. It happened when I was freed up by Clodoaldo in the centre circle, and I looked up-field to see that the Czech goalkeeper, Viktor, was miles off his line. I had noticed his tendency to do this earlier in the match, and as the Czech defence dithered, no doubt waiting for me to start running with the ball, instead I fired a powerful shot at their goal, some sixty-five yards away. It went high and fast towards its target, bending through the air as it went, and Viktor's eyes were wide with alarm as he scrabbled back towards his post. He would have had no chance had it been on target, but the footage doesn't change despite repeated showings and the ball slid inches wide. Journalists after the match asked me if I made this shot just to prove that I wasn't short-sighted. It was nothing to do with that! Even though it didn't go in, it galvanised the team and from then on it was all Brazil.

In the second half I scored a sweet volley after trapping a high pass on my chest, swivelling and shooting as it dropped; and then Jairzinho got two, the second of them a great individual effort. We had won 4–1, an excellent opening result, but now had to contend with the World Champions, England, in a match many people regarded as the clash of the tournament's titans.

England's preparation for Mexico had not been without its difficulties, not least because of a series of *faux pas* by their manager, Sir Alf Ramsey, who had not endeared himself to the Mexican public by making a number of ill-advised comments. But they had a very good team – and in Moore, Bobby Charlton and Gordon Banks, three players who would have walked into pretty much any Brazil side.

We met four days after the Czech encounter, also in the Jalisco stadium, in front of 66,000 spectators. It was another searing day, with a noon start because of television scheduling commitments (another cause of controversy throughout the Cup), but we knew the English would feel the heat and humidity more than we did. We were confident, but respectful. We knew it would be a tough match: Gerson was injured, the English defence was formidable, but Zagallo encouraged us to be patient, not to expect a samba-style dance to victory. As in many things, he was right.

The difficulty in breaching that defence was made very clear after only ten minutes' play by another famous 1970 moment – the save by Gordon Banks from my leaping header. Jairzinho had swept the English full-back, Terry Cooper, aside and delivered a perfect cross into the box. Jumping powerfully I met the ball cleanly and headed it down just inside the post. It felt like a textbook header, and as I watched the ball spin towards the net I knew it was a goal. But then, from nowhere – from the other post, in fact, which amounted to much the same thing – Banks flung himself towards the ball, managing in an effort of extraordinary agility to scoop it up, out, and over the bar. It was a phenomenal save, the save of that tournament and of most other tournaments you could care to mention. And not long after, he made another great save, this time from a free kick. It was a tremendous performance, and he kept England in with a chance.

But our patience was eventually rewarded, with a lovely team goal that began with Tostão beating three England players, including a lovely nutmeg on the otherwise flawless Moore, before sliding the ball calmly to me. Rather than shooting, though, as it was clear the English defence was expecting me to, I controlled the ball and passed it carefully to Jairzinho, who scored with practically our only other shot on goal in the game. We were 1–0 up, and that's the way it would stay.

Our third group game, against Romania, proved to be our worst performance. I scored twice and Jairzinho made up the third, but the Romanians should never have been able to get two through our defence. It was a bad game. We suffered from over-confidence, and were very nearly punished by a couragous and committed Romanian side. But at least we had made it through to the knock-out stages – played three, won three.

✯

In the quarter-final we played Peru, a team we knew well not least because they were now being coached by our old friend and former team-mate, Didi. He had proved himself to be as talented a coach as he had been a player, and Peru had done well not only to get to the Finals but to progress this far, beating Bulgaria and Morocco to reach the quarter-final and losing only to West Germany, always a strong side. That Peru side was good, but we were better, and we ran out 4–2 winners in the game on 14 June.

It was easily the most enjoyable match to play in so far – not just because of the Didi connection, or because I knew a lot of the Peruvian players personally having toured that country with Santos so many times, but because of the spirit in which it was played. It was all attack, attack, attack, and the game ebbed and flowed freely. Tostão and Rivelino in particular were magnificent, scoring three between them, with Jairzinho adding the fourth.

And so we progressed to the semi-finals, but as the Peru game ended we had no idea who our opponents would be. Before we had even showered or changed we huddled around a radio to listen to the closing moments of the other quarter-final between Uruguay and the USSR at the Azteca Stadium in Mexico City. Normal time had ended with the score tied at 0–0, and even extra time was now coming to a close too. But in the dying seconds little Cubilla, their talented right-winger, took the ball to the byline and crossed it back for Esparrago to score. Later there was much discussion about whether Cubilla had let the ball go out, across the goal-line, but the goal stood and the Russians were out. So, it would be Uruguay.

I remembered instantly my promise to my father back in 1950, and that terrible defeat against Uruguay in the Maracanã. I had sworn that Brazil would not have lost if I had been there, and now I had my chance for some kind of revenge. Brazil had not played Uruguay in a World Cup since then, so this 1970 match would be particularly special to me, and to the rest of the team. I remember the night before that game on 17 June, everyone going to our hotel in Guadalajara saying that even if we ended up losing the World Cup, what mattered most was that we beat Uruguay.

'They've been stuck in our throats for twenty years,' someone said, his voice thick with emotion. 'We've got to get them out. We've *got* to win.' The people who asked me about this match had no idea how important beating Uruguay was for me. I'd suffered as a nine-year-old boy, crying so much and promising that one day I'd avenge that Maracanã defeat. Journalists really hyped it up and it made us nervous. The 1950 result meant nothing to some of Brazil's players – Clodoaldo was only twenty years old now himself – but some of us remembered the agonies of 1950 and were there in Mexico.

When the time for the game arrived, it certainly wasn't easy to calm people down – there were a lot of nerves. I was amazed when the match started, it was as though all of us had been there on that July day twenty years ago and were now making all the same mistakes. Bad passes, weak defence, and we couldn't get through our opponents at all. After twenty minutes we were losing 1–0; a speculative and slightly mis-kicked shot from Cubilla, at an acute angle, surprising Félix in goal. I tried to pull things back by catching out the Uruguayan goalkeeper, Mazurkiewicz, pouncing on one of his short kicks out to his defenders, a habit I'd noticed and decided was vulnerable, but he recovered well and made a good save from my shot. We had other opportunities – the Uruguayans played hard, sometimes brutally, and we had lots of free kicks.

At one point Fontes trod on my ankle after he'd knocked me over in the penalty area. If my ankle had not been supported it would have broken. The Spanish referee did nothing. I did get my own back, though. Later in the match, I was running up the left wing and he was about to catch me from behind. I knew he was coming in to make a nasty tackle, so I caught him hard with my elbow. It was a violent blow. The referee gave a foul – in *my* favour. He could see that the Uruguayan had approached me with bad intentions. I was glad that I only hit him in the forehead because if I'd caught his nose or jaw I would have certainly broken it. I remember thinking, 'God! My elbow hurts!' Imagine what his forehead felt like . . .

Throughout my career, when players were violent towards me I always defended myself. Football is a game for men. But I was never deliberately violent. I was only ever sent off twice – and in both cases it was for arguing with the ref. I was never sent off for violent conduct. In 1970 the Uruguayans played defensively as well as violently: a game of brutal containment. Against Brazil they had just one attacker out front and the other ten players hanging back.

We stayed 1–0 down until the very end of the first half, when Clodoaldo, settled now after an early period of nerves, ran on to a great pass from Tostão and levelled the score. When we came out for the second half it was a different Brazil on show: we took control of the game, playing practical, quick, smart football. Jairzinho and Rivelino scored and we missed lots of other chances. One of my efforts has since become another treasured memory from 1970, albeit another goal-that-got-away: running on to a through-ball I dummied the goalie, sending him completely the wrong way by jinking to the left, *away* from the ball as it continued its course to the right, only to dart back to it beyond the keeper and shoot, but my strike went agonisingly wide of the empty net. Like the long-range shot against Czechoslovakia, it would have been so much more beautiful had it gone in, and I sometimes dream about both of them hitting the back of the net. I didn't play those shots thinking about how they would look, though – I just really wanted Brazil to win, I wanted more goals, and they seemed like good scoring options at the time. But sometimes life gets in the way, and it is important to be philosophical about these things.

We were a better team than the Uruguayans, just as we had been in 1950; the difference now was that, twenty years on, it was the better team that won.

✯

The side that would go on to be called the 'beautiful team', the best that ever played the game, was through to the World Cup Final, the fourth time Brazil had reached the summit of the world's greatest tournament. Our opponents would be Italy, twice World Cup winners, who had beaten West Germany 4–3 after extra time in their semi-final, gaining the upper hand after a terrible foul on Beckenbauer had shifted the balance of power in the match.

Most of those goals had come in extra-time: the Italians had a reputation for strong defence – what they called *catenaccio*, or 'door-bolt' – which made some of their games rather sterile. So now the implacable force would meet the immovable object, and although we were favourites the world was fascinated to see which would prevail – the watching audience on television was predicted at nearly 1 billion people.

Over 100,000 were actually inside the Azteca Stadium on that sweltering June day. Our line-up was unchanged from the semi-final: Félix, Carlos Alberto, Brito, Piazza, Everaldo, Clodoaldo, Gerson, Jairzinho, Tostão, Pelé, Rivelino. The Italians fielded some very good players of their own, including Angelo Domenghini up front, the full-back Fachetti, and Mario Bertini, who gave me a lot of trouble in the match but who was too clever ever to get caught by the referee. But their problem was that they needed to change their game-plan to beat us, they needed to come at us, and they did not. They sat back and tried to soak up the pressure, but we created too much pressure. Too many of us were on form that day, myself included – it was one of my best games in a Brazil shirt.

Our first goal came after only eighteen minutes, with Rivelino crossing into the box where I was waiting. I timed my jump to perfection and headed past the outstretched hands of their goalkeeper, Enrico Albertosi. Gerson and Carlos Alberto both had a lot of space, and we created problems throughout, with the Italians seemingly content to hang back and thwart our efforts. After thirty-seven minutes, though, it looked like their tactics might have been right after all – we had had all the play, but when Clodoaldo foolishly back-heeled into empty space it was snapped up by Boninsegna, who passed the desperate Félix and scored. Italy had poached an equaliser – could it be that *catenaccio* and counter-attack would win the day?

After forty-four minutes I had another shot on goal lined up which I was sure would hit home when the referee blew for half-time – I couldn't believe my luck, and dwelled on the decision during the interval.

But in the second half we reasserted our control, as Italy failed to press home any psychological advantage they might have had. Gerson made the most of the space afforded him and scored with a long, low shot from outside the box after sixty-six minutes; Jairzinho added another five minutes later, becoming the first person ever to score in every round of the World Cup Finals in the process. Italy began to make a series of desperate substitutions but the result was no longer in doubt, and we began to enjoy ourselves. The final verdict on who would win this contest between attack and defence was delivered four minutes from time. We knew that Italy were marking man to man, and that Fachetti, the left back, was following Jairzinho. So whenever Jairzinho strayed from the right wing there was a space there – which we called 'the avenue'. A few times in the first half we had tried to use the avenue but the goal didn't come. Then, near the end of the second half, Tostão got the ball, passed to Jairzinho and he passed to me. I saw Fachetti by Jairzinho and thought that no one was behind me and, since I knew Carlos Alberto would be coming in on his own, I passed to him. We had practised this move and it worked perfectly, Carlos Alberto driving the ball past Albertosi like a thunderbolt. The final score: 4–1.

Carlos Alberto and I knew each other brilliantly well, on

and off the pitch. We had spent five years at Santos together and had developed a good relationship. I had even introduced him to a famous actress, Terezinha Sodré. He was desperate to meet her, even though he was married at the time. I would tut-tut, but – to cut a long story short – he eventually married her. Carlos Alberto had a religious aunt in Rio, who he would bring to see me each time I got injured so we could pray together. We had a synchronicity, and that was most delightfully demonstrated in that final World Cup goal.

When the whistle blew there was pandemonium. People ran on to the pitch from all over, and in seconds our shirts and even our shorts had been whisked off by souvenir-hunters – I made sure to take my shirt off myself so that my head didn't go with it. I was hoisted aloft on a sea of fans and it was several minutes before we were able to go to the dressing-rooms to collect ourselves. I managed to find a quiet moment in the shower to give thanks to God and my family for helping me achieve this great victory. While I was in there I was disturbed by a journalist who had managed to get in to the dressing-rooms – I knew him, he was one of the writers who'd been spreading rumours about my eyesight. He knelt down in front of me, getting himself soaking wet, and begged forgiveness for what he'd written. I remember telling him that only God could forgive, and I wasn't God.

We then went back on to the pitch to collect the Jules Rimet trophy from the President of Mexico – as this was the third time we had won it, it had been decided it would now be ours to keep. The intensity of emotion as Carlos Alberto lifted the trophy above his head, tears of joy in his eyes, was like nothing I had ever known, except perhaps watching Bellini do the same thing in 1958. But this time I had a proper understanding of what it meant, what it would mean to all the people back home. And I had played in every game, come through unscathed, and felt as though I had achieved everything I had set out to achieve.

After the euphoria, was I left with any regrets about my World Cup career? Well, there is a silly little thing. I would have liked to have scored a goal with a bicycle kick. I scored them for Santos and, later, for the Cosmos. But never in a World Cup. I scored every other way – with my head, my right foot and my left, from a free kick, but never from an overhead kick. It's funny, but the goals that I missed in 1970 are remembered more than the ones that I scored – the shot from halfway, Banks' save, and the dummy round the goalkeeper. I would have preferred not to have made any of those moves but to have scored with a bicycle kick. It's a personal thing, without importance really, but it's what I feel.

7

The First Farewells

'His great secret was improvisation. Those things he did were done in one moment. He had an extraordinary perception of the game'

CARLOS ALBERTO TORRES

The immediate aftermath of the 1970 triumph in Mexico City was the familiar round of receptions, banquets and back-slapping – all very enjoyable but exhausting too. We had a celebratory meal and then a few of us took a call from General Emilio Médici, the President of Brazil. Brazil had been a military dictatorship since 1964 and Médici, who had been in power since 1969, was known as a football fan. He had even caused some discomfort in the national squad by saying before the World Cup that he wanted his favourite player, Dada Maravilha, to play in the team. That's what Brazil is like – before a World Cup, everyone wants to have their say, even the president.

Médici would congratulate us again in person a few days later, when we flew home to Brasilia for a victory reception at the presidential palace. He spoke movingly of his pride and joy in our bringing home the trophy: of course he saw some political capital in Brazil's footballing pre-eminence – it was good PR for the country and for his government too – but it was obvious that he was also a football lover, and on a very fundamental level was just delighted we had won.

At that time there was some criticism that the dictatorship was using football for its own ends. As I player I did not sense any political pressure from the government, although some of our technical staff were military men, like the reserve army captain Claudio Coutinho. During the preparation he had told us that winning was important because it would calm the people.

As the impact of our win began to sink in, so too could we reflect on what had been a wonderful tournament. The papers were full of pieces about how right it was that our free-flowing style had triumphed over the Italians' safety-first approach. And it had been an innovative competition, too – the 1970 World Cup was the first to allow substitutions, up to three players per side. This excellent idea came a little late for me, though – I could have used it more in Chile in 1962 or in England in 1966, when I'd had to stay on the pitch just to make up the numbers. The 1970 World Cup also saw the institution of yellow and red cards, an idea of referee Ken Aston's, who had taken charge of the infamous and violent 'Battle of Santiago' between Chile and Italy in 1962 and who later served as chairman of FIFA's referees' committee. This would prevent another occurrence like the farce of the 1966 World Cup match between Argentina and England, when the German-speaking referee sent off Argentina's Rattin, and a lot of time was wasted just because everyone had such trouble understanding each other.

Football itself had been 'the winner' of the 1970 World Cup: this seemed to be the consensus among the media. And I was perfectly happy for our team to represent the best spirit of the game. The challenge would be to maintain that spirit, and to spread it among other countries too – not easy when the pressure to win at all costs was becoming ever greater.

But in Rio, where we had flown from Brasilia for further celebrations, I had more immediate worries, not least getting hold of Rosemeri, who was then seven months pregnant with our second child. Very late one night I was finally put through to Santos, and it was wonderful to hear her voice again. She said she needed me at her side, so the next day I took an aero-taxi home. It then turned out that there was to be a further parade in São Paulo, but by then I was already on my way. I was later criticised for deserting the team but it wasn't like that at all: if it had been decided earlier that we'd all go and take part in the day's programme I would have been there too, with my team-mates.

Our son, Edson Cholbi do Nascimento – Edinho – was born on 27 August 1970. When I first held him in my arms I said that he could be whatever he wanted to be – he didn't have to be a footballer, that didn't matter to me. His mother Rose and I both just wanted what was best for our son. After all, every parent wants to give his child everything he didn't have, everything he had to struggle for. I was no different, and only thought that Edinho would go on to study – the same for Kelly and all our beloved children.

With a new mouth to feed I had already decided I needed to look to the future a bit more, and that it was time to fill the gaps in my education. I would at last go back to school. I wanted a degree, and following tradition as a freshman I had my hair cut – which is why in Mexico everyone had short hair, something that became known as the 'Pelé cut'.

When I was a young child I wasn't a good student – I've described earlier what a little pest I could be. As a kid, all I wanted to do was play. Many of us go through that phase, believing that life is a bed of roses and that we'll never have to grow up. I have great admiration for people who are able to dedicate themselves to their studies even when they're little. In 1970, by which time I was already an adult, the desire to study was still buzzing away in my head. That's the age when many of us realise how much we haven't done. I was more grown-up by then and understood how important academic qualifications would be to my life; and more than that, I began to feel the lack of a greater understanding, of a clear definition of myself as a person. Who was I? What was I? Just a footballer? No, it had to be more than that. I'd done many visits to schools, universities, hospitals and companies to talk about football. I felt I ought to make these performances better, more rounded. But I realised it wasn't my intelligence or instincts that were lacking, I just didn't have enough education. I had no grounding, or almost none. I met a lot of people who were better educated than me and decided I had to make up on all that lost time. It would be a good example to my children, and useful to me.

When you're a parent you know how important all this is, and how much time is squandered complaining about school. That was when I started thinking about quitting football. I was getting a bit tired of living on planes and sleeping in hotels. I wanted to study Physical Education, which would at least mean remaining within my own field. It wasn't a simple path, however.

It was Professor Julio Mazzei who turned out to be the man who most encouraged the realisation of this dream of mine, always telling me that I should study. When I told him I was considering it he was delighted, and told me that I could depend on his help. He used to tell me that it was not important if I was the best athlete in the world, what was important was to be the most *intelligent* athlete in the world. When we went on trips with Santos he used to bring books along and give us impromptu English and Spanish lessons.

Having already done primary school, to get to do Physical

Education at college I'd have to pass through secondary and further classes to prepare me for the college entrance exams. You don't get anywhere without a first step, however, and I had a real desire to reach my goal. It wasn't easy, with my football commitments and everything. I spent a whole year studying hard – any free time saw me at my desk, reading and writing. Professor Mazzei was like an elder brother, a second father. In fact, I ended up calling him 'Daddy'. That was the name his wife used, because his kids did, and so the name stuck for me too.

When I finally walked into the hall to take the exam Professor Mazzei noticed I was nervous – and it was no wonder! He turned to me and said, 'Relax, Pelé. Don't be nervous – you've worked hard, and studied a lot. You're well prepared, so don't even think about failing.' I remembered that trip to Santos when Waldemar de Brito said the same words to me as the Professor – the phrase 'Relax, Pelé' stayed with me. I passed and received a secondary diploma; this meant that I could go ahead and do the Preparatory exam I needed to pass in order to attend university. I studied for another year. But I was focused on my challenge, and Professor Mazzei was always at my side, doing just as he'd promised.

Finally I was ready. I took the exam in Aparecida, a nice city in the Paraiba valley on the São Paulo–Rio de Janeiro border. My old friend Zito – my fellow world champion from 1958 and '62, and sometime business partner – had a farm in Aparecida, and I had spent the night there before my wedding. When I woke up on the morning of the exam there was a horse saddled up, all ready to take me to the examination hall. I felt like a real Don Quixote, on horseback, trotting off towards another important moment in my life.

I managed to control my nerves and get through it, and when I left the hall I was sure I'd passed. A week later a letter arrived confirming this – at last, the door was open to go to college. I went back to my books, and the struggle went on. Professor Mazzei was more confident now and encouraged me every day. From now on the exams would be both written and practical. There was Brazilian history and maths as well as Physical Education. I almost failed in the 25-metre swimming test. You don't learn to swim by sitting on the bank of the river or sea just watching, and there'd been that time in Bauru when I'd nearly drowned; for the swimming test I'd have to train intensively. I passed. At last I was through the third stage in my battle to graduate.

The course at the University in Santos would last three years. As well as everything to do with physical fitness and an understanding of sport, there were lots of other subjects to study too, including psychology, physiology and history. I was heartened to discover that there were lots of other athletes on my course as well as me, as it was tough going and we all supported each other. Lessons began at 7.30 in the morning, and there really was no let-up. The professors had no interest in the fact that I was playing professional football in the evenings, I still had to keep up with the rest of the class. Finally I graduated with them – an amazingly emotional moment. I must again pay tribute to Julio Mazzei – my studies were crowned with success largely thanks to his near-paternal dedication.

I didn't get my degree in Physical Education in order to be a football coach – I have no desire to be a coach, and never have. I did it to set an example: when you want to be something, you have to fight for it. I only succeeded, from every point of view, because I decided I was going to study and followed through on that decision. I'd give the same advice to all young people, whether they're athletes or not – studying is fundamental. And determination brings success.

✯

The World Cup win in 1970 again made me think about retiring from football, beginning with the national squad, to spend more time with my family. I now had two children, and because I travelled so much Rosemeri was the one who'd had the greater burden of looking after them. Dondinho, my father, always told me that you should never stop when people ask you to stop. You should stop when you are at your best, because that is how you will be remembered. It's not a pleasant thing to witness one's own decline. And I was absolutely at the top; I had played my best World Cup, scored a thousand goals and was an international name. So I let it be known that I would be unavailable for selection for Brazil, and also prepared the ground for Santos to begin the search for a new Number 10. I was in no hurry to leave, but it was important to me to indicate my long-term intentions.

The last hurrah for Brazil came first, in two farewell games a week apart. The first match was on 11 July 1971, in Morumbi, São Paulo, against Austria. I only played in the first half, but during it I notched up the last goal I would ever score for the *Seleção*. I scored 77 in all – still a national record, I'm proud to say. The final farewell could be nowhere else but at the Maracanã. The game took place a week later, on the 18th, the opposition Yugoslavia. It was another extraordinary experience. For a start, there were 180,000 people crammed into the stadium – and it wasn't even a competitive match. The football was unmemorable, ending in a 2–2 draw, but I can never forget the send-off I received from the loving crowd. I found it hard to concentrate on the game, and only played the first forty-five minutes. When the match was over the entire stadium was chanting, *'Fica! Fica!'* ('Stay! Stay!'). I made a lap of the stadium, surrounded by kids, the crowd still imploring me not to go. My shirt, that hallowed gold and green, was in my hands but it could not stem the flow of tears.

Afterwards, perhaps predictably, I was criticised in some quarters for abandoning international football so early and while I was still in good shape. That's how it always is . . . It's hard to keep everybody happy.

My contract with Santos expired towards the end of the following year, and it seemed the club was determined to get their money's worth. The bird that laid the golden eggs was about to fly the coop, and they were really going to make him play, make him bank some money for the club . . . In an eighteen-month period we toured South America, the Caribbean, North America, Europe, Asia and Australia. Pretty much the whole world, in fact. Never in my life have I had my time so filled with airports, hotels and different countries. I had already played my 1,000th game for Santos, against Transvaal in Paramaribo, Surinam, and it seemed they were determined to get a few more hundred out of me before I went.

All the time my attitude to the club was gradually shifting. I was just enjoying it less. As well as the constant travel – something I'd sworn to give up after the birth of Edinho – there were lots of changes to the structure of the club being introduced at this time – changes to the management and to the team. First, there were new coaches – among them my former team-mate Mauro, who replaced the long-serving Antonio Fernandes (known as Antoninho, he was tragically killed in a car crash in 1973). Mauro was a real gentleman and had been captain of the World Cup-winning Brazil team of 1962. He was a good coach, who favoured a more cautious, defensive sort of playing – when he came to Santos it was already a side which didn't have the attacking power it had had in the past.

Then, there were new directors, and they fired Mauro after just six months. He was followed by Jair da Rosa Pinto, another ex-team-mate who had been at the club when I arrived in 1956, and had done good work as coach at the Rio team América. Jair knew that the team wasn't as strong as it had once been, but he wanted some attacking play nonetheless. One mistake he made, though, was dismissing Professor Julio Mazzei from running the physical fitness programme – unforgivable! When Jair left – also without having had much success – the ex-winger Pepe took his place. He was a Santos veteran and an old friend. And then the former Bangú man Tim, who had tried to sign me as a teenager, arrived in 1974. It was a merry-go-round, and did nothing for the continuity of the club, which was clearly in decline.

I was torn between quitting altogether or negotiating a new contract, on my terms. I decided to stay on for a bit longer as long as the club made it worth my while, and naturally this gave rise to all sorts of rumours about the ludicrous demands I was making, some of which bordered on libellous. During my time with the club Santos had banked over $20 million (worth much more nowadays, of course), and I don't think it is big-headed to say that a fair proportion of that had come because of me. It's just a fact that the countries and clubs we visited and played against paid Santos more if I appeared than if I didn't – sometimes up to twice as much. And it is also worth pointing out that in the years after I left, Santos didn't play a single game overseas.

Many people said that I was getting rich while Santos was poor and struggling – but of course it was just the opposite. I have always had my critics in certain quarters of the media, especially the Brazilian media, and during this period it seemed the knives were really out. After I spoke about the little children after the thousandth goal, many people thought it was demagogy but some politicians thought I was on to a good thing. It facilitated an episode when, together with some other players, I went to meet President Médici to complain about footballers' rights. This was an era decades before the Bosman ruling in Europe (which gives out-of-contract players the right to move to other clubs) and the situation in Brazil was disgraceful. It was like bonded labour. Once your contract with a club ended, you were not free to play anywhere else – you needed your club's permission. And the club could treat you with disrespect. There were no retirement plans, medical help or insurance. I was aware of what had happened to my father, and to Vasconcelos, neither of whom had had any job security. Footballers may have been treated like gods by the public, but in labour terms they were treated little better than slaves. I remember in Santos we had a midfielder for a while who started going out with the daughter of the director. One day he had an argument with her and the director insisted he was taken off the team. He was punished because he didn't have the rights that other people are guaranteed in other jobs. We went to see Médici and although he seemed to be sympathetic nothing was done. It was only almost three decades later that the legal status of footballers changed, after work that I did when I was Minister for Sport.

I was very aware of footballers' rights in general and my own rights in particular. I learned a lot, too, in my negotiations for a new contract at Santos. My proposal was simple. I wanted to play for a year on my terms – and then I would play for a year on a basic salary, with any fees and prize money going to charity. My fee for the year was reasonable, and I had the safety net of knowing that I could walk away if my demands were not met. The discussions went on for weeks, before they finally accepted.

So I would stay with the club I had played for all my life and try to enjoy the last few years with them. But it became harder all the time, as Santos changed and the people I knew best fell by the wayside. It felt lonely without friends and colleagues like our great captain Zito; or Lula, Antoninho or Mauro; Pepe, Coutinho, Lima and others, and especially Julio Mazzei.

In 1973 we began another year of travelling. We started in Australia again. We played in the countries of the Persian Gulf. We played in Egypt and Sudan, in Africa and Europe, we performed in Germany, France, Belgium and England. In England we played two matches and lost both, 2–1 to Fulham and 3–2 to Plymouth. I scored in each game, but my farewell on English soil was a sad one. The 'footballing machine' was losing its shine, although there were still the odd reminders of the glory days – I remember one match in particular, in June that year, when we were in the United States and played the Baltimore Bays in Baltimore. In this game I took a corner and the ball went directly into the goal without touching another player: a '*gol olimpico*' for the only time in my career.

That match against Baltimore had been suggested by the then US Secretary of State, Henry Kissinger. It may come as a surprise to learn that Kissinger was and is a great football fan, but it is true, and he would come to have an even more direct influence on my career. The Baltimore fixture was also Kissinger's way of helping to support Dr João Havelange's campaign to become President of FIFA. Kissinger could see the attention focused on Brazilian football and on me in particular, and saw it as a way of introducing the game to his own country. Kissinger's argument was impeccable: as a lover of football he wanted the game to be as strong in the United States as it was elsewhere, and this could only be achieved by bringing the best-known footballer of the time to play there, and with the country taking a turn to host the World Cup. Both would, eventually, come to pass.

Havelange asked me to help him in his attempt for the top job at FIFA, which was having elections in 1974. We travelled a fair bit together, to the US, Africa and Europe. I helped raise his profile and get the attention of FIFA delegates, especially in Africa. The trips were always eventful. On one occasion in France we were in a radio station auditorium doing an interview when some Brazilian political exiles tried to storm the stage. Havelange and I had to be bundled out the back door! In those days Havelange treated me like a son. He was successful and served as President between 1974 and 1998.

The idea of playing in the US had initially been sown in my mind two years earlier, when I met a man called Clive Toye and two of his business associates while Santos were on tour in Jamaica. Clive was head of a football team in New York called the Cosmos, and we got chatting one day by the pool of the hotel we were staying in. Clive had talked about the state of the game in America, how they were trying to rejuvenate their fledgling football league but needed star players to attract the crowds, who were still committed to their regular diet of baseball and American football. I had listened as Professor Mazzei translated, only half paying attention, as I couldn't really see what any of this had to do with me. But he had got my attention by concluding that the search for star players should also include the most famous player of them all, and that he would like to offer me a contract to go and play for the New York Cosmos.

'Money's no object,' he had said. 'Whatever it takes.' But it wasn't the money – I had already turned down huge sums from European clubs. And although I had not yet agreed the new deal with Santos I had every intention of ending my career with them. I said thanks, but no thanks, and Clive and his associates had left empty-handed.

Two years had passed and I hadn't given the Cosmos offer another thought, but my links with America were slowly becoming established. It was in 1973, for example, that I signed a contract with the Pepsi-Cola Company to work on a worldwide project of football workshops for children called the International Youth Football Programme, on which I would collaborate with Julio Mazzei. I decided to try it out for a year – and it turned out to be one of the best things I ever got involved with. After the first year was done, I signed for another five. It's not hard to imagine what my life became from that moment. I played football, and divided my time with the workshops – and studied and trained too.

The programme was a triumph, though. It cost nothing to the coaches, the schools or players. The Professor and I travelled to sixty-four countries, giving workshops all over the world. We produced a book and various posters of Professor Mazzei's teaching, and made a coaching film called *Pelé: The*

Master and His Method, which won eleven international prizes. The film project turned out to be a marathon, the brainchild of a PepsiCo creative called Giora Breil, but was well worth the effort and it is something I am proud of to this day. We shot a lot of the footage at the Santos ground at Vila Belmiro, using kids from the local neighbourhood.

Another thing happened in 1973: Garrincha was given his testimonial at the Maracanã. Even though I was busy I couldn't pass up the opportunity to play. Garrincha was the greatest right-winger I'd ever seen and had the pleasure to play alongside. It was good to see him back in the yellow jersey (the game was between a Brazil team and an FIFA invitation XI) after he had retired early because of an injured knee. He had also run into personal problems, especially with alcohol, and had lost his way. I had tried to help him out by suggesting to the Brazilian Coffee Institute that they give him some work, and in the early 1970s when he lived in Italy he did some promotional work for them. We all wanted him to get over his problems, he was an idol.

The saddest part of Garrincha's demise came a few years later. Everyone wanted to pay tribute to him, and so he accepted an invitation to go on a float during the Rio carnival parade. I've been invited fifty thousand times to parade in Rio but I never accept because if I go with one samba school, all the others get upset, so I don't think it is worth my while. Anyway, Garrincha was parading with Mangueira, one of the most popular samba schools. I was watching on television and when I saw him I wanted to cry. He was sitting there on a float, with no apparent notion of what was going on around him. His face looked worn out, like there was no life left. It was one of the saddest things I ever saw.

It's a crying shame. Everyone wanted to help but, in the end, no one could reach him. The same happened with George Best. We all wanted to save him, but no one could.

Garrincha died in 1983. I did not go to his funeral. The truth is that I hate seeing dead bodies, ever since I saw that glider pilot as a child. I prefer to pray on my own.

✯

I had hung up the boots of my international career – but there was pressure for me to change my mind for the 1974 World Cup in West Germany. One of the reasons was that I was still on great form at Santos. In 1973 Santos were Paulista champions and again I was the competition's top scorer. (In fact, we were joint champions that year, because of a unique mix-up during the deciding match, against Portuguesa. It was 0–0 after extra time and the match went to penalties. We were two goals up, and Portuguesa had two penalties left to take. But the referee, Armando Marques, lost count of this – and, in error, declared Santos champions. The crowd and the team started to celebrate. The Portuguesa coach knew that the ref had made a mistake, but also that it would have been difficult to win the remaining penalties and hope that we miss ours. So he quickly ordered his players out of the stadium and into the team bus. When Armando Marques realised his mistake, Portuguesa were nowhere to be seen. The Portuguesa coach had gambled well. The following day, the Paulista federation decided against a rematch and declared both teams the winner. I had been the last Santos penalty-taker and was frustrated I didn't have a chance to perform my spot kick – to score the winning goal in a championship final would have been sweet.) My record with Santos in the Paulista was a good one: since I played my first match I had been the tournament's highest scorer eleven times and Santos had been champions ten times.

The pressure to turn out again for Brazil came from many sides. President Ernesto Geisel, who took office in 1974, his wife and some military colonels wanted me back in the *Seleção*. But by then I had heard about what the military regime was doing to some students, some famous singers had been exiled and people spoke of torture too. Geisel's daughter came to see me to ask me to rethink. But I wasn't going to.

João Havelange, head of the CBD and soon to take up his post as FIFA boss, also urged me to go to Germany, and so did the Brazil coach, Mario Zagallo. He was worried that he hadn't found replacements of the quality of the old players. As well as my absence he was also missing Tostão, Gerson and Carlos Alberto. 'I'd like to be able to count on your talent,' Zagallo told me. 'You could solve the serious problem I have in attack.' If Brazil had Pelé they would be all set, he thought.

I have always had an enormous amount of respect for Mario Zagallo. After we had won the World Cup in 1970, I was grabbing a drink of water with Brito in the dressing-room when I felt a hand on my shoulder. Assuming it was just another journalist I didn't turn round, until Brito said, 'Hey, it's Zagallo, man.' I turned at once, and stood up. The coach and I put our arms out, and embraced, both of us crying. We hugged for some time, moved to tears by what had happened. I said to him, 'We had to be together to become champions three times – it could only have happened with you.' And I meant it – he had been there with me in 1958 and '62, and had made it happen as coach in 1970. Carlos Alberto Parreira, now the national coach but a member of Zagallo's Technical Commission in 1970, is another big fan, and rates him the greatest coach in the world. But I was adamant I would not play – I had set out my reasons back in 1971, and they had not changed.

I was still keen to attend the tournament, however, and considered a few options, among them an offer to act as commentator for a Brazilian television network. There was an outcry when this got out, though, as some people in that industry protested that I didn't have the necessary union affiliation, I wasn't experienced enough, and so on. So that was out. I was obliged to do some PR for Pepsi as part of the Youth Programme contract, and I had another compelling reason to be there at the start, as I had been invited with Uwe Seeler, the great West German player, to take part in the opening ceremony and exchange trophies – Uwe was to hand me the old Jules Rimet, which Brazil was to keep for good having won it three times; and I handed him the new solid-gold FIFA World Cup.

Despite missing several veterans of 1970, Zagallo was able to call upon Rivelino, Jairzinho and Paulo Cesar. But the team had not been playing as well; Zagallo had become a little more cautious in his approach; Clodoaldo got injured just before the Finals; and the general attitude didn't seem right – it lacked the rigour of our preparation in 1970, the intense focus on getting every little detail right and the hunger in the team to win. This was perfectly illustrated to me by a conversation I had with Paulo Cesar right before our first group match, against Yugoslavia in Frankfurt. I went to the training camp to wish them luck when Paulo Cesar cornered me to say he had a dilemma – but rather than worrying about some tactical aspect of the challenge of facing the Yugoslavs, it turned out a French club was trying to sign him and he couldn't decide whether to hold out for more money.

It was all a far cry from 1958, when I remembered Bellini, the captain, had responded to Dr Paulo's apology about there not being much money to go round as a win bonus; the CBD was then in a tough position financially. 'We're not here for the money,' Bellini had said. 'We came for the title – to win the championship – and we have. If there's any extra money then it would be appreciated, but don't worry about it.'

It seemed to me in 1974 that if the players were more concerned with their financial value *after* the tournament than with the tournament itself, the World Cup was as good as lost already. And so it proved. A dreary 0–0 draw against Yugoslavia saw few attempts on goal – Jairzinho had been pulled in from the wing to act as centre forward, and was clearly uncomfortable there. The next match, against a Scottish team galvanised by the tireless Billy Bremner, was hardly better, and also ended 0–0. The first win came against lowly Zaire, but we could still only manage a 3–1 scoreline – four days earlier Yugoslavia had thrashed them 9–0. We were lucky to qualify for the next stage, really – Scotland did not, despite gaining the same amount of points as us, and one more than Argentina, who went through.

Our first game of the second round was against East Germany, and again it was unconvincing, the only goal coming from a Rivelino free-kick, Jairzinho ducking in the wall to let it go past into the net. We also scraped home against Argentina to make it into the final four, but to get that far flattered the team. As an observer I had had the chance to see other countries play too, and it was clear Brazil had not yet met any of the stronger sides. That would change on 3 July in Dortmund, when Brazil played the Netherlands. This was the side of the great Johan Cruyff, the team that would define 'total football', and their flair and free-flowing style reminded me powerfully of how Brazil had played in the past.

It was too much for the Brazil team of the present, that was for sure, and the Dutch ran out 2–0 winners, with Cruyff scoring a stunning volley. We were out, and even went on to lose the third-place play-off to Poland. It was hugely disappointing and I felt the defeat as keenly as if I had been on the team.

The balance of power in world football was shifting. The Dutch; the young and brilliant team from France; the disciplined Germans, with such strong tactics and technique, who would go on to beat Cruyff and the Dutch in the final – it was clear that the Brazilian team had an era of totally new challenges ahead of them.

✯

It was a difficult period for me. In the street people would stop and say, 'You see what you've done? If you had been in the team Brazil would have won!' Yet I knew I had done the right thing. And at Santos, I also realised that my time was coming to an end. I decided that I would play my final game and told the club. They were not overpleased and tried to persuade me to rethink. I was still in good form, scoring goals and playing well. They wanted to squeeze out of me a few more weeks, months, years . . . But there was no changing my mind. At the end of September I told them the news: my last game would be the following week, against Ponte Preta, at the Vila Belmiro.

I always think it is a funny coincidence that for the first match I ever played in a Santos strip, against Cubatão back in 1956, I wore the club's away shirt. It has black and white vertical stripes, like Newcastle United and Juventus. Then I spent almost my whole career in the Santos home strip, which is all white. And for my final game – because of Ponte Preta's colours – I was again in the black and white stripes. There was a circularity to it all; it felt unusual to be in the second shirt, but it also felt right.

Usually when someone has a farewell game it all goes in a certain way: the cheers, the lap of honour, and so on. I had not planned what I would do. The match began. After twenty minutes I was in midfield and the ball was lofted over to me. Rather than chest it, or controlling it any other way, I caught it with my hands. It was a spontaneous decision. The idea just came to me there and then. The other players stopped and stared. I could hear the gasps of the crowd.

I think everyone understood at that moment that my career had come to an end. I jogged to the centre spot with the ball still in my hands. I then knelt down on the spot, with the ball between my knees. I lifted my arms out like aeroplane wings, as if I was making the sign of the cross. I wanted to thank all the people there, all the supporters, all Brazilians and, of course, God. I turned slowly to face all corners of the ground, saluting the fans as tears streamed down my face.

The crowd rose as one, a roar of approval, respect and regret sweeping towards me. I stood up and wiped my face, and then ran over to the stands – to the legions of Santos fans who had supported me in the eighteen years I had played in their colours. The tears kept coming. I could hardly bear to remain on the field. And then I walked away, convinced that – a few weeks shy of my thirty-fourth birthday – I would never play professional football again.

✯

Towards the end of 1974 I honestly thought I could look forward to a life of business and football while being a slave to neither. I still had my portfolio of interests, and others had been added over the years to complicate the picture; and I hoped that I would have some role to play in guiding the direction of Brazilian football and teaching the sport to children around the world. But I couldn't imagine turning out for a team again, week in, week out – and nor could I foresee the circumstances that would bring this about.

It was the business side of things that let me down again. Fiolax, the parts manufacturer I had a stake in, was in trouble, and when I hired someone to do a complete audit of all my affairs it was clear that I was again involved in a company that was losing me money hand over fist. The auditor did a great job of streamlining my assets, selling off a few businesses and properties that weren't paying their way, but Fiolax was a problem. Foolishly I had signed a note guaranteeing a bank loan for the company as well as its liabilities, despite the fact that I was far from a majority shareholder. When the loan came up and the company couldn't pay, the bank held me liable. There was also a fine to pay because of some breach of import regulations.

My total losses – the loan repayment, and now the fine – were massive: a couple of million dollars. I had to come to an agreement with my creditors, and I got some help from João Havelange, whose campaign for the FIFA presidency I had supported by doing a series of public appearances and some hard lobbying on his behalf before the vote.

But I was determined not to let Fiolax go bankrupt – again, I was worried about how this would be perceived – and I still had to find more money. There was one sure-fire way to make money: return to the game. And there were huge offers on the table. Juventus and Real Madrid were willing to pay $15 million. AC Milan and América, of Mexico, were also interested. It was making me feel confused because inwardly I knew that I didn't want to go to Europe. I would have had to play all year round, the pressure would be enormous, it would be the same kind of life that I had lived with Santos. And I had decided that it was time to move on.

Professor Mazzei saw that I was struggling with what to do. He suggested that I have another look at the Cosmos offer. It had first been made in 1971, and was still on the table. Clive Toye had even phoned me from New York after my final game for Santos to reiterate his interest. It was clear he was serious – but should we take them seriously? Julio Mazzei and I sat down and went through the advantages and disadvantages of going to America.

The main thing that worried me was how the news would be received in my own country. After all, I had retired not just from the national team but from the game itself; I had been criticised for not playing in the 1974 World Cup, when I was fit enough to do so and might have helped Brazil win the trophy (although I've always believed my participation would have made no difference to our result). How could I now go back on my word? And to go and play abroad, to boot? There were other complications, too – my English back then wasn't great; and it would be disruptive for the family, especially my daughter, Kelly Cristina.

Professor Mazzei highlighted the plus points about going to the US. First, it was all about promoting football. The US was the richest, most powerful country in the world and yet football there was in its infancy. It would be a great opportunity to change habits – I could have a much greater impact on many more people than I could by going to play in a country where football was already established. It really felt like the start of something, like something exciting and fun to be part of. Secondly, it was an opportunity for me and my children to learn English, which Professor Mazzei had always said would be very important in whatever I wanted to do in the future. And thirdly, the money was very, very good. It was to be the biggest sports contract that had ever been signed.

After discussing the decision with Rosemeri, who said she would support me either way, I concluded it was the best thing to do. I would go to New York, and bring a little samba to the Big Apple. When I retired, something inside me had died. Playing football again would be like therapy.

Santos v. Corinthians, 1971.
Rivelino lunges in the tackle.

31

Proud parents: Dondinho and Celeste in 1971.

32

The second farewell: running out for Santos for the last time, against Ponte Preta at the Vila Belmiro, 2 October 1974.

Twenty minutes into the match I caught the ball with my hands and jogged over to the centre circle, where I placed it on the ground and knelt before it. It was at this moment that everyone realised my career with my beloved Santos had come to an end.

Debut for Cosmos at Downing Stadium,
Randall's Island, 15 June 1975.

Playing against the great George Best
during his spell for Los Angeles Aztecs, May 1976.

The last goal: scoring for Cosmos during my farewell match, in which I played one half for Cosmos and one half for Santos, 1 October 1977.

36

'Now there are two of the greatest': with Muhammad Ali after my final game.

37

The tears flowed again,
but as the rain came down
this time I didn't bother
wiping them away.

39

Life after football – well, almost. Commentating on West Germany v. Poland during the 1978 World Cup in Argentina.

40

The world of pitches became a world of offices. But I never found business as straightforward as kicking a football.

Professor Julio Mazzei with Franz Beckenbauer at Cosmos. My friend and mentor in so many ways, Julio went on to coach the New York club after I retired.

41

With Michael Caine on the set of *Escape to Victory*. Ossie Ardiles, a World Cup-winner himself with Argentina in 1978, watches in the background.

42

Fathers and sons: with Edinho and Dondinho in 1993.

Overcome with emotion during my marriage to my second wife, Assíria Seixas Lemos, 1994.

44

A speech as Brazil's Minister for Sport, with Assíria and President Fernando Cardoso, 1995.

45

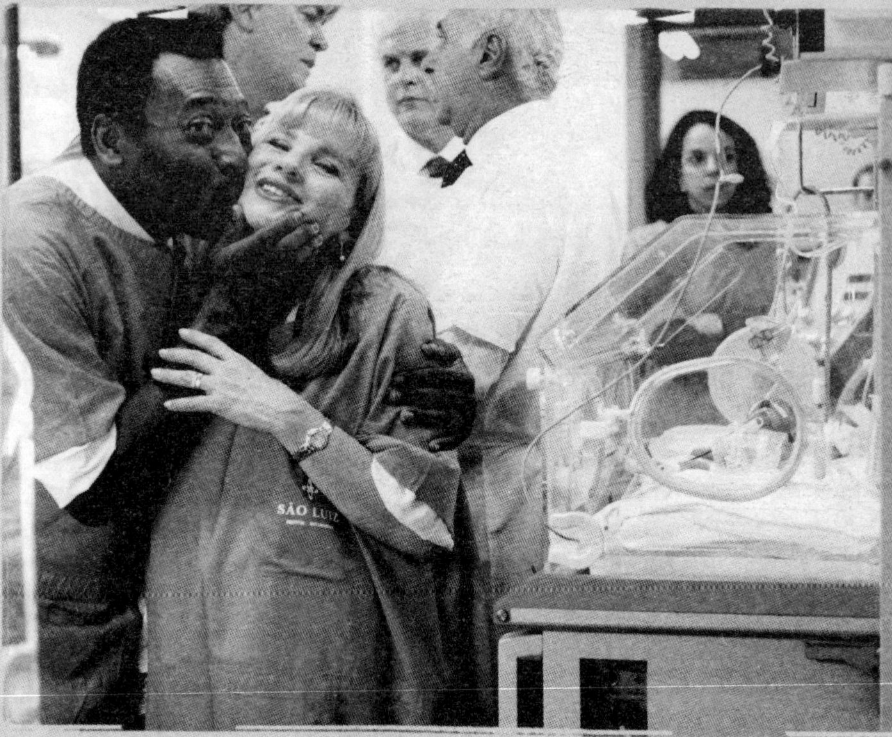

46

At the birth of our twins, Joshua and Celeste, in 1996.

47

President Bill Clinton shows off his juggling skills during a visit to the Mangueira Samba School in Rio de Janeiro, 1997.

48

In December 1997 I had the great honour of being made a Knight Commander of the British Empire during a ceremony at Buckingham Palace.

49

Giving an imprint of my feet for the new Hall of Fame at the Maracanã, during celebrations for the stadium's fiftieth birthday in 2000.

With Assíria on a business trip to China early in 2002.

50

51

And later that year, also in Asia, I watched Brazil lift the World Cup for a record fifth time, after Ronaldo had scored both goals in our 2–0 win over Germany.

Another honour – carrying the Olympic torch during its first-ever visit to South America ahead of the Athens Games in 2004.

Icon. **With Nelson Mandela** in Pretoria, South Africa.

8

Cosmonaut

'Pelé has elevated the game of soccer to heights never before attained in America and only Pelé, with his status, incomparable talent and beloved compassion, could have accomplished such a mission'

PRESIDENT JIMMY CARTER

The decision itself to go to America was only the start of the process, however – actually reaching an agreement with Cosmos took months. At least six months, in fact, of telegrams, phone calls, meetings and messages between lawyers, consultants and tax officials of every stripe. There were offers and counter-offers, and the negotiations dragged on and on, all in the strictest confidence as we wanted to keep the possible transfer under wraps until the deal was done. The company that owned Cosmos, Warner Communications, pulled strings wherever they could, and even got the US Secretary of State, Henry Kissinger, to issue a formal invitation to play in his country to help with the development of football, in case it would help oil the wheels of Brazilian bureaucracy.

I knew that Kissinger was doing all he could behind the scenes to make it possible for me to move. He was a useful ally, and Havelange also played a part, taking several meetings with Steve Ross, the then boss of Warner. Eventually all the details were thrashed out, and the contract was finalised. I was to play for Cosmos for two years, as an employee of Warner Communications, and an associated sub-licensing agreement guaranteed me 50 per cent of any revenue the club received from the use of my name. The contract gave me almost $9 million for the transfer. It was a lot of money in those days – and yet still I had my doubts about going. 'Do they really expect me to play just as I've been playing until now?' I wondered. I was nearing my mid-thirties; they must know I was past my peak as a player. I managed to convince myself that what they wanted was for me to promote football in the US to the rest of the world – and that it was my name they were hiring as much as my skill as a player.

Before I moved to New York, the US was the one place I could go in the world without fear of being mobbed. The US had a national football team, it was true, but the game wasn't well developed at the grass-roots and at the pro level it was insignificant compared to baseball or American football. It is often forgotten, however, that a US team had made the semi-finals of the very first World Cup in 1930 – losing to Argentina. And in 1950, the team had a famous, and totally unexpected, 1–0 victory over an England side featuring Billy Wright, Alf Ramsey, Wilf Mannion and Tom Finney. Until the establishment of the NASL in 1967 there wasn't much by way of a truly national professional league – all previous attempts had been restricted to a particular region, usually around New York and New England. But it was changing fast, football was becoming more popular by the day, and I was excited to be a spearhead for the sport in a country of a couple of hundred million people.

I had been to the US a few times before. In 1968, I had even been awarded the title Citizen of Kansas City when Santos flew there to play the Kansas City Spurs. While most Americans didn't know who I was, there were lots of immigrants from football-loving countries who did – and they helped fill up the stadiums during the Santos tours. I liked the US, and Rosemeri – who had been with me to New York a couple of times – had fallen in love with the city. So she was very excited about moving. One of the conditions that I had insisted on was that Julio Mazzei also be hired by the Cosmos as assistant coach and fitness adviser. His wife, Maria Helena, came too and she was great company for Rosemeri as we got settled.

Finally the lawyers withdrew, the ink on the deal dried, and Warner were ready to unveil their new star. The date for the announcement of Cosmos' new signing was set for 11 June 1975; the venue, a glamorous celebrity hangout called the 21 Club. The press conference was attended by what seemed to be half the world's media. It was a real indication of the level of interest and curiosity my transfer had aroused. With Professor Mazzei translating, I dealt with the barrage of questions as best I could. Clearly, improving my English was going to be a priority!

So too was getting to grips with the challenges I would face as a Cosmos player. I was keen to get a glimpse of my new team-mates as soon as possible, and once the formalities were out of the way, we went to watch a couple of games. At the Downing Stadium on Randall's Island, New York, their temporary home ground, we watched them lose 1–0 to Vancouver, and then we saw them lose by the same score away to the Philadelphia Atoms.

It was clear there was a lot of work to be done. After joining the NASL in 1970 the team had had an up-and-down time of it, winning the championship for the first time in 1972 but then coming last in 1974, losing fourteen of their twenty games that season. They were really just a college team. I knew the coach, the Englishman Gordon Bradley, as he had played for the New York Generals in their 5–3 win over Santos in 1968, marking me very successfully and keeping me off the score-sheet. He had played in the English First Division for Sunderland as a teenager before suffering a knee injury, and had then moved to North America, playing in Toronto and Baltimore before joining the Cosmos as player–coach in 1971.

He had been a good player and was a very decent man, but it seemed to me and Julio Mazzei that he was lacking a lot of raw material. The squad just didn't have the talent in depth required to sustain a period of pre-eminence, and the essentially part-time nature of the playing calendar meant that the general levels of fitness were nothing like those I was used to at Santos. It was also worrying to discover, as we did over the course of the next few weeks and months, that there were other teams in the league who not only had better players, those players were better trained and had higher levels of fitness than our squad as well. It was difficult at the beginning. I can remember saying to myself, 'Oh my God! What have I let myself in for?'

My league debut came just a week after the press conference at the 21 Club, against the Toronto Metros at Randall's Island. Not only did we win 2–0, the regular home attendance of 8,000 went up to 22,500, more than capacity, and we would average more than 20,000 fans at home for the rest of my time at the club – a strong indication that my arrival had sparked interest in the game. Again, I don't wish to sound conceited in pointing out that ticket sales dropped markedly if I was injured or on the bench: it is simply a statistical fact, and proof of the strategy that Cosmos and Warner Communications had invested in. I had come to get Americans interested in football, and I saw it as my job to be as visible as possible.

We struggled in that 1975 season, though, winning six and losing seven of the remaining fixtures. It didn't help that I got injured in a match against the San José Earthquakes, and we failed to make the play-offs. We were due to tour Europe and the Caribbean at the end of August for a month, and I was concerned that we would be made to look foolish unless we strengthened the squad. After discussions with Gordon Bradley and Clive Toye the club agreed to bring in two South American players who were currently at Santos, the Brazilian Nelsi Morais and the Peruvian international Ramón Mifflin. Both of them were good players, experienced and skilful, and I felt happier having them on the plane as we headed off to Sweden for our first match against Malmö.

Although we lost 5–1, the scoreline flattered the opposition and I was encouraged by the way we had played. The next match brought back memories of 1958, as I returned to Gothenburg for a match we won 3–1, in which I scored twice but which was marred by a bad injury to Nelsi Morais. I had an even stranger trip down memory lane when we arrived in the city. Ilena, the girl I had met during the 1958 World Cup, read of my visit in the local newspaper and then showed up at my hotel. It was embarrassing because I didn't recognise her at all – she was a mother and had brought her daughter with her, who was already a beautiful woman. We chatted and had our picture taken together. I have not seen her since but I'm sure that Ilena is now a grandmother and her granddaughter is probably as delightful as she – and her daughter – were at that age.

After a close game in Stockholm we went on to Oslo and Rome, by no means carrying all before us as Santos had done, but with no disgrace either. The team was starting to gel, and by the time we got to the Caribbean for the final leg of the tour I felt much more confident about our prospects for the 1976 season. We played Santos in Jamaica, and had great fun in a free-wheeling 12–1 win over a Puerto Rican side. My ongoing commitment to the PepsiCo Youth Programme meant I had to miss the last game, against a Haitian team, but having been so concerned before we set off on the tour, I felt much happier leaving it.

✯

I was taking to New York and New York was taking to me. Crowds were flocking to Cosmos games and soon it seemed that everyone knew who I was. Once I went to a baseball game with Dick Young, a well-known sportswriter who was sceptical about football taking off in the US. When people realised that I was in the stadium there was pandemonium because everyone wanted to see me. I remember Dick saying, 'I was wrong – you really are famous.'

With the club's help, Rosemeri had tracked down a great apartment for the family on the east side of Manhattan and the children were quickly adapting to a new country, a new city, a new language. Edinho, my son, took to the culture. At the Cosmos we would mess about with a football together. But at school he started to play basketball and baseball. Later on, when he was sixteen, I can remember going to his graduation ceremony. The principal called me up and asked if I could give him a sports prize. I assumed it was for being the best footballer, but when I was up on the stage I realised that it was for best baseball player. It was a big surprise, and – for a split-second – somewhat frustrating!

As part of my contract with Warner I had lots of publicity engagements. I had to go to many baseball and American football games, to give interviews, be photographed – that sort of thing. I can remember that when I went to watch baseball I would often fall asleep. Between pitches there is nothing going on; everyone just sits there eating popcorn and chatting. I used to think, 'What kind of *boring* game is this?' American football is a little bit faster, but still.

It was during this time that I first used the phrase 'beautiful game'. American reporters used to always ask me about 'soccer'. I would reply that it isn't soccer, it's 'football'. But I would add that it is not what they considered football, which was American football. I said that the football I – and the rest of the world – played was a *jogo bonito*, a 'beautiful game'. The phrase was my way of explaining to Americans the difference between soccer and American football. It must have resonated since the 'beautiful game' is probably my most commonly repeated phrase.

I was a sportsman and took that seriously, but it was a very different style of life to the one I had lived in Santos. Santos was a small town compared to New York. Santos wasn't even one of the biggest cities in Brazil – and New York was the capital of the world. During the 1970s the city was going through an exciting period – it was the age of the big disco nightclubs, and the Cosmos were part of it. I met so many musicians, actors and celebrities that I can hardly remember them all. Because Warner, as well as owning the Cosmos, owned music and film businesses there were always Warner cocktail parties linking us all together. I met Frank Sinatra, Mick Jagger, Rod Stewart, Woody Allen, the list is endless. I went to Michael Jackson's eighteenth or nineteenth birthday party and I had my portrait painted by Andy Warhol. Once I bumped into Steven Spielberg in a restaurant and he told me: 'I'm going to film you playing football on the moon. Because that's the only place you haven't played football yet – on the moon!'

On another occasion I was going to the Warner office in the Rockefeller Center and there was a huge commotion with people wanting my autograph and shouting my name. I went into the elevator with another man. He then turned to me and I saw it was Robert Redford: 'No one paid any attention to me!' he said, and burst out laughing.

It was also at this time that I began to drink. I'm joking – I have never been a drinker. I've never even let a caipirinha pass my lips – and that is the Brazilian national drink. I have always been very careful to look after my health. I have never drunk, never smoked and never taken drugs. People used to tell me that it is fine to drink alcohol socially, and even that wine is good for the heart. My reply was always that since I'm from Três Corações, I have three hearts, and so I would end up drinking three times as much as I should.

However, at the Cosmos this changed. We used to start training for the season in March, when it was barely past winter. The team doctor, noticing that the Latin players were suffering because of the cold, used to say that we could have a small dram of whisky before starting the training sessions. I couldn't believe what I was hearing. Could you imagine a Brazilian doctor suggesting a tipple before going on to the pitch? To me it was ludicrous. The doctor said it would help us warm up. Well, I tried it out. That's when I first tasted whisky. Now I let myself drink it every now and again, on special occasions, such as when raising a glass in a toast.

Even though I am very careful with my diet, in my travels I have tried every type of food you can imagine. Whenever a foreign place wants to pay tribute, inevitably I am asked to taste the local delicacy. I have eaten goat's knee, testicle, monkey brain and dog. When I saw the scene in that Indiana Jones film when he is served up weird dishes I thought, 'I've been through exactly the same thing!' I'm lucky because I seem to like everything. I like meat, fish, vegetables . . . and I like to start the day with two boiled eggs. That's because of Dondinho – he had it drilled into me that boiled eggs are good for you.

At the start of the 1976 season the Cosmos were more of a serious outfit. Gordon Bradley moved 'upstairs' to an administrative role as another Englishman, the former Evertonian Ken Furphy, replaced him as coach. We also moved from Randall's Island back to the Yankee Stadium, the Cosmos' first home. Furphy didn't waste time in recruiting players from his native land, bringing in five First Division players including three from one of his former clubs, Sheffield United. The squad was getting stronger all the time, and Professor Mazzei's new training programmes were starting to bear fruit, but I wasn't entirely convinced by Furphy's tactics. He was much more fixed in his views than Bradley, and urged the team to adopt a more cautious, defensive playing style. I was moved to midfield, which I felt was a bit of a waste of everyone's time, given that I had been brought to the club to score goals. And the style didn't exploit the talents of the squad at that time – as well as myself we had good forwards in Brian Tinnian and Tony Field, and became even more powerful when we were joined by the Italian international striker, Giorgio Chinaglia, who I knew well having played against him several times before, and rated highly.

Despite a thumping 6–0 win in Giorgio's first game, a match against Los Angeles Aztecs in May in which both he and I scored twice, Furphy remained unconvinced that an attacking strategy was the way forward, and the results remained mixed. Furphy just refused to commit more than one player to attack, and time and again one of us found ourselves in a good forward position but with no support. We won four and lost four of the next eight games. Clearly this wasn't working, and after the last of these, a 2–3 defeat to the Washington Diplomats, Furphy was eventually replaced, with Gordon Bradley taking over as coach once more.

Things improved immediately, and we ended up finishing second in the Northern Division of the NASL. We had made the play-offs, and faced Washington again in the first round in August. I scored in our 2–0 win at the Shea Stadium, leaving us to face the Tampa Bay Rowdies, one of the strongest teams in the league. Tampa hadn't been beaten at home all season, and we would need to be at our very best to overturn this record. But despite a great effort on the part of our players it wasn't to be, and we ended up losing 3–1. I had pulled a goal back after their first, but some poor refereeing led to a moment of confusion on the pitch which was cleverly exploited by the former Watford star Stewart Scullion. And then, as we absorbed this blow, Rodney Marsh added their third.

It was a disappointing end to a season of hard work, but at the same time much progress had been made, both at Cosmos and for the sport in America more generally. I really felt vindicated that I had made the right decision in coming out of retirement. I had turned out twice for an 'American All-Stars' team in May, against Italy and England, and although we lost both games it showed that the US was starting to register on the international scene. And throughout the year I had been the focus of great interest as a story for newspapers, magazines and on television, as well as continuing my work on the Youth Programme. In fact I had travelled as never before for this scheme, almost always with Professor Mazzei, and during 1976 we had visited, among many other places, Japan, India, Uganda and Nigeria – almost causing a diplomatic incident in that country when we were caught up in an attempted *coup d'état*. The president, General Mohammed, was assassinated during our stay, and although the plotters were soon caught a period of mourning was declared, which led to the airport being closed and a curfew imposed. Arthur Ashe was also in Lagos, for a tennis tournament, but he was moved from our hotel to the US Embassy. We were unable to leave our hotel for six days, prompting Rosemeri back home to place a series of frantic calls to various embassies as well as Cosmos and PepsiCo to get me out. Fortunately calm was eventually restored and we were allowed to leave – although when I did go, the Brazilian ambassador insisted I wear an aviator's uniform as a disguise.

I also took the opportunity to sign various new advertising contracts. It was important to me to be a good businessman in the US, and I knew I should make good use of my contacts with such powerful individuals as Steve Ross from Warner and the record company executives Ahmet and Nesuhi Ertegun, who had been involved in the Cosmos' creation. My family were studying a lot, and happy with our surroundings. Kelly Cristina, Edinho and Rose all spoke perfect English. I felt that my move to the States had been all to the good for me and my family, and for Brazil too.

✯

Towards the end of the 1976 season I had returned to the 21 Club to be presented with a gold-encrusted boot to commemorate my 1,250th goal in professional football. Although there was nothing like the fanfare, or the pressure before it, that had accompanied the 1,000th goal, it still felt like a remarkable milestone, and I realised that day just how far I had come from playing barefoot in the streets of Bauru.

I had so much to be thankful for, not least my continuing good health. I've always been in excellent shape – God has been generous to me, even in that. For years the person who took charge of my physical condition was the able Julio Mazzei, who has been a real brother to me, as I hope this book has made clear. The Professor was a maestro in his field, a pioneer, a professor of physical training always fascinated by the latest techniques. But although we worked hard to maintain my fitness and health, I was lucky to be blessed with a physique tailor-made for sport, especially football, to begin with. Julio once told me he thought I could have been Olympic champion in the decathlon, such was the all-round nature of my attributes: 'Without any training you can run the hundred metres in eleven seconds, jump a metre eighty, and in the long jump do six metres fifty,' he said. 'Your body responds perfectly to everything in sport.'

No, I had been lucky in inheriting some good genes, and in meeting someone who encouraged me to work hard to preserve and exploit the physical prowess they gave me. But I was also aware that it could not go on for ever. Even so, I signed a one-year extension to my contract. I didn't know whether 1977 would prove to be my final season as a player, I just wanted to do the best for the club, and was excited by the further changes that were taking place, all of them, it seemed, underlining Cosmos' position as a force to be reckoned with in American soccer.

As with the previous year, there was a change of coach and of home ground – Eddie Firmani, fresh from his success with

Tampa Bay, took over from Gordon Bradley; and at last we found a more permanent home at the Giants Stadium in New Jersey. But most exciting of all was the arrival of some heavyweight talent – first Franz Beckenbauer, the World Cup-winning West German captain, joined us from Bayern Munich; and then my old friend and Santos team-mate Carlos Alberto came to Cosmos in July. Other signings included Jomo Sono, Vitomir Dimitrijevic, Rildo and many others. And new local talent began to emerge too – like Bob Smith, Gary Etherington and the Canadian, Bob Iarusci.

It would prove to be a great season. With attendances going up every game, and media coverage increasingly fevered, we won our last eight home games to finish second to the Fort Lauderdale Strikers. In the subsequent play-offs we got the better of them, however, thrashing the Strikers 8–3 in front of a sell-out crowd of 78,000, as well as defeating the previous year's nemesis, the Tampa Bay Rowdies. After defeating Rochester home and away we went on to the Soccer Bowl, the match for the NASL Outdoor Championship. Played in Portland, Oregon on 27 August, we beat the Seattle Sounders 2–1, with Giorgio Chinaglia getting the winner nine minutes from time in my last competitive match – a wonderful finale.

The end was in sight now. I had played 111 matches for Cosmos, scoring 65 goals. Our farewell tour saw us playing in Japan, in Venezuela, in Trinidad and Tobago, in China and India. On my return I knew I would have to face the emotional turmoil of my very last game, a match against my beloved Santos in which I would play one half for each side.

On 1 October 1977, three weeks before my thirty-seventh birthday, some 75,000 people gathered at the Giants Stadium to watch my farewell to the game that had given me so much joy, over twenty-one years packed with incident and excitement. Millions more watched on television. I scored for Cosmos in the first half, but couldn't repeat the trick for my old Brazilian friends in the second, and Cosmos won 2–1. The end had come, and it was as charged with emotional intensity as my previous farewells for Brazil in 1971 and Santos in 1974 – again, the tears flowed down my face as I received the cheers of the crowd, but this time, as the rain came down, I didn't bother wiping them away.

It was the end of my career for only the second club with whom I'd ever had a contract. I made a speech on the pitch and ended it by saying the words, 'Love! Love! Love!' Later, the Brazilian singer Caetano Veloso wrote a song inspired by that moment where the chorus goes, 'Pelé said love, love, love.' Of all the songs written about me I think that one touches me most.

Carlos Alberto tried to cheer me up, but I was really overcome. The players carried me around the pitch. Afterwards my father, Waldemar de Brito and I were standing under an umbrella, and I had a sudden, vivid recollection of that journey the three of us had undertaken over twenty years earlier. In the VIP box I thought about my mother, Dona Celeste, and what she'd make of this extraordinary spectacle. My thoughts blurred between the past and present. Once again I thought of God, who had given me the talent to play this beautiful game and who had protected me from serious injury.

There was a great party at the Plaza afterwards, a wonderful occasion made all the more special by the presence of so many people close to me. As well as Dondinho and Waldemar there was my mother and other family and friends; former World Cup-winning captains like Bellini, Mauro and Carlos Alberto from Brazil; Bobby Moore, England's champion in 1966;

Germany's 1974 hero Franz Beckenbauer; and the great boxing champion Muhammad Ali, who had cried when he hugged me after the match, saying, 'Now there are two of the greatest.'

✯

Why did I retire? Even though I was thirty-seven, Julio Mazzei said I was in good enough shape to carry on. I quit because I was doing what I had always done. The storyline of my life dictated it. I had become champion at Santos, in the army team and for Brazil. I had left all of them at the top. Now I was champion at the Cosmos too. It was time to leave.

Also, the NASL had got a lot tougher. It was now a serious league. Our rivals had brought in more strong reinforcements from Europe. I thought to myself it was a very good time to stop.

I also felt that I had played my part in what I had set out to do. Football had really caught on in the US. Even though the NASL fell apart a few years later, a seed was sown and now soccer is the largest sport for Americans aged between six and twenty. That makes me feel very proud. It has some way to go as a professional sport there – because of the competition from American football and basketball – but it is now established at grass-roots level throughout the country. The USA were quarter-finalists at the 2002 World Cup; I'm convinced that had it not been for me and the Cosmos creating such an interest thirty years ago this would never have happened.

Stopping gave me a chance to reflect on what I had achieved in my career. I had played 1,367 matches in all, scoring 1,283 goals. That felt like enough.

I did play again – for a few tribute games, like Franz

Beckenbauer's Cosmos farewell in 1980. To celebrate my fiftieth birthday, in 1990, a big party was organised at the San Siro in Milan for which a giant birthday cake was built on the middle of the pitch. In that game, I played for a 'Friends of Pelé' Brazilian side against a team of players from the Italian league. I even considered putting myself forward for the 1986 World Cup in Mexico – I would have been a player at forty-five years old, bagging the record as the oldest as well as one of the youngest players in the Finals. Brazil's coach in 1986, Telê Santana, said it wasn't impossible, especially with judicious use of substitutes. But it was just a moment of longing to put that magical yellow shirt on again.

I knew that I would really miss the days when stepping out on to the pitch was a regular part of my life – and I do. I miss the ball, the thrill and the energy in the stadium, the fight to get a good result, the joy and sorrow in victory and defeat.

But now it was time for me to exchange the world of pitches for a world of offices. Or at least, that's what I thought.

9

Citizen of the World

'Most of today's fans have never seen him play, and yet they feel he is somehow part of their lives'

HENRY KISSINGER

On 27 September 1977 the United Nations gave me a certificate declaring that I was now 'A Citizen of the World'. I was very moved by the honour, which came at a time when I was looking ahead to what I would do after football. My retirement was imminent, and although I had various business and sponsorship commitments I knew I wanted to do something more than just lend my name to the highest bidder for the rest of my life. It sounds grandiloquent to say that becoming a 'citizen of the world' helped focus my thoughts – after all, everyone on the planet is a citizen of the world in their own right – but it was a humbling reminder that I had come to occupy a different place in people's attentions and affections. In kicking a ball around a pitch, and scoring some goals, I had somehow come to embody a little of what so many millions of people around the world loved about football, this beautiful game. I had been lucky to be blessed by God with a talent for it, and lucky to have loving and supportive parents, and lucky to have played alongside and against some of the best players in the world, who helped me hone my skills. Football had been my job for over twenty years, and now it was time to use the fame it had given me in a positive way.

Football's world governing body, FIFA, was an obvious

organisation to become more involved with, not least because I knew its President, João Havelange, well and had helped in his campaign to become elected. I was invited to join FIFA's Fair Play board, a cause that has always been close to my heart. I had applauded the introduction of the red and yellow card system at the 1970 World Cup, and saw my work for FIFA as a way of encouraging higher standards of refereeing and stronger punishments for players who went out to hurt their opponents rather than just trying to relieve them of the ball. I had certainly had my share of this treatment, especially in 1966, when I felt that I had no protection from the referees in that year's World Cup. Although I have had my share of bookings – many of them perfectly deserved! – I have always had the highest admiration for those players who conduct themselves well on a football field: the former England striker Gary Lineker, who went through his whole distinguished career without once getting even a yellow card, is a good example not just to professional footballers but to children around the world.

As well as the Fair Play work I also came to perform a more general, almost ambassadorial role for FIFA, which took me all over the world as a figurehead for football and which I grew to enjoy very much. Following the UN honour described above I also became a 'Goodwill Ambassador' for UNICEF, the United Nations' Children's Fund, which was established in 1946 to help children who were suffering from hunger or disease. Since then it has become a permanent part of the UN's Charter, working to protect the basic rights of children to things like education and healthcare. I took part in fund-raising events for this cause and I'm proud that to this day I'm still involved with the organisation's work. Much later, in November 2001, I was able to combine these two interests by appearing at the launch of a partnership between FIFA and UNICEF to dedicate the 2002 World Cup to the children of the world. I was proud to take part – I was a child too, once, and a country that has no children has no future.

✯

I was trying to do my bit on that score, too, and in 1978 Rosemeri and I had our third child together when the lovely Jennifer was born. Unfortunately I was away in Argentina at the time – I had been offered a television contract to commentate on that year's World Cup, which I thought would be good experience for a possible future sideline, and I was very sorry to have missed her birth. When I got back from Argentina, however, it was clear that my absence had been the straw that broke the camel's back. Rose and I had a heart-to-heart, and I realised things were about to change. She was very upset that I hadn't been there with her at the birth, and told me she could no longer bear my being away so much all the time – as well as my new ambassadorial commitments, there was all the advertising work and my ongoing soccer clinics for Pepsi. It was all too much, she said, especially now I wasn't actually playing any more. She wanted a divorce.

It was true, the countless activities did take up a huge amount of my time. I was often away for up to eight months a year. I knew that it wasn't easy for her being both mother and father to our three children, and I knew that, deep down, she was right. Life would have to go on, and we'd just be friends. I'd still be a father, though, and I'd still play an active part in all my children's lives.

And so, in the week of Jennifer's birth, after twelve years of marriage, we officially announced our separation. We were divorced in the Dominican Republic, but I have never stopped taking care of anything Rose wanted. Maybe sometimes it wasn't enough, but she and my children know what has been done for them. She had the chance to go and live in New York and study, and my children will always be able to count on my support.

Some years later, much to my sadness, Rose decided she wanted to publish a book about our relationship, despite the protests of our three children as well as me. One of the unfortunate things she wanted to write about was the fact that I had had a short fling when we had been together, although before we were married, and that this had led to the birth of a daughter, Sandra Regina Machado. She was born in 1964 – Rose and I got married in 1966. Sandra is the daughter of Anísia Machado, a household maid. When Anísia first brought Sandra to my house to meet me, by which time I was already married, my initial reaction was to deny that I was the father – after all, Anísia and I had only been together once, no more than that. I was shocked, and it was obvious that I couldn't keep the girl – there was no proof that she was my daughter. Subsequently, after many discussions and misunderstandings, it was proved that she is indeed my daughter, and a court ruled that she is able to use my surname: Nascimento.

But the story didn't end there. Sandra too decided to write a book, *The Daughter the King Didn't Want*, which I found hurtful. I had many reactions during this whole story, as it was years before Sandra got in touch – not until 1991, in fact. My sister Maria Lúcia went to talk to her, and got the sense that she was more interested in money than in being close to me. As far as I'm concerned, though, the matter is closed; I'm prepared to respect the judge's decision, and accept that Sandra is my daughter.

There was one affair, though, that did happen while I was married – for a very short while in 1968 I was seeing a journalist from Rio Grande do Sul called Lenita Kurtz. And this too led to the birth of a daughter, Flávia Christina Kurtz, although this time there was no legal case involved. Flávia sought me out – to make contact, not to hassle me for money – and the moment my mother saw her she knew right away that there was no need for a DNA test: this was her granddaughter, all right. Flávia, who's now married, gets on well with me, and sometimes comes to visit us at my ranch, Sossego, in Juquiá.

Separating from Rose was one of the most difficult moments of my life. I really missed not spending time with my kids. I decided, however, to carry on living in New York. I signed up for another contract with Warner, this one for ten years, to do promotional and other work. Being in New York, and being single again, there were distractions. I still had some of those hormones that had driven me crazy as a boy. There were many girlfriends and parties. I can remember bumping into George Best a few times and we became mates. He used to always chide me: 'What kind of King are you? You don't drink, you don't smoke!' I used to always joke back that I was sure he wasn't European – that he must have had some Latin in him.

One of the more infamous relationships I had after Rose was with Maria da Graça Meneghel, a beautiful blonde model of German ancestry known as Xuxa. I first met her when she was sixteen years old. We were doing a photoshoot in Rio for the magazine *Manchete* – in which I appeared with her and two other models. I invited her to see a concert, but because she was so young I had to ask her father's permission. I invited her as a friend, but she eventually became more than that. She would describe our relationship as colourful . . . I always used to joke back that it was black and white.

I helped Xuxa's career get off the ground by introducing her to some friends of mine who made films that in those days were seen as quite spicy. She landed the lead role in one of them and this led to an invitation to pose for *Playboy*. She became a cover-girl in late 1982 and her new celebrity status resulted in Manchete TV offering her the job of presenting her own show the following year. It was a kids' show. Once she was working with children, however, I didn't think her past as a glamour model was cool. I said this to her, her parents and the staff at *Playboy*. So we made a deal – I would give the mag an exclusive interview, and in return they would give me the originals of the entire *Playboy* shoot. I went into the magazine's offices and they handed over the negatives, which I then handed to her parents. Xuxa was very pleased and I think it was a weight off her shoulders that these pictures were out of circulation. She was very good at her job as a children's presenter and went on to be very successful as a singer, TV and movie star. I'm proud of her because in those days it was very difficult for women to get a break in TV. I used to go on her show and play the guitar, or dress up as Santa Claus for her Christmas specials. We were together for six years, but it wasn't a very intense relationship – it was more a a friendship. I lived in New York and she was in Brazil.

I was also fortunate enough to date a couple of beauty queens – Deise Nunes de Souza, who I went out with in 1986; and Flávia Cavalcanti, who I saw around the end of 1989, had both been crowned Miss Brazil. Flávia was from Ceará. At times it was a really serious relationship – she even took to wearing a wedding-ring, though I didn't want to get married – but by the time of the 1990 World Cup in Italy we had already split up.

After me, Xuxa went out with Ayrton Senna, the motor-racing champion. People have often speculated that Ayrton and I had issues with each other because of Xuxa, but that is ridiculous. His career took off when I was living in New York, so I didn't really know him – for geographical reasons. I am now good friends with his sister, Viviane, who runs the Ayrton Senna Institute.

Ayrton died on 1 May 1994. I remember hearing about his death and, like every Brazilian, was shocked and saddened. I also remember the date for another reason – the day before, I had married Assíria.

✱

Born in Recife, Assíria Seixas Lemos had left Brazil to study theology at a Baptist college in New York at the age of eighteen. She later studied psychology, and it was in New York that I first met her in 1985. We had mutual friends, it turned out, and would often spend time together. I liked her and admired her from the start, although she was still married at that time – she and her first husband would have a daughter together, Gemima, named after Assíria's mother. She was settled in New York, I was then based in Santos but was travelling all over the world, and so we decided to put off any serious decisions about our relationship for the time being. I was going out with a doctor from Rio called Luciene, but I realised I couldn't stop thinking about Assíria. We would meet up whenever I was over in New York, although we would often go for long periods without seeing each other. She had her own life, her own goals and plans, she loved New York and had no intention of going back to Brazil.

Towards the end of the 1980s her marriage broke down, and we started to see each other more often. One moment Assíria and I were friends; the next, we were lovers.

✯

A life is only rich if you fill it with experiences. I've had my share, like any man who has experienced first love, second, and third . . . And like all of us I dreamed of having a family, children, health and happiness. I have been lucky to have found all four. I loved my first wife, Rose, and my children. I would go on to love again, and have more children. As I get older I devote myself more intensely to all of them, and more calmly; but I do like to look back on the loves in my life, the experiences I've lived through. My life has been filled with emotions, with energy, and indeed it remains so to this day. I never meant to hurt anyone, but it can happen when you love so many people. I've always been in love with something or other, that's what drives me – that's what gives me the fuel to travel so much and work so hard.

As a child in Bauru I loved the arts; I loved performing, and I loved playing up, too. I was crazy about setting up those little circuses in the yard of our house. I was a fearless boy, constantly looking for new thrills, and that sort of entertainment made me want to be an artist in my own right one day. People say there was a lot of art to what I did on the football pitch, which may be true. What there certainly was, when I was on the pitch, was a musicality. Without a doubt the way Brazilians play football is intimately connected with rhythm, melody and beat. I have always loved music. I play the guitar a little and have composed songs that have been performed by Brazilian greats like Elis Regina, Jair Rodrigues, Sérgio Mendes and Wilson Simonal. I have recently started recording with Gilberto Gil, the pop star who is Brazilian Minister of Culture. One of the things I hope to do in the future is release a CD of all the songs I have composed.

I also hope to appear on a theatre stage before I die. There is definitely something of the performer in me – playing football at the highest level requires it. During my sporting career, in fact, I always imagined I would end up acting. I had always loved going to the cinema in Bauru, and not just to hang out with the girls there. One of my earliest memories of the movies was seeing with my family *The Passion of the Christ*, the first one, in black and white.

I love watching films. Sometimes I can watch three or four films a night. On a long-haul flight, maybe five. Suspense and action flicks are my favourites. And I have been fortunate enough to be involved in my own small way with the movie business, making films with Carlos Hugo Cristensen, Oswaldo Sampaio and Luiz Carlos Barreto – films like *O Rei Pelé* (1962; I played myself), *A Marcha* (1972), *Isto é Pelé* (1975; again, as myself) and *Os Trombadinhas* ('The Child-Thieves', 1979). I especially liked *Os Trombadinhas*, and collaborated on the story for it. It was about the problem of abandoned children; a subject I cannot repeat often enough is close to my heart. I hoped the film would help get them off the streets, make something useful of them, for them and for society.

But my best-known foray into the acting world was without doubt the 1981 John Huston film *Escape to Victory*, starring Michael

Caine and Sylvester Stallone. My involvement came about as a spin-off from my contract with Warner Communications, who owned the Warner Bros studio. The film, set mostly in a prisoner-of-war camp during the Second World War, revolved around a propaganda plan by the Nazis to stage a match between their best players and an all-star Allied team from POW camps – but the prisoners end up using the match as the cover for a daring escape plan.

As well as acting as technical adviser for the football scenes I played a Corporal Luis Fernandez, and when we were shooting the film I'd come on to the pitch with the same passion that I had brought to real games. The director, John Huston, used to shout, 'Pelé, relax! It's a film, it has to be contained within the scene, the emotion has to be controlled . . .' He was a cinematic genius – I learned so much from him. I learned too that the 'stars' don't always work democratically. Stallone, for example, wouldn't let anyone else sit in his chair on the set, and the story went round that he insisted on his character being the player who scored the winning goal. Since he played the goalkeeper, Hatch, this didn't really work, hence the scene where Stallone saves a penalty at the end.

We shot a lot of the film in Hungary, because there was a stadium in Budapest that looked the part – big enough to stage the climactic match, but without modern floodlights. There were lots of other players involved, too – Ossie Ardiles, fresh from his World Cup-winning experience with Argentina; another World Cup-winner in Bobby Moore, who had been at my farewell Cosmos game, and who I thought wasn't a bad actor; and a group of Ipswich Town players drafted in as extras. I got to show off a little in the final reel – my character gets hacked down by a German player only to return limping to the pitch late on to score the equaliser with a spectacular bicycle kick.

I spoke to Freddie Fields, who produced *Escape to Victory*, when I was in Los Angeles last year, and he brought up the idea of filming a sequel. Stallone said he was up for it. I told Freddie to send me the script, but I haven't heard from him since then. There is no lack of proposals on the table, it's just a case of choosing the right one. Benedito Ruy Barbosa, who wrote my first book more than forty years ago, has a good idea about a retired footballer who has a bit of a chip on his shoulder about the profession. He says he wanted me to play the main role, but that I'd have to paint my hair white. Let's see . . . Movies will always be part of my life, whether making them, watching them or simply replaying the film of my memory.

✯

Despite all these extra-curricular activities, football was still a constant in my life. My involvement with the soccer clinics came to an end in 1983, but of course I kept a close watch on the domestic scene and also on Brazil's fortunes, which throughout the 1980s were mixed. At the World Cup in Spain in 1982 there were some excellent performances, not least from a brilliant midfield that included Socrates and Junior, but it seemed the team was all midfield, it wasn't as balanced as the teams I had played in. The defence was undone in the final second-round game against Italy, which Brazil only had to draw in order to make the semi-final, when Paolo Rossi finally came to life and scored a superb hat-trick. We lost 3–2, and were out.

In 1986, as I have already described, I fleetingly considered a return to the top flight as the years away from the buzz of pulling on a Brazil shirt took their toll. But the tournament that year lost a little of its shine because of a falling-out I had with João Havelange, the FIFA President. During my time in America with the Cosmos, one of the long-term goals had been to bring the World Cup to the United States, as this would be the best way to kick-start the development of the sport there. And it looked as though this might be a strong possibility after 1982, when it became clear that the designated hosts for 1986, Colombia, weren't in a position either financially or politically to stage such a big tournament. When Colombia gave up the 1986 competition I really hoped it would go to America, and many of us who had been working towards that end shared my confidence. Even Henry Kissinger, in conversations with Havelange, had been led to believe it was on the cards.

But it was not to be. The United States was passed over in favour of Mexico, who had staged the tournament barely a dozen years earlier. Of course, I have nothing against our Mexican friends, it was simply that we'd assured people that a World Cup would provoke quite significant developments in football in the US, and it seemed the perfect moment for them to take this major step. Havelange strenuously denied that any pressure had been brought to bear by powerful interest groups in the Mexican media, but many were surprised that the US bid wasn't even given a hearing when the FIFA committee met in Stockholm in May 1983. The Americans would have to wait another eleven years before they got their chance.

The second Mexico World Cup will be forever remembered as Maradona's tournament. But there were good performances from the Brazilians, too, especially Josimar, and we were unlucky to go out on penalties in the quarter-final against France, after a terrific match. And in 1990 it was even worse, as a defensive

Brazil side under Sebastião Lazaroni failed to make much impact and were beaten in the second round, losing 1–0 to Argentina in Turin. Even after the first group game against Sweden it was clear the team was in trouble, and I knew they would be exposed as soon as they came up against some decent opposition. I enjoyed seeing the exuberance of Cameroon, though, and part of me envied their veteran striker Roger Milla, still playing at thirty-eight. I look forward to the day when the competition is held in Africa, and an African team lifts the trophy. Amazingly, Milla would play again four years later, in the World Cup Finals of USA '94.

✯

When Assíria and I decided to get married, we did it twice. We had a service in Las Vegas and then another one at the Episcopal Anglican Church in Recife. Religion has always been important to Assíria – she has been a practising Christian since she was a little girl, although she also has Jewish ancestry. She recently discovered that she has Jewish blood on both her father's side and her mother's – both families had emigrated to New York, then called New Amsterdam, after the expulsion of the Jews from Brazil during the Portuguese Inquisition. She was delighted at this discovery, as she has always been strongly attracted to the Jewish people and Judaism, and had long been fascinated by the Jewish community in New York. She even told me at one point that she really wanted to live in Israel, but didn't have the money at the time to make it happen.

As well as the Church, Assíria has always lived for singing. Her mother, Gemima, was a soloist at their church when she was growing up, and she used to love listening to her voice, and would copy her when she sang. She herself sang in the church choir for the first time when she was seven, and then as a soloist at thirteen. It was as necessary to her as the air she breathed. My wife says she never intended to sing professionally, that singing for her was simply a manifestation of how God was present in her life. But that is what she does now, and her work is wonderful – she sings Gospel music really well, and has travelled right across the world for people to hear her. It makes me so proud.

She took up singing again after a trip with me to Brasilia, to the city's evangelical church. When people learned she was there they asked her to sing, and she hasn't looked back since. Her greatest audience was at the Maracanã, and when she's been abroad she's sung for audiences of over 70,000. This year she was nominated for a GMA award, the Gospel music equivalent of the Grammys. She still gets nervous when she's about to go out and sing, however, but she prefers larger audiences. 'Singing for four people is terrible, when you can see the whites of their eyes! It's easier with a larger audience, when you can't make out the individual faces,' she says.

I love to hear her sing Gospel. She has recorded two CDs, and I've been asked to be on one of them. I never saw the harm in it – we were all speaking and singing to God, as far as I could see. I don't believe anyone can remain agnostic their whole life. It's just the truth that as you get older you start believing more. It's a right everyone has, since God has given each of us free will to do what we want to do. Believing in God, being religious, has only done me good.

We were married twelve years ago, and I know the change wasn't an easy one for her. She left the city that her heart had chosen for her, to marry a Brazilian, and a very famous one. All the things she didn't want, in fact – her plans for life had been quite different. When a princess marries a king, she moves into his castle, lives with his servants, his friends – everything!

As she herself says, for six years she was living in a desert. 'It was a radical change in my life. I had no one in Brazil, all my family was in New York.' She spent a fair bit of time feeling isolated, depressed. She didn't know who to trust. It was all very hard to deal with. There weren't many people who welcomed her; she'd come to spoil everything, to take control of the king's house and his life, so people thought, and they didn't like that. Her faith in human nature was disappointed several times during that period: 'Real friends are few and far between; in time I started going back to church, something which always made me happy.'

A little over two years after we were married, we reversed the vasectomy I had had so we could have children, and she became pregnant with our twins, Joshua and Celeste – the girl received the name as a tribute to my mother. They're ten now, and they're delightful, and they get on really well with Gemima, Assíria's daughter from her first marriage. Celeste is thrilled by her brother and sister, and vice versa. 'Gemima is Edson's daughter, you know?' she says. Gemima has been with me since she was two. She calls me daddy, and we love each other as father and daughter.

At home in New York we spoke only English. Now we are back in Brazil we speak Portuguese. They are all bilingual. I try to be a good father, a good companion to my twins. I'm mature now – when I got married the first time I was very young, and travelled a lot. Whenever she can, Assíria comes with me when

I travel, but now she spends more time on the children and on her own career as a singer. And I go with her whenever I can. We respect one another.

✯

In order to improve my financial security I decided to move more formally into the sports business. In 1990 I established the company Pelé Sports & Marketing with Celso Grellet and Hélio Viana. Celso was experienced in sports administration and had been instrumental in bringing modern marketing techniques to Brazilian football, and when we met we thought he could do the same for me. Viana I had met when he was working for the Rio mayor's office and we became involved in a community project together. The idea of PS&M was to manage my profile and also to further the interests of football in Brazil. As well as dealing with my personal contracts with multinationals like MasterCard, the company would invest in tournaments and television rights.

It sounded so simple. Unfortunately, it was anything but. We began negotiations with the Brazilian Football Confederation (CBF) about TV rights for the 1994 Brazilian championship. Two of my associates went to a meeting with the CBF. I was not present. Later, my associates told me the CBF had asked for a $1 million bribe. I was outraged and of course didn't pay it. I told the press what had happened in a famous in-depth interview in *Playboy*, in which I accused the CBF of corruption. I now know that the allegation wasn't true, but I had created a political storm that grew out of control. Ricardo Teixeira, the CBF president, was fuming and I tried to get in touch with him to explain myself but did not manage to.

The scandal broke a year before the 1994 World Cup in the US.

João Havelange, the FIFA President, took Ricardo's side (Ricardo had married Havelange's daughter, so there was a family connection as well as an administrative one) and I was not invited to the World Cup draw. I was very disappointed because I felt I had done so much to get the US to host the event. I was also saddened because Havelange was acting without having full knowledge of the situation. I considered him a father-figure. We had a long-standing, mutually beneficial relationship – everyone knew this. I had shown my gratitude in the early 1970s by flying with him to Africa to help his campaign for the FIFA presidency. The press, understandably, kicked up a huge fuss about our rift. But the truth is it was all based on a misunderstanding.

After the draw furore, I was indeed invited to the World Cup. I did some punditry and also a huge amount of publicity work for MasterCard. I was their ambassador and I took part in 126 events, earning myself a tidy sum. This was very good for me – and the World Cup was very good in another, important way. Brazil won the title for the fourth time, much to my joy, with my old friend Zagallo as technical co-ordinator and Carlos Alberto Parreira as coach. I had not been confident about their chances to begin with, but they played well, Romário especially, and came through a classic quarter-final against the Netherlands 3–2, with all five goals coming in a breathless second half. After a more cautious performance against Sweden the team was through to another World Cup Final. Italy, our opponents, had struggled to make their own way there, conceding goals to Bulgaria, Spain and Nigeria in their last three games, but they had one of the best players in the world at the time in Roberto Baggio. Sadly for Baggio he would prove to be villain rather than hero, missing a penalty in the shoot-out after extra time had ended with the score still 0–0. It wasn't a classic final, and it was an awful way to decide who would be champions, but I jumped for joy when Brazil's captain, Dunga, lifted the trophy.

✯

Many great players retire and stay in the game as coach. That career was not for me. Even though I had been a player for twenty years and worked with many talented coaches, I was never interested in taking that path. I think I would have been a good coach, because of my experience, knowledge of the game and dedication. I'm not sure I would have had the same luck that I had as a player – and I'm not sure how I would have dealt with the players making mistakes. I think I am too much of a perfectionist.

I wanted, however, to put back something into the game – especially in Brazil where football is so important, but is also so disorganised. It is as much a jungle as the Amazon itself. I thought that I could use my status as a force for good.

At club level, Santos brought me on board. For a while I was International Relations Adviser, a role I enjoyed even though the club was going through a difficult time financially. In late 1994, however, the then President of Santos, Miguel Kodja Neto, had me removed from this post after I had criticised his handling of the club's finances – more than a million dollars had been lost through the 'Telebingo' game he created, and there were a number of excessive transfer fees and salary hikes. But the club's Governing Council then fired Kodja Neto himself, and I returned when Samir Abdul Hak came in to take his place. In a period fraught with challenges he managed to pay off the $2 million the club owed, and still managed to build a training centre. I did all I could to help Santos during that difficult time.

In-fighting like this left me cold. I have no interest in party politics, none whatsoever. However, I understood enough about the way football was run to realise that the only way to change it was to do so at the highest possible level – in government.

✯

The problem with football clubs in Brazil is that they live in a legal limbo between amateurism and professionalism. On the one hand they are so bureaucratic that to sell a can of drink in the restaurant you need authorisation; on the other you can sell a player for millions and no one knows where the money goes. The situation is a breeding ground for corruption. And that is one of the reasons why the national league is in such a state and the best players move to Europe.

After the dictatorship ended I had been sounded out by most Brazilian presidents to become Minister for Sport: first by Tancredo Neves in 1985; then by his successor José Sarney and then by Fernando Collor when he won the 1989 election. I had always refused. When, however, Fernando Henrique Cardoso was elected in 1994 the call came again, and I decided that the time was right to accept.

There were a few conditions that I made. I needed a guarantee of political independence. As you can imagine, every which party wanted me to join their slate. I did not want to ally myself with anything but the job in hand. Fernando Henrique, on announcing my appointment, said, 'Our country's national hero has been chosen by the ministry. He is the symbol of

Brazil, a man who has come up from his roots and triumphed.' My life changed completely. I took office in 1995 and moved to Brasilia, the first black man to become a government minister in Brazilian history.

Well, I say I moved to Brasilia. My family moved into an apartment there, and I would be in the office from Monday to Wednesday. The rest of the week I would be travelling. Whatever life choice I made, I always seemed to travel more and more. Brasilia is a very different place to anywhere else I have lived. There is nowhere really to go. And it is full of politicians. When I was a footballer, I surrounded myself with footballers. We were all friends. But in Brasilia, you don't know who your friends are, or who is using you for their own ends. It can be a dangerous place.

When I first got there I was the New Big Thing. Everyone wanted to have their picture taken with me. As soon as they realised I wanted to shake up the system, however, life got a lot more complicated. There were two pillars to the reforms I wanted to make. First, I argued that clubs must become proper businesses so that they could be run in an ethical, transparent way. Secondly, I wanted footballers to be 'free agents' – so that, for example, once a contract with one club was over, the club had no residual rights over them. In Europe this was the issue of the day – thanks to Jean-Marc Bosman, a Belgian player unable to leave his club even though his contract had expired, who was taking his case through the courts. Bosman eventually won, and the law was changed, giving players in Europe more of a say in their own destinies. I wanted to bring in parallel legislation in Brazil.

I must have been naïve to think it would be easy. As soon as I suggested that the presidents of football clubs would have to produce annual audited reports, they turned against me. Of course they didn't want to do this, since the lack of transparency explained how the millions of dollars made from selling players vanishes into offshore bank accounts. The presidents of the clubs had lots of money and were also politically very influential. The football lobby became my biggest foe. The club presidents had very close links with many congressmen – one was even a congressman himself! It was upsetting going against the football establishment, because it meant that they started saying bad things about me. They made me look like I was against football – but that was the opposite of what was true. *They* were destroying Brazilian football. I was trying to make our national sport stronger. If the big clubs were properly managed they would be able to keep most of the players here, but instead they are leaving every day.

I also had my differences with CBF president Ricardo Teixeira and FIFA boss João Havelange. I wanted the national league to be run independently, like the Premiership in England. But they were against it since it would be an erosion of their power. My aim was not to hurt anyone; I had no personal vendetta – I merely wanted to create structures that would benefit footballers and football fans.

I did not realise that being in politics is one battle after another. It was a steep learning curve. There were allegations of corruption in my ministry and I had to sack fourteen people. That was tough. But I think I did make a difference. One of the best things we started was a programme with local governments to provide sports centres. We called them 'Olympic Villages' – central government built them and local authorities provided teachers. Our first one was in Rio in the Mangueira *favela*. They worked brilliantly; kids stopped getting into crime because they had a better way to spend their time.

Now, you would have thought that this would have gone down very well in the corridors of power. After all, we were putting money into public projects that were benefiting poor communities. In fact, the opposite happened. We were building dozens of them throughout Brazil when Congress started to cut our budget – which was pretty tiny in the first place. I put it down to pork-barrel politics and jealousies. What most depressed me about Brasilia was that some politicians were more interested in helping themselves than they were interested in helping young people.

I was an ex-player, so I also wanted to improve the lot of footballers. In Brazil most players earn almost nothing – even if the famous ones in Europe are paid millions. Footballers are a group of workers and as such the labour law that governs their rights should be fair. I put my energies into helping the ministry's lawyers draft a Brazilian version of the Bosman ruling. Yet this was a struggle too. The clubs were against it because they were worried they would spend lots of money developing a player and then lose out if the player could transfer to another club for free as soon as his contract expired. Something that demonstrates what I was up against was the fact that never in my time in Brasilia did the Professional Athletes' Union organise any event in my favour. On the other hand, the football lobby set up an office in Brasilia and were a formidable force. Brazilian footballers have not yet learned to work together to improve their lot. That's sad.

I don't want to sound too bleak. There were good men in the government too. In my three years in the ministry there were moments of real unity in our common struggle to realise our vision of a better Brazil. And of humour too. I remember one day the Minister for Health, Adib Jatene, asking me, 'So how's the Ministry of Sport?'

'No, you've got it wrong,' I said. 'Mine is the Ministry of Health. Yours is the Ministry of Sickness.' He roared with laughter. There were good people there.

I got to travel a lot too, often at the President's side. We were warmly received by world leaders and royalty. In England in 1998 I was awarded an honorary knighthood by Queen Elizabeth II, at Buckingham Palace. It was a real thrill being honoured in that way. Just as in 1968, when I met her at the Maracanã, people kept saying I had to behave according to the protocol, but again it hardly mattered – the Queen and her husband were completely relaxed; so much so that as we approached she asked right away if maybe I could come and play for Liverpool, which I took to be her team. When we left, the whole entourage (including President Cardoso and his wife, Ruth) and I went to Stamford Bridge, the Chelsea ground, to help launch a new football initiative in schools, where we were warmly welcomed by the Duke of Kent and members of the new British government. They were excited by the support they'd received – it was just what I'd hoped to do for children in Brazil. It was obvious that my worldwide renown could be useful in establishing understandings between Brazil and other governments.

After lots of debating my Bill was finally passed by Congress, and on 29 April 1998 Fernando Henrique formally ratified what is known as the 'Pelé Law'. I'm not sure if the law deserves my name, since almost everything I wanted to put in it was taken out as it went through parliament. Clubs are not required to be businesses, and so the lack of transparency (and corruption) continues. The most important clause that was kept in, and of which I am very proud, is the Brazilian Bosman ruling – which came into force three years later. I feel that I helped liberate footballers from slavery.

✯

I left the ministry in 1998 so I would be free to take up a role as commentator for that year's World Cup in France. Brazil reached the final – two finals in succession for the first time since 1962 – where they met the host nation. Again, my old colleague Mario Zagallo was coach. The final, which we lost 3–0, was overshadowed by what happened with Ronaldo. I wasn't there but we heard that he had had a fit shortly before the match and was taken to hospital. He did some tests and was then given the all-clear. I think it was a mistake to play him. I even told Zagallo so. They believed that he could recover from the fit, but in my opinion if the team doctor says someone is in bad shape, you don't let them play. There were other good players who could have come on, like Edmundo, who was in terrific form.

The defeat led to two congressional inquiries into the state of Brazilian soccer. They even called Ronaldo up to explain what had happened to him. While I applauded the intentions of the inquiries – to shed light on the dark and corrupt side of the game (which is what I had tried to do as minister) – they ended up being a national embarrassment. The politicians just wanted media attention. What they had set out to prove was not proved at all.

It was at that time that I was heavily criticised in the press for hugging Ricardo Teixeira. I'd like to set the record straight.

I have never had any personal issues with Ricardo. Sure, we have had our disagreements, but on that day I was called to a meeting with João Havelange, Ricardo and the new Minister for Sport. Once the meeting was over we hugged, in the usual way that Brazilians do. Since there are powerful voices in the press who do not like Ricardo Teixeira, they accused me of sleeping with the enemy. But why shouldn't I shake his hand just because a few journalists don't like him? That's not my problem. I do not have personal objections to him. What is important for me is that my conscience is clear.

10

Family

'Parents always do the best they can for their children, and he certainly has. But we still make mistakes'

ASSÍRIA ON PELÉ AND PARENTHOOD

When my first son, Edinho, was born I wondered – like all dads do – whether he would follow in the footsteps of his father (and grandfather, for that matter) and become a professional footballer. He was a good sportsman as a kid, although since he grew up in New York he spent more time playing American sports like baseball and basketball. That's not to say we wouldn't mess about playing football too, like all fathers and sons – especially Brazilian ones. Edinho was a good outfield player. Then one day there was a kick-about game and he went in goal – I thought just for the fun of it. But when we were back in Brazil one year for the holidays he went for a trial at Santos – as a goalkeeper! And they signed him.

Edinho was at Santos for five years. He was good. What he lacked in height – he is 5 feet 10 inches, small for a goalkeeper – he made up for in agility, strength and speed. In 1995 he was Santos' keeper when they were runners-up in the Brazilian national league. (This was a better placing than Santos had ever achieved when I was in the team! But then the national league only started in 1971, so I didn't have many chances at that trophy.) I always thought that it was very ironic that my son became a professional goalkeeper. My career was all about humiliating the wearers of the number one shirt. Was God having some kind of joke?

Friends used to tell me that Edinho had chosen the position as a way of avoiding comparisons with his father. This makes sense, I can understand the motive – my brother Zoca suffered from the same dilemma, and ended up quitting the game as a result – but I'm not so sure it tells the whole story. I think he really wanted to be a goalkeeper. And also, I was a pretty good goalie too. I was always the reserve keeper for Brazil and at Santos, and I loved playing in that position. Making a good save could sometimes be almost as satisfying as scoring a goal.

There is a game I used to like playing with Edinho. I would take ten penalties against him and then he would take ten against me. I never ever lost to him. In fact, I used to play this game when training with the national team. I used to win against everyone. Only one person beat me – and then on only one occasion: Carlos Alberto, because he was a master penalty-taker. The others always lost.

Unfortunately, Edinho's career took a turn for the worse in 1996. He broke his knee and was out of action for a year and a half. He used to joke with me, saying that I had played for twenty-five years and had never been seriously injured, yet he played for four and did in his knee. 'Son,' I used to joke back to him, 'I treated keepers badly all my career. I used to hurt them terribly. Now you are one yourself, you are reaping everything I sowed.'

During Edinho's recuperation he went to Ponte Preta on loan. But convalescence wasn't easy and he never got back to his best form. He retired in 1999. It was a shame since I really think that he had enough talent to have made the national team.

All he needed was more experience, and a bit of luck. But, just like my father – a knee injury curtailed his career in its prime.

After leaving football Edinho started competing in motocross races. For a while he even produced a motocross show on Brazilian terrestrial TV. But fate would have other things in store for him.

✯

Back in 1970, the year Edinho was born, I wrote some words which would come back to haunt me: 'Young men always think they're better than their elders. Sometimes this leads to their doing things they shouldn't. I'd like to warn young people that any kind of excess is harmful – starting with smoking and drinking. I think that young people can belong to groups and yet retain their own individuality, not be led by imitation or influence. The bad kids lead the good ones into vice and ruin through drugs . . . Young people have to do the things they want to do, without being influenced by their peers. Wherever you go in the world you'll find good kids drawn into vice by bad company. It's important that you're able to keep away from these people.'

Thirty-six years have passed since I wrote those words, but I could never have imagined how pertinent they would become, how prescient. Edinho too has suffered the consequences of getting involved with the wrong people.

I don't know how this happened; I wish I did. I don't know how much the way his life has turned out has been influenced by his upbringing, although it must have been. I have already written about how I regret being away from home so much during the 1970s, and how this contributed to the breakdown of my first marriage. I know it was hard for all of my family then, living in New York, learning English, trying to fit in. As one man living with three women – his mother and two sisters – Edinho always behaved very differently from the young Americans all around him. He was a normal kid, though – sweet, sometimes anxious, occasionally wilful: a typical adolescent. He grew up, married, he had two daughters, he had friends and he played football. I've always supported him in everything he's done, as long as it was reasonable, and I've never forced him to do anything that he didn't want to do.

In October 1992, however, he was involved in an illegal car race – very early one morning, through the city streets, endangering the lives of innocent drivers and pedestrians as well as those of the people taking part in this stupid and pointless activity. There was, with a terrible inevitability, an accident. A man called Pedro Simões Neto, a motorcyclist, was hit and killed.

Eventually the case came to trial, and Edinho was sentenced to a year and a half in an open prison, even though he hadn't been directly responsible, as he wasn't the one driving the car. Then, in 2005, there was a second trial, and the jury unanimously accepted the evidence and testimonies that proved he hadn't played any active part in the death of Pedro Simões Neto. We were all thrilled. From the moment it had happened, I had been sure that Edinho hadn't been responsible. He'd been there, yes, he'd been in the car; but someone else had been driving. He learned a tough lesson from this, but it didn't prevent him making a few undesirable friends who just wanted to use him and the connections he had through being Pelé's son. There are few true friends in the world without any self-interest.

One of the people that Edinho hung out with, or who

attached himself to Edinho, was a man known as Naldinho. He is actually the son of Pitico, a former Santos team-mate who I also got to come over to play for the Cosmos with me. Naldinho was accused of being involved in drugs and money-laundering, and was arrested one day in a state-wide operation. As an associate of Naldinho, Edinho was arrested too: on 6 June 2005 narcotics agents raided his house in Santos, where he lived with his wife Jéssica and two daughters. They weren't able to find anything they could describe as illegal, but alleging an infringement of Article 14 of Law 6368 of the Association of Narcotics Trafficking, the police thought they ought to take Edinho in. The arrest was based on casual telephone conversations with people, which were no proof of any association, let alone of a crime. No evidence was brought to show that Edinho was involved with any illegal activity. Why would there be any? What need would he have to launder money?

When I was told what had happened, it was like a nightmare, and one from which I couldn't wake up. But the sadness of all those around me and the worry we felt was too real to be a nightmare. I became aware that I was experiencing something that I'd never imagined possible, that I had a son who'd been arrested for drug trafficking. How ironic that it should happen to me, someone who had spent his whole life campaigning against drugs.

After a few days of confusion Edinho was taken to a maximum-security prison at Presidente Bernardes, a town in the interior of the state of São Paulo. He would end up being there for two months. Those sixty days when Edinho was in the maximum-security prison were definitely the worst of my life. He was being treated like a monster, locked away from society, as if he were some sort of pervert who could do harm to the world.

That's how bad my pain and suffering were. I felt shame, fear, doubt, sadness and hatred, and had crazy thoughts, wishing I had the superpowers of a Spiderman or a Superman to change the course of this awful story and see him whenever I wanted to, and talk to him, tell him a bit more about life, about people. We often look at our children as though they are grown-ups, and then we realise that they're still just children, that they still need a word from someone older than them, from their real father. I missed my father Dondinho during this strange time – he had passed away in 1998 but I felt now that I needed him more than ever, as though I too were still a child. I wanted him to take my hand and walk with me, showing me the path I should take through this new and awful experience.

My mother Dona Celeste was strong, as ever, but her age meant that we had to be careful with her, with the disappointment of it all, seeing her son, Pelé, who had been such a cheeky kid, now so angry, vulnerable, impotent. There are things we just can't do for other people – this was one of them. My mother's pain was twofold – for her son, and for her grandson. It was horrific. We were all going through such a difficult time, we all worried about each other, and Edinho was so far away.

My fatherly heart was put to its greatest test. I cried a lot. I couldn't sleep, and asked myself if it was fair that such things should happen to me. I'd never drunk, never smoked, always fought against drugs – why should I have to face these tribulations? It was no use being famous – it just made things more complicated. Everyone was careful not to over-protect Edinho – or at least to be fair. If he had been released people would have said it had been arranged just because he was my son – Pelé's son. If anything had happened to him in prison, the police could be blamed for it. It was all a very delicate situation for them. I felt that the right thing to do would be to release him – no doubt about that at all. I had moments of disgust, of bitterness, of guilt, despair, rage – emotions just the opposite of those feelings I've experienced at those wonderful moments in my life as a sportsman. Beside me, Assíria and our family and a few friends gave me the strength to play on – against the most difficult opponent I have ever had to face.

I hired lawyers, and put myself on the front line. But I had no experience with anything of this kind – my struggles had all been on the football pitch. But now I had to defend my son. It was a tough challenge to face, but there was nothing else for it. I was still Pelé, but at that moment I was only Edinho's father. I put myself in front of the cameras and gave the interview that Brazil and the world expected of me. To hear what I had to say about what had just happened was as important as that moment when I scored my thousandth goal. Not everything in life is as easy as it looks: all I wanted to do that day was hide myself away, run away from everything or cry in my mother's arms, rest my head on my wife's shoulder. I wanted all my children close to me, I desperately wanted Edinho to be there to hug him and show him that, yes, we often make mistakes, but that I believed in him and wanted to guide him through this.

I had to gather my courage, for Edinho's sake, and before going to the press I thought about how wonderful my life had been, how often I'd spoken to them about all the good news I'd given to Brazil, a place so in love with football that has always cherished me as an idol. I saw a film playing out in my mind, and it didn't take me long to realise that this was the right thing to do, it was important and consistent with my life-long struggle against drugs and alcohol abuse. I have fought tirelessly and I fight still, hoping that one day the fight will be won. The abuse of drugs is clearly a sensitive and complicated subject, but it is giving the world a sort of incurable cancer that's destroying our society. I believe it is possible to prevent this, and I'll fight for it until the day I die.

Eventually Edinho was transferred to the Tremembé Penitentiary, which was better, as it was closer to home. I kept travelling, not just to fulfil demanding contracts and spread the anti-drugs message around the world: I felt a need to keep myself busy. I thought that things would pass more quickly like that, and realised that there was no way I could stop my ordinary life, I couldn't weaken and give up. I understood that no one would be able to live my life for me, nor I anyone else's, however much I might like to.

I got to know the Progress Centre of the Tremembé Penitentiary as soon as Edinho was sent there. I was reassured that he was closer to us now, in a place that was more pleasant and with a better range of activities for inmates. His daughters could visit him without experiencing the trauma of a maximum-security prison – they'd never seen him there, at Edinho's request. While it wasn't ideal, I derived some comfort from seeing Edinho somewhere more fitting.

After blaming myself for some time about the whole affair I came to the conclusion that I couldn't bear the guilt for this alone. I had gone off in search of my profession, fulfilment, a goal and a dream. I had thrown myself completely into everything I did. The only thing Edinho and my other children lacked was the constant presence you might expect of an involved father. I regret it, but it was an inevitable consequence of what I did for a living. My choice, yes, but no easier for that. But I know that apart from this, they lacked nothing.

I wouldn't think of judging my son. I have an enormous

longing for him to be acquitted and released, and to be able to resume his life, but that isn't up to me – not Pelé, not Edson. Now only the justice system can look at the evidence and determine that he is not guilty, that he is not associated with opportunistic friends who are involved in drugs – though having friends who are involved in drugs isn't in itself enough to keep him locked up. I just pray that God will keep an eye on him, as he always kept an eye on me.

There's so much sadness in me because of this sorry saga, such questioning. But I have no doubt that God will continue to illuminate my path as he has always done. If he has given me this pain, it is because he knows I will be able to deal with it, somehow; he knows that I have the heart of a sportsman, the triple heart of Três Corações, that will be able to bear this suffering. I believe too that we have to accept such trials when they are presented to us, and deal with them as best we can – you can be sure that's the only way to make it pass more easily. There's no point losing sleep over it, crying inconsolably, hating the whole world.

As for me, how many times have I believed in people who have turned out to be less than friends? How many times have I shared my home, my family, my table or my free time with people I later understood were envious, who wished me ill and even did me financial harm? It's so sad to experience this sort of disappointment, but it happens. Many times I've been wrong to put absolute faith in people, but life never stops teaching you. When I think like this, I see that he and I and all of us can make mistakes.

In December 2005, to our joy, Edinho was released – the Ministry passed a preliminary order which would allow Edinho to remain at liberty for the duration of his trial. Having him back home for Christmas was the best present I have ever received, and we spent a lot of time together, talking. He was frail, and very emotional. He cried a lot. He knew there was still much to resolve concerning the trial, but he's sure that he has learned a painful lesson, he's absolutely clear on what he has and hasn't done. He's still prepared to work with the Ministry of Justice and says there's a lot of this story that still hasn't been properly told. He wants to prove his innocence of any criminal association with Naldinho, whom the police have identified as one of the main traffickers on the southern coast of São Paulo.

Just before New Year I went with Edinho to visit a clinic that treats people with substance abuse problems. It's outside São Paulo, about an hour away. This was at my son's own request – he wanted to take stock of his life, and realised he needed to address his problem with marijuana. I understood that this was what he wanted, and it was the right thing for me to do to go with him to see the place, which we looked into a lot before committing to it. Edinho accepts that he wants to live a better and healthier life, he's ready to be cured – and that willingness is itself half the battle.

But despite our hopes that this was the beginning of the end, in February 2006 there was a new twist and Edinho was arrested again, along with six others. I can only hope that he is found innocent; and that once the case is decided one way or the other, that he grows up once and for all, and through this physical, moral and spiritual pain learns that he is lucky to have us as his family and his only true friends.

Despite Edinho's problems, or perhaps because of them, as a family we try to see each other as much as we can. I am lucky to have several homes in which we can get together. In New York I have an apartment, an office and a villa upstate in East Hampton. My first two daughters still live there. Kelly Cristina is thirty-nine now and married to Arthur Deluca. She works in theatre, and speaks various languages. She gave me my first grandson, Malcolm Edson. Jennifer, who is twenty-eight, is there too. She works as an auditor in a digital film company. I still enjoy New York – after living there full-time for a decade and on and off for another two, it's really my second home – and I try to spend the summers there.

When it's cold in the northern hemisphere I like to be in Brazil, where it is always warm. Assíria, the kids and I have moved back to São Paulo, where I also have an office and an apartment. Joshua and Celeste go to school here. On weekends we go to what feels like my *real* home, in Guarujá, on the coast near Santos.

I still travel a lot, but I try to arrange my trips so that I spend as little time away from my family as possible. Nowadays there's nothing I'd exchange for the happiness of being with them – not only is it wonderful, but I learn so much and enjoy myself a lot too. I think the family is at the root of everything. All I know is that as I get older, things about us begin to look different. Now I'm the person who needs them most of all.

My family are the heart of everything. If it hadn't been for them I wouldn't have achieved what I've achieved – I have no doubt about that. My parents were perfect – my uncle, brother and sister, everyone who passed through my life has been important. I always think of them with immense affection.

I have seven children and seven grandchildren (three by Kelly, two by Edinho and two by Sandra). There is also Assíria's daughter Gemima from her first marriage, whom I consider my daughter too. I even have dozens of godchildren – I've lost count of the number of times I've been asked to be godfather to a child, right across the Americas. I haven't always been able to maintain contact with the children or parents, but there are kids in Chile, Peru, Colombia and Mexico as well as Brazil who call me godfather.

There is one more place I own that I want to tell you about. It is my ranch in the interior of the state of São Paulo – between Registro and Juquiá, about one hundred miles south-west of the capital. I bought the land in 1960 – it was Macedo, the Santos masseur, who first told me about it. We have eleven hundred hectares, four hundred head of French cattle and a thousand pigs. I've had an artificial lake put in, where we raise carp and other fish to sell. We get up to 70 tons a year – the equivalent of 40,000 fish. It's a wonderful place, a real haven.

I am calmest when I am there. This is where I am able to forget about the pressures of being Pelé, and I can for a time just be Edson. I rest, I relax. Thoughts about life, my obligations and the responsibilities I've gained, disappear. I like looking after the fish, the horses and even the pigs. I'm in touch with nature, and I enjoy the peace and quiet tremendously. I sit in the shade of a tree and lose myself looking out to the fields, at the animals and the scrubland. At other times I sit there with my guitar and try out a song or two.

My twins Joshua and Celeste love going there. The house I built there has six bedrooms and a wing for guests, friends and staff. Whenever we can, the family get together at the weekend for a barbecue and beer. I've got two battery-powered cars that I keep there, just like the ones they use on football pitches to transport injured players. I go horse-riding with my younger children, with them on their ponies. One of my favourite things in life is our conversations on these trips – I ride in the middle, with the twins on either side. I know that I wasn't able to be around so much for Kelly, Edinho and Jennifer – when they were young my career wouldn't allow it, so I suppose in a way I am trying to make up for that.

I also love playing football with Joshua, my young son, who's already turning into a young man. It reminds me of the time I spent with my dear father, Dondinho, doing the same with me. Time just flies by, and we barely notice. Before too long Joshua will be doing it with his own son. Joshua is my near-constant companion during my free time.

I will be sixty-six years of age in 2006 – and I still feel young at heart. Everyone always lives long in my family, so I expect to have many years ahead of me. Ambrosina, my grandmother, died aged ninety-seven in 1976, and my father was eighty-six when he passed away in 1998. When I do go, I will be buried in a tower block. Santos has the world's highest vertical cemetery – a tall multi-storey building with graves on each of the floors. I have bought an entire floor for my family. Already that's where my father, my aunt (Maria, who died aged ninety) and my grandma are. I bought it because it was built by a business partner of mine. You can see the Vila Belmiro pitch from the window – that was not a factor in deciding to be buried there, but I guess it's a happy coincidence.

But before then there is still much to do, although I look forward to the day when I can slow down a little. Fame has many rewards, and I'm grateful for them, but it would mean nothing without my family.

11

Icon

‘Pelé is one of the few who contradicted my theory: instead of fifteen minutes of fame, he will have fifteen centuries’

ANDY WARHOL

I always say that I am a Brazilian from Três Corações: a Brazilian with three hearts. I am very proud of what my country has contributed to world culture. We are a racial melting-pot, a country where all the races have mixed in a special way. Despite the unfairnesses I have described in other chapters, there is a wonderful sense of equality here too. We are a musical people, and we have faith. We are by nature optimistic. No matter the difficulties, the suffering or the disillusionment, we always have faith that things will get better. We believe.

I know that my compatriots love Pelé, but they are tough with him too. I'll explain these contradictory feelings with two stories. A few years ago I was being driven through the streets of São Paulo. We stopped at some traffic lights when two armed thieves jumped out at us. One of the men pointed his gun at the driver and asked him to open the window. But when they saw who was inside, they gave me the thumbs-up, apologised and walked away. They couldn't face robbing a hero.

On the other hand, sometimes I have the opposite effect. I have gone through immigration at airports all over the world without a passport. People know who I am and let me through. Even in the US there have been times when they have let me in without checking my documents, and that happens to hardly anyone. And, once I'm in customs, no one ever looks in my luggage. Yet here in Brazil, every now and then the customs people open my bags and have a root around. The rest of the world treats me differently than my homeland does.

Why is this? I think that Brazilians are very demanding with their idols. Sometimes it is as if they are more concerned with pulling you down than building you up. They like supporting the underdog, instead of the winner – it's a cultural thing, something ingrained and psychological. When I get sad, I always think of Dona Celeste reminding me: 'You can't please all of the people all of the time.'

I often wonder if other countries are the same with their own heroes. I'm not sure. I have travelled a lot and seen many things. In America, for example, Elvis Presley and Martin Luther King have wonderful memorial museums. But in Brazil there is no Pelé museum. There is something not right about that, it seems to me. Pelé is in Madame Tussauds in London – but here in Brazil there is nothing.

My travails in trying to create a Pelé museum reflect some of the problems I face in Brazil. A few years ago there was a plan to build such an institution on some disused land in Santos. It was a fantastic project. It would have created hundreds of jobs and increased tourism too – since the city doesn't really have anything else but the beach to attract visitors. The São Paulo state governor approved the proposals and we were all set. Then a local councillor appeared on the scene and scuppered the whole thing. He said it was because of environmental issues, but really it was petty local politics. The councillor and the mayor were members of opposing parties and even though the museum was of benefit to everyone, the councillor didn't want the mayor to get the credit.

A similar thing happened down the road at Guarujá. We wanted to build a football school in a run-down area where there were already some football pitches. Local politicians thwarted it by insisting on a whole load of impossible and pointless bureaucracy. This kind of small-mindedness makes me really frustrated.

I always told my mother that she gave me three hearts: one for my family, one for those who admire me, and the other for those who are envious. I know that sometimes I have ruffled feathers because I speak from the heart. Like when I invoked Brazil's little children after the thousandth goal, and was accused of being a demagogue. I know I also made enemies when I was Minister for Sport, because I was trying to change things, since many powerful people had a vested interest in the status quo. Certain sections of the press also like to have a go at me – it's a love–hate thing.

Since I am a celebrity, of course, everything I say is scrutinised. That's part of the deal. The resulting furores don't always reflect what I actually said, of course, but they usually sell papers. In the late 1970s I said that Brazilians had to vote properly. This caused a scandal because I was accused of insulting the Brazilian people, of saying that they didn't know how to vote, implying that they were stupid. In fact, my words were twisted out of all proportion. We were still in a dictatorship, without direct presidential elections. Our leaders were chosen for us. What I said was that it had been a long time since proper elections, and that I supported a change towards greater public participation in the political process. Journalists like to create a storm out of nothing.

I have learned to tread as carefully as I can. Sometimes, this is not carefully enough. It serves journalists' purposes to stir things up: sensationalism sells more papers. I have lost count of the number of times I have said something to help someone, and the press have gone to that person and reported just the opposite. For example, this year I was in China and a journalist asked me if I thought Ronaldo would regain his best form for the 2006 World Cup. I replied that he would – the Cup was three months away. He had been injured. He had had personal problems, such as the end of his marriage. When the focus of your life is not football, then of course this affects your game. But I said that these things are temporary, he had not forgotten how to play football and that he would recover in time for Germany.

I was being positive and encouraging about one of Brazilian football's great stars. Yet when asked to comment on my comment, Ronaldo said that I should have kept my mouth shut about his personal life, that I only talk rubbish.

A similar scenario had taken place a few years back with Romário. But when Romário found out what I had really said, he called me up and apologised. Ronaldo should have called me up too, to ask me what I had really said. But I forgive him.

I have learned that people often have selective memories. A few years ago, when Ronaldo was recovering from his major knee injury, I visited him at his home. I remember he had a picture of Buddha on his wall, since his wife at the time, Milene Domingues, was Buddhist. I told him that I too had had a bad injury once, in 1966, that I spent three months receiving treatment, yet my best World Cup was in 1970. I got to know Ronaldo's father. We spent all afternoon praying. And he became world champion. Did he ever tell the press anything about this?

Since 1956 I have been the subject of books, articles, films, documentaries and more. The public knows me by now. They know what I am like. They know I don't like to sit on the fence. I make predictions. And if I predict something that doesn't happen, then so be it. In 1961 I said I would never marry and in 1965 I said I might retire to Bauru. Okay, so we are not always in control of our own destinies! More importantly, I am not the owner of any ultimate truths. And it's much better to have an opinion than not to answer any questions – people wouldn't accept that; I'd be accused of arrogance.

✯

One of the ways I try to keep perspective on things is to remind myself that what these people are responding to isn't *me*, necessarily, it's this mythical figure that 'Pelé' has become. This is why I refer to Pelé in the third person. I know some people don't like it, but for me I feel I have to 'raise up' Edson in order to 'bring down' Pelé.

It's not easy to separate Edson from Pelé psychologically, try as I might, and of course the two are inextricably linked. I often find myself caught in this conflict between both personalities. I remember the dramatic occasion of my farewell game at the Giants Stadium in 1977. For a moment I thought, 'That's it, I'm going home now, I'm just going to be Edson from now on.' Big mistake.

I knew in myself that I didn't want to play, or need to play any more. But Pelé had taken on a life of his own; he overtook everything. Everybody in the football world wanted to keep him around. And so I carried on being 'Pelé'. Maybe the fact that the name is such an easy word to say clearly (although the English mispronounce it slightly: the last syllable sounds closer to 'lair' than it does to 'lay') helped it become so widely known.

I'm proud Pelé is still here. After all, Pelé the footballer went to many places, scored many goals, won many trophies. What I did on the pitch was shown across the world on television, in newspapers, magazines, photos, in every medium possible. I have been honoured in hundreds of different ways in different countries around the world and the more you receive, the stronger the mythology becomes. Pelé cannot stop – he has commitments all over the world and he will fulfil them all. As Pelé I know I can make a difference.

I am sometimes asked why I have never changed my haircut. In the 1970s I never had a 'black power' afro, nor have I ever shaved it off like many footballers now. My hairstyle was always a tribute to my father. His cut his hair like this and when I was a boy he cut mine in the same way. Apart from when I went back to college I have never changed it and I never will. I think the hairstyle has helped consolidate Pelé's image. Because I have neither gone bald nor grey, it has been a constant all my career. Whereas other footballers are constantly changing their looks, apart from a few wrinkles I have stayed looking pretty much the same since I was a sixteen-year-old boy.

As I get older, however, I'd definitely like my life to be a bit more like Edson's, and to make Edson and Pelé better friends. As I approach my eighth decade I have to find the balance that will make both Edson *and* Pelé strong and happy. Edson is the simple things: family, peace, calm, the countryside, fishing, riding, watching my kids grow up and enjoying my grandchildren; Pelé – well, you know him well now.

I sense the dichotomy between Edson and Pelé every time I take out my MasterCard – bear with me, please, this is not a cheap plug! On one side is the image of me doing a bicycle kick together with the signature of Pelé, and on the other is my real signature, of Edson Arantes do Nascimento. It is a perfect representation of what I am – both identities are separate and both are parts of me. They are the two sides of what I am.

It is also a good example of how Pelé has become more than a sportsman. The name is an international brand. Every day my office receives requests from companies from all over the world asking me to endorse their products. All sorts of things: I've even been asked to advertise toilet paper, but that's one I didn't accept.

Companies have wanted to associate themselves with me since I was a teenager. The first time I was approached to give my name to a product was when I had just started at Santos. A drinks company from inland São Paulo asked my father if I would lend my name to a line of *cachaça*, the sugarcane spirit that is the national drink and the main ingredient of caipirinhas. My father was very keen because as a payment they would buy us a proper house. But when Dondinho told me I was shocked. 'Dad, how can I do this when I don't even drink? I'm a sportsman, an athlete,' I said. He understood immediately and went and cancelled the contract.

I am happy to endorse products but I do have rules: no alcohol, tobacco or religion. As you can imagine, beer and cigarette companies are constantly trying to get me to change my mind. I have been offered insane amounts of money, but I always refuse. One whisky company wanted to put my face on one of their bottles. Can you imagine that?

Cigarette companies have tried all sorts of imaginative ruses.

Once I was invited in to meet a board of tobacco executives. They asked me if I wanted to take part in an advert for their company in which I would make it clear that smoking is *bad* for you. I was somewhat baffled, but told them to continue. They had already prepared a dummy commercial. In it I was running around telling the camera that I was healthy because I looked after my diet, that I was an athlete and that I didn't smoke or drink. I was then surrounded by lots of children and I approached them to say: 'Look here, none of you should smoke. Smoking is not good for you, it's not good for sports people. But, if one day I decided to take up the habit – then I would smoke *these* cigarettes.'

I was gobsmacked! Were they serious? Their concept was that even though smoking is bad, their brand was the *least* bad. I thought it was absolutely mad. They had shown me the advert hoping to get approval and asked me to name my price. I said thanks, but no thanks. There is no way I would do anything like that.

When I endorse a product I will only say things in which I believe. I'm not afraid of being controversial. Certainly, many eyebrows were raised when I decided to talk about erectile dysfunction for Pfizer, the makers of Viagra. This came about because Pfizer got in touch with me saying that young people were dying because they were using Viagra incorrectly. They were taking it for fun, like a recreational drug, perhaps mixing it with alcohol, which could cause heart problems. Pfizer wanted me to encourage men to take it properly by going to see a doctor. They told me that they had done a lot of market research about which athlete would get the message across best, and that I was their first choice. Once they explained what it was about, I was happy to do it.

Endorsements are one thing, but there's only one product that I have actually given my name to: Café Pelé. This came about after I helped the Brazilian Coffee Institute promote Brazilian coffee around Europe in the late 1960s. The suggestion of a Pelé-branded coffee came up. I thought it was a good idea because coffee is an important Brazilian export commodity, and I could see that I was the perfect ambassador for it. Café Pelé has been a huge success and is still around today. In fact, in Russia and the other countries that were behind the Iron Curtain it is the number-one coffee brand.

Café Pelé has also given me a bit of a shock recently. I knew that it was also popular in the Middle East – but I didn't know to what extent. When Saddam Hussein was captured by US forces in 2003, he was apparently hiding in a hole with only three possessions – a machine gun, a suitcase full of dollars, and a packet of Café Pelé!

I have recently decided to launch a Pelé brand properly. Many sportsmen are doing this and I feel it is an exciting new business opportunity. I have a chain of gyms called Pelé Club and the Pelé brand will be broadening out into licensed products such as perfume, clothes and watches. I am also setting up the Pelé Foundation, a children's charity, which will receive a percentage of all profits.

The Pelé brand logo can only be one thing: my signature. When I first gave an autograph – back in the late 1950s – I could barely write properly, but I think it worked out well. I used to sign myself Edson Pelé. Then the first part dropped. My signature has hardly changed since then. In fact, I think the name became a brand decades ago – the style, unintentional though it was, is iconic: the large 'P' and the little circle above the second 'e'. In fact, the circle above the 'e' is a mistake. I was told it should be an acute accent, not a little circle. I said it's a little ball, like a little football, and then it started to catch on.

I sometimes wonder what Bilé, the São Lourenço goalie who'd played alongside my father, would have made of all this. Would I have still existed if he had not? I learned not long ago that he died some years ago at the age of fifty-three. His friends say he was proud to know that the name Pelé had been based on his own. He's undoubtedly a part of my life, of my story. I hope he rests in peace.

✯

What kind of person am I? Pelé, I always say, has no colour or race or religion. He is accepted everywhere. And Edson? Well, I'm Brazilian, and we are a calm, good-humoured people, by and large. I'm almost always in a good mood. My friends will tell you that when I wasn't playing football I was usually just messing around.

I am very competitive too – I think you have to have a competitive streak if you are to compete in sport at the highest level. It doesn't take much for me to accept a challenge. I remember one time in 1968, when I was on tour with Santos in America, we were sitting by the pool of our hotel in Kansas City after dinner one evening, enjoying the lovely cool air. With us was Clayton Espinhel, one of the directors of Santos, who all of a sudden put this challenge to me: 'I'll give you fifty dollars if you swim across that pool.' I didn't have to think twice, and surprised him by pausing only to take off my shoes before diving in. The people who were with us were also astonished – I think they were unsure of whether I needed the money that badly or just couldn't resist the challenge.

I hate losing in anything. Ever since I was a kid I have played 'button football'. It is a game, a little like Subbuteo, in which you make a football team out of buttons, or discs thick like poker chips, and flick them around a table. I mentioned in Chapter 3 that my button team had been Corinthians. Zoca and I always played button football at home – all we ever needed was twenty-two buttons and a flat surface. And you know what? He always used to beat me. It drove me absolutely mad. We still play together when we can and he still beats me. It causes me so much frustration. It really winds me up. I shouldn't be bothered, after all I have achieved, but it really does.

As we get older we often get a bit bolshier, and our wishes start becoming demands. I know that my greatest failing is my stubbornness: if you ask Assíria what I'm like at home, she'll tell you some good things and some bad things. I don't think I'm any different from anyone else, a normal person, flesh and bone, with emotions, loves, pain, with courage and with sins – and why should I be any different? I was born knowing nothing about life; now I know a bit more, but I'll die still learning.

At home, I like everything to be kept nice and clean. I am a bit bossy in that respect. At work, I have a bugbear about timetables. When I can't meet them I get bad-tempered. And when people get things wrong, the same happens. I trust people, until they make a bad mistake, and then I scrub them out of my address book, out of my list of friends . . . I don't think this is to do with temper, it's more a desire not to be taken advantage of.

I think my stubbornness is an aspect of another trait: my perfectionism. I always want to do everything properly. And I also only believe things are wrong when I see them myself. This has caused me problems and continues to do so. I first went into business with a friend, and I ended up paying through the nose when it went wrong. The second time, again, was to help a friend and that too cost me a fortune.

When I was in New York, Warner boss Steve Ross would tell me that I should never mix business and friendships. He said: 'You can't use your heart in money matters; business is business.' I know I am too trusting – call it naïvety or whatever – but I ended up repeating my previous mistakes.

I had set up Pelé Sports & Marketing with a friend, Hélio Viana, with the intention of being a positive influence on sport. Yet, again, the partnership turned into a disaster. One of the company's business deals concerned a UNICEF benefit event that we were planning to stage at the Maracanã. The proposal was to put on a game between a European and a South American all-star team, and have famous singers and bands too. An Argentinian business partner got us a $700,000 bank loan to begin working on the project, but the event didn't happen and there were problems in retrieving the money. Once I found out about this I ordered an audit of my company. It uncovered maladministration, and so I closed the company down. The press seized on this and the negative publicity was terrible.

I had not been aware of the details of what was going on in the company – because I put my trust in people. I trusted him so much we had divided the company so he had 40 per cent and I had 60 – a father wouldn't give so much even to his own son! The whole PS&M fiasco cost me a packet and still takes up time and money because of my legal action against Hélio Viana. One of the reasons why I still work so hard is that I have so many lawyers to pay.

I have learned important lessons, though, and I think I have become stronger because of my disillusionments. I still feel like I'm here on an apprenticeship, improving my spiritual growth and my growth as a human being. I know that when I die there will still be a lot I don't know about life, because life teaches us so much. But I still have faith in my fellow human beings – and will continue to do so.

Another important thing to know about me – which maybe explains why I am so willing to trust people – is that I am a very sentimental person. More than that, I am an absolute cry-baby. I cry a lot. Remember the image of 1958, when Brazil had just won the World Cup, and I bawled my eyes out and put my head on Gilmar's shoulder? Well, I've been crying ever since.

I'm always very emotional. I cry when I sing a sad song. I cry when I see poor children in the street. Sometimes I get sad at how the world is and I ask God why it is that way. After my time at the Ministry of Sport, when I had problems, I asked Him why he put me there unless He wanted me to do good. Why do millions of Brazilians get up early every day and commute for hours to get to exhausting and poorly paid jobs, when the people in power are a bunch of crooks? I've travelled all around the world and seen countries with less natural resources than we have here, but where there are proper health and education systems. Brazil is so rich in so many ways, but the country is full of *favelas*, public health is in a pitiful state, education likewise and still so many people steal from the poor. Why does it have to be that way? It makes me so sad.

When I think of the problems in my country I think of what I can do to help. In 2005 the 'Little Prince' Pelé Institute was established in Curitiba, in the south of Brazil, after doctors at the Little Prince hospital told me about their struggle to raise money for a paediatrics unit, looking after children and adolescents. I signed up at once, and will help them raise the $20 million necessary to build the 12,000-square-metre building needed to carry out the Institute's work. My ultimate aim will continue to be about helping young people. I've never forgotten what I said after my thousandth goal.

In 1999 I had a chance to start training youngsters. I returned to Santos to supervise the junior levels. It was something I had always wanted to do and I relished the opportunity. It was great – I was working with Clodoaldo, Manoel Maria and Ramos Delgado, team-mates from the old days. Two days a week I would go to take part in the sessions. Straight away we noticed we had a talented group of youngsters. Manoel Maria asked me to check out one player in particular. 'There's a kid who is dead good, very skinny but great with the ball,' he said. The name: Robinho. I picked him out and told the press that he had a great chance to make it as a professional.

My role there was not just technical. I paid with my own money to install a building with a locker room at the training ground, since the kids had nowhere to change. I also asked to speak to Robinho's father. It's important to make sure that footballers have stable home lives. And we sorted out a dentist for him. There were other talented lads: Diego, who is now in Portugal; Alex, now at PSV Eindhoven, and Paulo Almeida. People said Robinho reminded them of me, because we started at the same club and were physically similar. I didn't make the comparison. When I saw him I saw a great player in his own right.

My other commitments meant that I was unable to continue my Santos work. But I set up a kids' football team in the city, called Litoral, which is looked after by Clodoaldo and Manoel Maria. Now there are about 500 children who play and train there.

People ask me when I'm going to retire. I'm not going to.

I'm never going to be that person who spends the rest of their days with a fishing rod on the riverbank. For a start I feel responsible for the hundred people who work for me, spread out between my houses and my offices in São Paulo and New York. But I do want to calm down, to do fewer adverts and spend less time on planes. In the last year, I was probably travelling for 60 per cent of the time. That is going to stop.

My energies will be more focused towards training young players. I will have more of an involvement at Litoral, and I would like to set up more football schools – not just for the most talented kids, but open to all.

✯

I don't play football professionally any more, of course – you know that. But I do have a five-a-side pitch at home on my ranch, and won't say no to a game, a kickabout like the ones we had when I was a kid, with family, close friends or people who come to visit. In summer, when it can get really hot in Brazil, we sometimes end up playing into the night, into the early hours – I love being able to exercise without having to put up with the heat of the sun. Football, in Brazil, crosses all social boundaries.

At home I also like to play tennis, although a year ago I broke my wrist when I misjudged a shot and hit the floor with my racket. One game I have never played is golf – although it is not through want of opportunity. I must have had more than 500 offers. Loads of former players – like Beckenbauer, Platini, Bobby Charlton – they are always trying to get me to take it up. Maybe I will one day.

As well as playing tennis I like to watch it. And, of course, I try to watch as many football matches as I can. I'm still a big fan myself and take a real interest in developments in the game. FIFA have me – together with about forty other former players – on one of their boards. I have an active, creative mind and I am always thinking of ways to improve the sporting spectacle. I have some suggestions, which I have already brought up at FIFA meetings.

First, I would change the rule regarding the wall at free kicks. The way it is at the moment is blatantly unfair. Just say I dribble past one player, two, three – maybe I dribble past the whole team and there is only the full-back and keeper in front of me. If the last defender fouls me, and I win a free kick, then all his team-mates are allowed to make a wall between me and the goal. They were all behind me, yet they are allowed to reassemble in front of me. Is that fair?

My solution is that either the wall should consist of only one player (the defender who committed the foul, say) or there should be no one there at all – in this way a free kick would be like a penalty kick from outside the box. I think it is a good idea, because as well as being fair it encourages attacking play. I would have loved that rule to be in place when I was a footballer. In fact, this is a rule that could only have been thought up by an attacking player!

Second, I do not see why throw-ins cannot be taken with one's feet as well as one's hands. When a keeper has a goal kick, he is allowed to kick it or throw the ball. Why can't other players do this when the ball goes out? The argument against my proposal is that players would be able to kick the ball straight into the middle of the box. But I think this would be a positive thing. Just say a game of football is in its closing minutes, and one team is trying to waste time by making sure the ball goes out. If you have a throw-in, you won't be able to threaten the goal. But if you could shoot the ball directly into the box, then who knows . . .

My third proposal to change football would be to have five officials per game, including one behind each goal to adjudicate on goal-line controversies.

I am often asked what I think of other footballers. Will there be another Pelé? (My answer is always no; Dondinho and Celeste have closed down the factory.) Who are the best? What I always say is that in my many years' playing I watched thousands of players, including the best in the world – how could I possibly single one out? It would be grossly unfair. I find it especially difficult to say who the best Brazilians are. I always just mention a few without going into too much detail. Instead I prefer simply to say that we play the best football in the world, and that's the way it will continue – Brazilians love football, Brazilian children all share the same dream I had. If the administration of Brazilian football was properly organised, we would win the World Cup at every age level every year.

But I can write about the players I've seen and liked, and there have been lots. I was lucky to catch Puskas, for instance. I only played against the Hungarian once, for Santos when he was at Real Madrid, but I could tell he was gifted. In Germany they had Vogts, Müller, Seeler – and how can I fail to mention the Kaiser, Franz Beckenbauer? He was everything to German football – player, captain, coach, champion. I remember advising him to stay on as coach of Germany when he was having doubts about whether he wanted to continue – he wanted to know what I thought, as we'd been friends since our Cosmos days.

Italy too has always had some great teams and great players. The Italians who spring to mind include Trapattoni, Fachetti,

Rivera, Burgnich, Zoff, Baresi and Roberto Baggio. The first great French footballers I encountered were that marvellous triumvirate from the 1958 World Cup – Piantoni, Fontaine and Kopa. But they have been succeeded by other talents, among them Platini, Giresse and Tigana. Nowadays France exports fine players too, including Zinédine Zidane at Real Madrid, and Thierry Henry at Arsenal. For Portugal Eusébio and Coluna were very good, and that country also gave us Luis Figo. And I have to mention the brilliant Argentine players I've seen, like Maradona, Batistuta, Ramos Delgado, and the amazing Di Stefano.

Everyone always makes a fuss about the rivalry between Maradona and me. We are friends, not enemies. When he asked me to take part in his TV programme I was happy to accept. The press, again, like to hype up the differences – especially in the eternal bar-room conversation about who was the better footballer. For what it's worth, I think that when you are judging footballers you need to consider everything – who shoots best with their right foot, who shoots best with their left foot, who heads the ball best, who runs most and so on and so on. And on that test, there really is no comparison. That's reality. But football fans aren't interested in reality, they are interested in passion.

On to the English. Stanley Matthews was an exemplary player – a sportsman with amazing technique. He played to his utmost, and didn't depend on tricks. His skills once helped England defeat Brazil 4–2 at Wembley, when he was forty-one years old. My old team-mate Nilton Santos had marked him that day, and although Nilton had been tipped as unbeatable, he had to concede at the end of the match that Matthews had got the better of him, saying, 'Mr Matthews, you are the king.'

I also admired Gordon Banks, Bobby Charlton and Jimmy Greaves in my playing days, and now the baton has passed to Owen, Rooney and Beckham; all are world-class.

And while I'm talking about the English I should mention another friend, who has also passed away: Bobby Moore. He played like a lord and marked straight; I always had enormous respect for him. I'll never forget that famous match we played against each other in Guadalajara during the 1970 World Cup. Once the whistle had blown, I remember waiting in line to shake hands with the England team. I tried to speak the tiny amount of English I knew. It all came out at once: 'I'm happy, you play good, yes, good luck . . .' We exchanged shirts as souvenirs. During the match some thieves broke in to my room back at the training camp and took the ten team shirts I had been allocated for the World Cup, which caused us some trouble – we even considered asking Bobby to return the one I'd given him so I'd have something to wear against Romania. We didn't have to in the end, although the stolen shirts were never found.

Football is unpredictable. That is one of its joys. If it was based purely on merit, however, then Holland should have won in both 1974 and 1978. The fantastic Cruyff heads the list from the Netherlands, but Marco van Basten was one of the best I've seen. And Ruud Gullit was a favourite, who went on to become a good coach. Pluskal, Masopust and Lala for Czechoslovakia also really impressed me. I faced these and others in Chile and Mexico; what matters most with these Czech players was their sporting spirit.

I should reiterate that I'm not making a list of the *best* players – that's something people find very confusing. I prefer to say that I *like* the players I've named – and a couple of hundred others I haven't mentioned.

As I have said, it's hard to mention any Brazilians, as even if I were to make a hundred lists I wouldn't satisfy even one of our fans. Although I'm happy to talk about generations. I think that, individually, our best team was the one from 1958: as well as myself we had Garrincha, Nilton Santos, Didi, Vavá . . . Collectively speaking, however, 1970 pips them to it. The only stars were myself, Jairzinho and Tostão. But the team was much better organised. The current generation is also very special, with great players like Ronaldinho, Juninho Pernambucano and Kaká.

The world has changed, but I think that Brazil still play the same kind of football that they always did. Maybe the game is slightly faster nowadays. And contrary to what many people think, Brazil can play defensively. Back in 1970, we were seen as an attacking team, because of the goals we scored, but in actual fact when the ball went into our own half we all went back. Only Tostão stayed up front. Brazil still play defensively now. A technical difference is that in those days we had marvellous crossers like Rivelino and Gerson. We don't have players like that any more, and the ball usually comes forward from the midfield along the ground.

When Brazil won the World Cup for the first time it was a great surprise. To me it will be no more of a surprise if the 2006 World Cup is won by an African team, or even by another country that's not known for its international pedigree in football. The United States made the quarter-finals last time and the South Koreans made the semis. Ronaldo has a chance this year to beat my Brazilian record of goals scored in World Cups. If he helps Brazil retain the trophy then he can score as many goals as he likes!

*

Throughout my career it has been a privilege to meet so many people from all walks of life. When, not long ago, my wife Assíria and I found ourselves in Germany with Pope Benedict XVI, it struck me that he was actually the third pontiff I had met, having previously been received by Pope Paul VI, one time in the Vatican library itself. The library is kept exclusively for heads of state, royalty and other VIPs – and being in there did make me feel like one myself. He knew a lot about football, and wanted to talk about it. Someone else who loved football, who'd played in Poland in his youth, was Pope John Paul II. I'll never forget the genuine warmth he displayed when I once gave him a model of the Cristo Redentor, Rio's 'Christ the Redeemer' statue.

I'm not a politician but I've met more than my share. I have met every Brazilian president from Juscelino to Lula, and every US president from Nixon onwards. Jimmy Carter received me in the Oval Office, and I gave him an autographed football. The same for Ronald Reagan, who introduced himself by saying, 'Good to meet you. I'm the President of the United States; you don't have to tell me who you are – I know you're Pelé, everybody knows!'

Often heads of state want to meet me. I don't always say yes. When Bill Clinton invited me to have dinner at the White House in 1997 I turned him down because I had another engagement. My friend Celso Grellet was horrified: 'No one turns down an invitation from the President of the United States!' he said.

'Take it easy, Celso,' I replied. I reminded him that my engagement was with the Mangueira Samba School in Rio de Janeiro, who wanted me to be a part of their project encouraging children to take up sport. Because I was Minister for Sport at the time I knew that President Clinton would soon be coming to Rio, and would be visiting them too; he did come, and we had a bit of a kickabout as he practised his football skills – not showing any great expertise, it must be said, but he was clearly enjoying himself. When the ceremony was over, President Clinton invited me to dinner – informal, without any journalists or advisers attending. Then I did go, and it was great to spend that time with him.

As well as presidents of countries in all five continents, I have met all sorts of film stars and famous athletes. And the person I was most impressed with? Probably Nelson Mandela, a true icon. Just as importantly, I have met tens – if not hundreds – of thousands of fans. One thing I always try to do when I'm in public is to remain friendly and polite when people come up to me to say hello. I know how good it is to be with them – after all, I have idols of my own, like my father, or Zizinho, the great Brazilian player of the 1950s I wrote about earlier. So when someone does come up to me in an airport, or at a party, at an event or on a plane, I try to give them the attention they expect of me. People who are idolised mustn't disappoint their public – we wouldn't be half of what we are without them. I'm well aware of that.

I have disappointed some fans, however – such as the Greek man who turned up at my hotel and offered me his daughter in marriage. (The same thing also happened in Nigeria.) I said I was very flattered but had to turn him down. Once I remember I was in England and a fan asked me to come to his house, where he had a wall signed by famous people. I apologised and said I wouldn't be able to go. The following day he turned up with a chunk of masonry. 'You couldn't come to my wall, so I brought it to you,' he said. In Yugoslavia, a fan has even turned his house into a Pelé museum.

When I arrive somewhere on an official visit the local press usually finds out or is told that I'm coming, and I'm met at the airport with absolute mayhem, people waiting for me and photographers there to record it all. I enjoy it, though I have to confess that every once in a while, when it hasn't been a particularly good trip, or it was too long, or I'm tired or desperate for a shower, to rest in a clean bed, it would be lovely just to arrive like a normal person and go off to my hotel. When I've recharged my batteries, though, then yes, I'm up for anything.

The rule one must live one's life by is to respect other people, whoever they are. When I played for Santos I always respected the fans. I always tried to do my best. I always tried my hardest to entertain, to make sure that the crowds left the stadium happy that they had watched a spectacle. I used to pray to God: 'If You are going to make this match a draw, then please can it be a score draw like 3–3 or 2–2 and not 0–0. The result is the same and it costs You nothing!'

The life of a top footballer has changed so much since I was in the game. In my day, there weren't so many flash cars, expensive watches or clothes. The only modern thing you could get in Santos was a pair of jeans. I was never one for gratuituous demonstrations of wealth anyway. Even now I drive a normal car, a Vauxhall Zafira. My two Mercedes Benz – I was given one in 1973, and the other in 1986 – are in my garage. Some people like to buy art, or helicopters or yachts. I'm not bothered by conspicuous consumption. I have been given hundreds of expensive watches, but I don't wear them. Luxury is living well, about having comfort within your own home. I have no expensive, guilty pleasures.

I don't like to call attention to myself when I don't have to. I rarely travel with a bodyguard. Just with a business colleague or my wife. President Lula gave me a red diplomatic passport but I never use it. If I did there would always be a reception, with embassy personnel, police, security and the like. When I arrive at an airport ideally I would do so on the quiet, unannounced, like an ordinary guy.

✵

Looking back over my life like this has reminded me of so many wonderful experiences. It is exactly half a century since I left Bauru, a little boy in his first long trousers. I have received so much admiration, affection and respect from so many people all over the world. My family has always kept me grounded. My life has been the same rollercoaster since I was fifteen. I have got used to it now! I am always surrounded by people. I don't get lonely.

Sometimes, though, I miss being the small boy from upstate São Paulo who had never seen the sea. I miss the simplicity of a life where happiness was playing football in a street full of friends. I miss the taste of fresh mango that I picked from the tree in the yard. I have vivid, wonderful memories of growing up.

A part of my childhood which is still with me is my *pião*, my wooden spinning top. I always have one with me in my brief-case, alongside my papers and pens. When I find myself alone in a hotel I take out the top, coil the string around it and then spin it to the floor. When it is on the ground you pick it up and keep it spinning in your hand. I'm very good at it. (Zoca may beat me at button football but I am better than him with the *pião*!) I love watching the top balance on my palm. It is meditative – and I am reminded of the innocence of the boy I once was.

But now I am a man, in his seventh decade. I have achieved more than I could ever have imagined. I've had everything a man could hope for. It has been a thrilling life. The joys have outnumbered the sorrows, many times over. I would like to thank everyone who has helped me become who I am, who I have been, both as Pelé and as Edson. Without the energy I have drawn from you, I would never have reached where I am today.

APPENDIX

Pelé's Goalscoring Career

Note

This match-by-match summary covers Pelé's goalscoring career as a professional player, up to his retirement from Cosmos on 1 October 1977. It includes a number of 'lost' Pelé matches that have only recently come to light, in the course of research for projects like *Pelé Eterno* and ongoing work on the historiography of Brazilian football. This latest research suggests that he did indeed score the 1,000th goal before the famous match v. Vasco da Gama on 19 November 1969, although it is still described as such in the text as that was how it was perceived and celebrated at the time. Similarly, the 1,000th game of Pelé's career was celebrated at the time as Santos v. Transvaal on 28 January 1971, but it now seems likely this milestone had been reached nine days (and three matches) earlier.

After his retirement from Cosmos Pelé also played in eight exhibition matches:

22 April 1978	Fluminense v. Nigeria	3–1
26 April 1978	Fluminense v. Racca Rovers (Nigeria)	2–1
6 April 1979	Flamengo v. Atlético Mineiro	5–1
24 September 1980	Cosmos v. NASL All-Stars*	3–2
21 July 1983	Sudeste XI v. Sul XI	1–1
9 May 1984	Cosmos All-Stars v. Cosmos	2–6
4 January 1987	Brazil Seniors v. Italy Seniors	3–0
31 October 1990	Friends of Pelé XI v. Brazil	2–1

*Franz Beckenbauer's farewell game.

Pelé's goalscoring career

Match	Year	Date	Pelé's team	Goals for	Opposition	Goals against	Goals by Pelé	Total goals
1	1956	7 September	Santos	7	Corinthians (Santo André)	1	1	1
2	1956	15 November	Santos	4	Jabaquara	2	1	2
3	**1957**	12 January	Santos	1	AIK (Sweden)	0	0	2
4	1957	9 February	Santos	2	Portuguesa de Desportos	4	1	3
5	1957	17 February	Santos	5	América (Joinville)	0	0	3
6	1957	19 February	Santos	3	América (Joinville)	1	0	3
7	1957	12 March	Santos	2	Grêmio (Porto Alegre)	3	0	3
8	1957	14 March	Santos	5	Grêmio (Porto Alegre)	0	0	3
9	1957	17 March	Santos	5	Rio Grandense	3	0	3
10	1957	19 March	Santos	3	Pelotas	2	0	3
11	1957	22 March	Santos	2	E. Club Brasil (Alagoas)	2	0	3
12	1957	24 March	Santos	1	Guarani / Bagé XI	1	1	4
13	1957	27 March	Santos	3	Renner (Porto Alegre)	5	0	4
14	1957	31 March	Santos	4	Flamengo / Juventude XI	1	1	5
15	1957	7 April	Santos	4	Vasco da Gama	2	0	5
16	1957	11 April	Santos	5	Corinthians (São Paulo)	3	1	6
17	1957	14 April	Santos	6	Guarani (Campinas)	1	2	8
18	1957	26 April	Santos	3	São Paulo FC	1	1	9
19	1957	1 May	Santos	1	Corinthians (São Paulo)	1	0	9
20	1957	5 May	Santos	0	Flamengo (Rio)	4	0	9
21	1957	9 May	Santos	2	Portuguesa de Desportos	4	0	9
22	1957	11 May	Santos	5	Botafogo (Rio)	1	0	9
23	1957	13 May	Santos	1	Botafogo (Ribeirão Preto)	3	0	9
24	1957	15 May	Santos	3	Palmeiras (São Paulo)	0	2	11
25	1957	19 May	Santos	7	Londrina (Paraná)	1	2	13
26	1957	26 May	Santos	2	Fluminense (Rio)	2	0	13
27	1957	29 May	Santos	4	América (Rio)	0	1	14
28	1957	1 June	Santos	2	Vasco da Gama (Rio)	3	1	15
29	1957	9 June	Santos	7	Lavras (Minas Gerais)	2	4	19
30	1957	19 June	Santos / Vasco XI	6	Belenenses (Portugal)	1	3	22
31	1957	20 June	Santos	3	Rio Branco	2	0	22
32	1957	22 June	Santos / Vasco XI	1	Dinamo (Yugoslavia)	1	1	23
33	1957	26 June	Santos / Vasco XI	1	Flamengo (Rio)	1	1	24
34	1957	29 June	Santos / Vasco XI	1	São Paulo FC	1	1	25
35*	1957	7 July	Brazil	1	Argentina	2	1	26
36	1957	10 July	Brazil	2	Argentina	0	1	27
37	1957	14 July	Santos	5	XV de Novembro (Piracicaba)	3	1	28
38	1957	21 July	Santos	1	Corinthians (São Paulo)	2	0	28
39	1957	23 July	Santos	3	Benfica (Portugal)	2	1	29
40	1957	25 July	Santos	7	Ponte Preta (Campinas)	2	3	32

*Pelé's debut for Brazil.

Match	Year	Date	Pelé's team	Goals for	Opposition	Goals against	Goals by Pelé	Total goals
41	1957	28 July	Santos	3	Arapongas (Paraná)	1	0	32
42	1957	31 July	Santos	4	Jabaquara	6	0	32
43	1957	4 August	Santos	2	Ferroviária (Araraquara)	3	0	32
44	1957	11 August	Santos	4	Botafogo (Ribeirão Preto)	2	0	32
45	1957	15 August	Santos	8	Guarani (Campinas)	1	4	36
46	1957	18 August	Santos	5	Portuguesa de Desportos	2	0	36
47	1957	20 August	Santos	2	Salvador XI (Bahia)	2	0	36
48	1957	8 September	Santos	1	Palmeiras (São Paulo)	2	1	37
49	1957	11 September	Santos	7	Nacional (São Paulo)	1	4	41
50	1957	15 September	Santos	2	São Paulo FC	3	1	42
51	1957	22 September	Santos	1	AA Portuguesa	1	1	43
52	1957	25 September	Santos	9	Ypiranga	1	3	46
53	1957	29 September	Santos	6	Juventus (São Paulo)	1	1	47
54	1957	2 October	Santos	1	Esporte (Recife)	1	0	47
55	1957	4 October	Santos	0	Náutico (Recife)	0	0	47
56	1957	6 October	Santos	2	Sampaio Correia (Maranhão)	1	2	49
57	1957	8 October	Santos	2	Esporte (Recife)	1	1	50
58	1957	10 October	Santos	1	Canto do Rio	0	0	50
59	1957	20 October	Santos	2	Botafogo (Ribeirão Preto)	4	0	50
60	1957	23 October	Santos	2	AA Portuguesa	2	0	50
61	1957	26 October	Santos	4	Palmeiras (São Paulo)	3	1	51
62	1957	3 November	Santos	3	Corinthians (São Paulo)	3	3	54
63	1957	4 November	Santos	0	Bandeirantes (São Paulo)	3	0	54
64	1957	6 November	Santos	3	Portuguesa de Desportos	1	0	54
65	1957	10 November	Santos	3	XV de Novembro (Piracicaba)	0	1	55
66	1957	17 November	Santos	2	São Paulo FC	6	0	55
67	1957	24 November	Santos	5	Jabaquara	1	3	58
68	1957	27 November	Santos	6	XV de Novembro (Piracicaba)	2	2	60
69	1957	1 December	Santos	6	AA Portuguesa	2	4	64
70	1957	3 December	Santos	2	São Paulo FC	2	0	64
71	1957	8 December	Santos	2	Ponte Preta (Campinas)	1	1	65
72	1957	15 December	Santos	6	Portuguesa de Desportos	0	2	67
73	1957	22 December	Santos	1	Corinthians (São Paulo)	0	0	67
74	1957	28 December	Santos	4	Palmeiras (São Paulo)	1	0	67
75	1957	29 December	Santos	10	Nitro Química	3	1	68
76	**1958**	19 January	Santos	4	Bragantino	1	1	69
77	1958	26 January	Santos	4	Prudentina	0	1	70
78	1958	30 January	Santos	2	Atlético (Minas Gerais)	5	1	71
79	1958	2 February	Santos	2	Atlético (Minas Gerais)	0	1	72
80	1958	5 February	Santos	2	Atlético (Minas Gerais)	2	0	72
81	1958	7 February	Santos	4	Botafogo (Ribeirão Preto)	2	2	74
82	1958	26 February	Santos	5	América (Rio)	3	4	78
83	1958	2 March	Santos	2	Botafogo (Rio)	2	0	78

Match	Year	Date	Pelé's team	Goals for	Opposition	Goals against	Goals by Pelé	Total goals
84	1958	6 March	Santos	7	Palmeiras (São Paulo)	6	1	79
85	1958	9 March	Santos	2	Flamengo (Rio)	3	1	80
86	1958	13 March	Santos	2	Portuguesa de Desportos	3	1	81
87	1958	16 March	Santos	2	São Paulo FC	4	0	81
88	1958	22 March	Santos	0	Vasco da Gama (Rio)	1	0	81
89	1958	23 March	Santos	2	Noroeste (Bauru)	3	0	81
90	1958	27 March	Santos	1	Corinthians (São Paulo)	2	1	82
91	1958	4 May	Brazil	5	Paraguay	1	2	84
92	1958	14 May	Brazil	4	Bulgaria	0	0	84
93	1958	18 May	Brazil	3	Bulgaria	1	2	86
94	1958	21 May	Brazil	5	Corinthians (São Paulo)	0	0	86
95*	1958	15 June	Brazil	2	USSR	0	0	86
96	1958	19 June	Brazil	1	Wales	0	1	87
97	1958	24 June	Brazil	5	France	2	3	90
98†	1958	29 June	Brazil	5	Sweden	2	2	92
99	1958	16 June	Santos	7	Jabaquara	3	2	94
100	1958	20 July	Santos	2	Juventus (São Paulo)	0	1	95
101	1958	23 July	Santos	6	XV de Novembro (Piracicaba)	0	4	99
102	1958	27 July	Santos	2	Botafogo (Ribeirão Preto)	2	2	101
103	1958	31 July	Santos	1	Comercial (São Paulo)	1	1	102
104	1958	3 August	Santos	0	América (Rio Preto)	0	0	102
105	1958	6 August	Santos	4	Portuguesa de Desportos	3	1	103
106	1958	10 August	Santos	0	Noroeste (Bauru)	1	0	103
107	1958	13 August	Santos	4	Ferroviária (Araraquara)	3	1	104
108	1958	17 August	Santos	1	São Paulo	0	1	105
109	1958	20 August	Santos	4	Ponte Preta (Campinas)	0	1	106
110	1958	24 August	Santos	1	Palmeiras (São Paulo)	0	0	106
111	1958	28 August	Santos	5	XV de Novembro (Jaú)	2	1	107
112	1958	31 August	Santos	2	AA Portuguesa	1	0	107
113	1958	4 September	Santos	3	Taubaté	0	1	108
114	1958	7 September	Santos	4	Ypiranga (São Paulo)	1	0	108
115	1958	11 September	Santos	10	Nacional (São Paulo)	0	4	112
116	1958	14 September	Santos	1	Corinthians (São Paulo)	0	1	113
117	1958	17 September	Santos	8	Guarani (Campinas)	1	1	114
118	1958	21 September	Santos	2	Prudentina	2	1	115
119	1958	25 September	Santos	1	Internacional (Porto Alegre)	5	0	115
120	1958	28 September	Santos	0	Grêmio (Porto Alegre)	4	0	115
121‡	1958	1 October	Santos	8	Ypiranga (São Paulo)	1	5	120
122	1958	5 October	Santos	2	Taubaté	3	0	120

*Pelé's first match in the World Cup Finals.
†1958 World Cup Final, Solna Stadium, Stockholm.
‡The first time he scored five goals in a senior match.

Appendix

Match	Year	Date	Pelé's team	Goals for	Opposition	Goals against	Goals by Pelé	Total goals
123	1958	11 October	Santos	3	Noroeste (Bauru)	0	0	120
124	1958	15 October	Santos	6	AA Portuguesa	1	3	123
125	1958	19 October	Santos	5	XV de Novembro (Piracicaba)	0	2	125
126	1958	20 October	Santos	6	Jabaquara	2	3	128
127	1958	26 October	Santos	4	Botafogo (Ribeirão Preto)	0	3	131
128	1958	29 October	Santos	1	Portuguesa de Desportos	1	0	131
129	1958	1 November	Santos	0	XV de Novembro (Jaú)	0	0	131
130	1958	5 November	Santos	3	América (Rio Preto)	1	1	132
131	1958	9 November	Santos	1	Ferroviária (Araraquara)	2	0	132
132	1958	16 November	Santos	2	Palmeiras (São Paulo)	1	1	133
133	1958	19 November	Santos	9	Comercial (São Paulo)	1	4	137
134	1958	23 November	Santos	2	Ponte Preta (Campinas)	1	0	137
135	1958	27 November	Santos	4	AA Portuguesa	3	1	138
136	1958	30 November	Santos	4	Nacional (São Paulo)	3	1	139
137	1958	7 December	Santos	6	Corinthians (São Paulo)	1	4	143
138	1958	10 December	Santos	7	Juventus (São Paulo)	1	3	146
139	1958	14 December	Santos	7	Guarani (Campinas)	1	4	150
140	1958	18 December	Santos	2	São Paulo FC	2	2	152
141	1958	21 December	Santos	1	Coritiba	1	1	153
142	1958	23 December	Santos	4	Cruzeiro (Minas Gerais)	2	3	156
143	1958	30 December	Santos	3	Paulista XI	0	2	158
144	**1959**	4 January	Santos	3	Sports Boys (Peru)	0	2	160
145	1959	6 January	Santos	4	Sporting Cristal (Peru)	0	2	162
146	1959	9 January	Santos	5	Deportivo Municipal (Peru)	1	0	162
147	1959	11 January	Santos	3	Emelec (Ecuador)	1	2	164
148	1959	15 January	Santos	3	Saprissa (Costa Rica)	1	2	166
149	1959	18 January	Santos	2	Comunicaciones (Guatemala)	1	1	167
150	1959	21 January	Santos	2	Costa Rica	1	0	167
151	1959	29 January	Santos	4	Guadalajara (Mexico)	2	3	170
152	1959	5 February	Santos	2	León (Mexico)	0	0	170
153	1959	8 February	Santos	4	Atlas (Mexico)	1	1	171
154	1959	12 February	Santos	5	América (Mexico)	0	2	173
155	1959	15 February	Santos	3	Uda Duklas (Czechoslovakia)	4	0	173
156	1959	17 February	Santos	3	Curaçao	2	0	173
157	1959	19 February	Santos	4	Deportivo Español (Venezuela)	0	0	173
158	1959	22 February	São Paulo*	1	Rio	5	1	174
159	1959	25 February	São Paulo	0	Rio	1	0	174
160	1959	10 March	Brazil	2	Peru	2	1	175
161	1959	15 March	Brazil	3	Chile	0	2	177
162	1959	21 March	Brazil	4	Bolivia	2	1	178

*The state side, not São Paulo FC.

Match	Year	Date	Pelé's team	Goals for	Opposition	Goals against	Goals by Pelé	Total goals
163	1959	26 March	Brazil	3	Uruguay	1	0	178
164	1959	29 March	Brazil	4	Paraguay	1	3	181
165	1959	4 April	Brazil	1	Argentina	1	1	182
166	1959	9 April	Santos	4	Botafogo (Rio)	2	1	183
167	1959	12 April	Santos	3	Flamengo (Rio)	2	1	184
168	1959	15 April	Santos	2	Colo Colo (Chile)	6	0	184
169	1959	18 April	Santos	1	Fluminense (Rio)	1	0	184
170	1959	21 April	Santos	2	Portuguesa de Desportos	0	0	184
171	1959	23 April	Santos	2	Bahia	1	0	184
172	1959	26 April	Santos	4	São Paulo FC	3	2	186
173	1959	30 April	Santos	3	Corinthians (São Paulo)	2	1	187
174	1959	13 May	Brazil	2	England	0	0	187
175	1959	17 May	Santos	3	Vasco da Gama (Rio)	0	1	188
176	1959	19 May	Santos	5	Santa Cruz (Recife)	1	3	191
177	1959	23 May	Santos	3	Bulgaria 'B'	3	2	193
178	1959	24 May	Santos	2	Bulgaria 'A'	0	1	194
179	1959	26 May	Santos	1	Royal Standard (Belgium)	0	0	194
180	1959	27 May	Santos	4	Anderlecht (Belgium)	2	2	196
181	1959	30 May	Santos	1	Gantoise (Belgium)	2	0	196
182	1959	3 June	Santos	3	Feyenoord (Netherlands)	0	1	197
183	1959	5 June	Santos	2	Internazionale (Italy)	3	2	199
184	1959	6 June	Santos	6	Fortuna (W. Germany)	4	1	200
185	1959	7 June	Santos	3	Nuremberg (W. Germany)	3	0	200
186	1959	9 June	Santos	4	Servette (Switzerland)	1	1	201
187	1959	11 June	Santos	6	Hamburg (W. Germany)	0	1	202
188	1959	13 June	Santos	7	Niedersachsen (W. Germany)	1	3	205
189	1959	15 June	Santos	5	Enschede (Netherlands)	0	3	208
190	1959	17 June	Santos	3	Real Madrid (Spain)	5	1	209
191	1959	19 June	Santos	2	Sporting (Portugal)	2	1	210
192	1959	21 June	Santos	4	Botafogo (Rio)	1	1	211
193	1959	24 June	Santos	4	Valencia (Spain)	4	1	212
194	1959	26 June	Santos	7	Internazionale (Italy)	1	4	216
195	1959	28 June	Santos	5	Barcelona (Spain)	1	2	218
196	1959	30 June	Santos	4	Genoa (Italy)	2	0	218
197	1959	2 July	Santos	0	Vienna (Austria)	3	0	218
198	1959	5 July	Santos	2	Real Betis (Spain)	2	1	219
199	1959	18 July	Santos	2	Fortaleza (Ceará)	2	2	221
200	1959	19 July	Santos	0	Pernambuco	0	0	221
201	1959	23 July	Santos	7	Jabaquara	0	1	222
202	1959	26 July	Santos	8	XV de Novembro (Jaú)	2	3	225
203	1959	2 August	Santos	4	Juventus (São Paulo)	0	3	228
204	1959	16 August	Santos	1	Taubaté	1	1	229
205	1959	19 August	Santos	0	Ferroviária (Araraquara)	0	0	229

Appendix

Match	Year	Date	Pelé's team	Goals for	Opposition	Goals against	Goals by Pelé	Total goals
206	1959	21 August	6 GAC*	9	Docas	0	3	232
207	1959	23 August	Santos	4	Noroeste (Bauru)	3	3	235
208	1959	26 August	Santos	3	Corinthians (São Paulo)	2	1	236
209	1959	27 August	6 GAC	7	QG 2a RM Coy (Army)	0	3	239
210	1959	30 August	Santos	3	América (Rio Preto)	2	1	240
211	1959	5 September	6 GAC	0	AA Portuguesa	0	0	240
212	1959	7 September	Santos	5	Portuguesa de Desportos	0	3	243
213	1959	10 September	Santos	4	Guarani (Campinas)	1	2	245
214	1959	11 September	6 GAC	8	Santos	4	3	248
215	1959	13 September	Santos	3	Botafogo (Ribeirão Preto)	1	1	249
216	1959	17 September	Brazil	7	Chile	0	3	252
217	1959	20 September	Brazil	1	Chile	0	0	252
218	1959	27 September	Santos	1	São Paulo FC	2	0	252
219	1959	28 September	6 GAC	4	Armed Forces XI	2	1	253
220	1959	1 October	Santos	3	Comercial (São Paulo)	1	0	253
221	1959	3 October	Santos	7	Palmeiras (São Paulo)	3	3	256
222	1959	6 October	6 GAC	3	Armed Forces XI	2	0	256
223	1959	11 October	Santos	1	Coritiba	0	0	256
224	1959	12 October	Army 'A'	4	Army 'B'	3	0	256
225	1959	14 October	Santos	8	América (Rio Preto)	0	4	260
226	1959	25 October	Santos	5	XV de Novembro (Piracicaba)	2	2	262
227	1959	27 October	Army	6	Navy	1	3	265
228	1959	29 October	Santos	6	Noroeste (Bauru)	1	0	265
229	1959	1 November	Santos	6	Comercial (Ribeirão Preto)	2	1	266
230	1959	4 November	Santos	4	Comercial (São Paulo)	2	1	267
231	1959	5 November	Army (Brazil)	4	Army (Uruguay)	3	0	267
232	1959	8 November	Santos	0	XV de Novembro (Jaú)	1	0	267
233	1959	11 November	Santos	5	Juventus (São Paulo)	1	2	269
234	1959	15 November	Santos	4	Nacional (São Paulo)	0	2	271
235	1959	17 November	Santos	4	Grêmio (Porto Alegre)	1	0	271
236	1959	18 November	Brazil	4	Uruguay	1	1	272
237	1959	22 November	Santos	5	Portuguesa de Desportos	1	3	275
238	1959	24 November	Army (Brazil)	2	Army (Argentina)	1	0	275
239	1959	25 November	Santos	0	Grêmio (Porto Alegre)	0	0	275
240	1959	29 November	Santos	1	Palmeiras (São Paulo)	5	1	276
241	1959	6 December	Santos	5	Ferroviária (Araraquara)	2	2	278
242	1959	10 December	Santos	2	Bahia	3	1	279
243	1959	13 December	Santos	4	São Paulo FC	3	2	281
244	1959	20 December	Santos	2	Guarani (Campinas)	3	0	281
245	1959	23 December	Santos	2	Taubaté	0	0	281

*The Sixth Group of the Motorised Coast Artillery (Pelé's army team).

Match	Year	Date	Pelé's team	Goals for	Opposition	Goals against	Goals by Pelé	Total goals
246	1959	27 December	Santos	4	Corinthians (São Paulo)	1	2	283
247	1959	30 December	Santos	2	Bahia	0	1	284
248	**1960**	5 January	Santos	1	Palmeiras (São Paulo)	1	1	285
249	1960	7 January	Santos	2	Palmeiras (São Paulo)	2	0	285
250	1960	10 January	Santos	1	Palmeiras (São Paulo)	2	1	286
251	1960	19 January	São Paulo	2	Bahia	0	0	286
252	1960	24 January	São Paulo	7	Bahia	1	3	289
253	1960	27 January	São Paulo	4	Minas Gerais	3	1	290
254	1960	31 January	São Paulo	2	Pernambuco	4	0	290
255	1960	3 February	São Paulo	4	Rio	1	0	290
256	1960	10 February	São Paulo	3	Pernambuco	1	2	292
257	1960	14 February	São Paulo	2	Rio	1	0	292
258	1960	16 February	Santos	2	Universitario (Peru)	2	0	292
259	1960	18 February	Santos	3	Sporting Cristal (Peru)	3	0	292
260	1960	24 February	Santos	2	Alianza (Peru)	1	0	292
261	1960	26 February	Santos	2	Universitario (Peru)	3	0	292
262	1960	6 March	Santos	2	Medellín (Colombia)	1	1	293
263	1960	9 March	Santos	1	América (Colombia)	0	0	293
264	1960	12 March	Santos	1	Milionários (Colombia)	2	0	293
265	1960	13 March	Santos	4	Calli (Colombia)	0	1	294
266	1960	16 March	Santos	1	América (Colombia)	0	0	294
267	1960	20 March	Santos	6	Liga Universitaria (Ecuador)	2	0	294
268	1960	19 April	Santos	2	Portuguesa	2	0	294
269	1960	21 April	Santos	1	São Paulo FC	1	0	294
270	1960	24 April	Santos	0	Vasco da Gama (Rio)	0	0	294
271	1960	29 April	Brazil	5	United Arab Republic (Egpyt)	0	0	294
272	1960	1 May	Brazil	3	United Arab Republic (Egpyt)	1	3	297
273	1960	6 May	Brazil	3	United Arab Republic (Egpyt)	0	0	297
274	1960	8 May	Brazil	7	Malmö (Sweden)	1	2	299
275	1960	10 May	Brazil	4	Denmark	3	0	299
276	1960	12 May	Brazil	2	Internazionale (Italy)	2	2	301
277	1960	16 May	Brazil	5	Sporting (Portugal)	0	0	301
278	1960	19 May	Santos	4	Royal Standard (Belgium)	3	1	302
279	1960	25 May	Santos	5	Poland	2	2	304
280	1960	27 May	Santos	9	TSV Munich (W. Germany)	1	3	307
281	1960	28 May	Santos	6	Anderlecht (Belgium)	0	0	307
282	1960	31 May	Santos	10	Royal Neerschot (Belgium)	1	4	311
283	1960	1 June	Santos	3	Roma (Italy)	2	1	312
284	1960	3 June	Santos	0	Fiorentina (Italy)	3	0	312
285	1960	7 June	Santos	5	Stade Reims (France)	3	1	313
286	1960	9 June	Santos	4	Racing (France)	1	1	314
287	1960	11 June	Santos	5	Gantoise (Belgium)	2	2	316
288	1960	12 June	Santos	3	Antwerp (Belgium)	1	0	316

Match	Year	Date	Pelé's team	Goals for	Opposition	Goals against	Goals by Pelé	Total goals
289	1960	14 June	Santos	4	Eintracht (W. Germany)	2	2	318
290	1960	15 June	Santos	4	Berlin (W. Germany)	2	1	319
291	1960	17 June	Santos	3	Stade Reims (France)	1	1	320
292	1960	19 June	Santos	2	Deportivo Español (Spain)	2	0	320
293	1960	23 June	Santos	3	Toulouse (France)	0	2	322
294	1960	25 June	Santos	1	Valencia (Spain)	0	0	322
295	1960	2 July	Santos	3	Barcelona (Spain)	4	1	323
296	1960	9 July	Brazil	0	Uruguay	1	0	323
297	1960	12 July	Brazil	5	Argentina	1	1	324
298	1960	17 July	Santos	6	Ponte Preta	3	1	325
299	1960	21 July	Santos	1	Portuguesa de Desportos	1	0	325
300	1960	24 July	Santos	2	Guarani (Campinas)	2	0	325
301	1960	27 July	Santos	8	Jabaquara	3	3	328
302	1960	31 July	Santos	1	Corinthians (São Paulo)	1	1	329
303	1960	3 August	Santos	5	Botafogo (Ribeirão Preto)	1	1	330
304	1960	7 August	Santos	0	Comercial (Ribeirão Preto)	2	0	330
305	1960	10 August	Santos	4	Noroeste (Bauru)	1	3	333
306	1960	14 August	Santos	1	Corinthians (Pres. Prudente)	0	1	334
307	1960	15 August	Santos	3	Jaú	2	1	335
308	1960	21 August	Santos	3	Palmeiras (São Paulo)	1	1	336
309	1960	31 August	Santos	1	São Paulo FC	1	0	336
310	1960	4 September	Santos	0	Ferroviária (Araraquara)	4	0	336
311	1960	8 September	Santos	0	AA Portuguesa	0	0	336
312	1960	11 September	Santos	0	XV de Novembro (Piracicaba)	0	0	336
313	1960	15 September	Santos	5	Juventus (São Paulo)	2	3	339
314	1960	17 September	Santos	0	América (Rio Preto)	1	0	339
315	1960	21 September	Santos	3	Jabaquara	2	0	339
316	1960	24 September	Santos	3	Juventus (São Paulo)	1	2	341
317	1960	28 September	Santos	3	Portuguesa de Desportos	4	1	342
318	1960	23 October	Santos	4	Ponte Preta (Campinas)	1	1	343
319	1960	6 November	Santos	2	XV de Novembro (Piracicaba)	0	2	345
320	1960	9 November	Santos	1	AA Portuguesa	0	1	346
321	1960	13 November	Santos	3	Noroeste (Bauru)	1	2	348
322	1960	15 November	Santos	6	Goiânia	1	0	348
323	1960	20 November	Santos	4	Botafogo (Ribeirão Preto)	2	1	349
324	1960	23 November	Santos	5	Corinthians (Pres. Prudente)	0	1	350
325	1960	30 November	Santos	6	Corinthians (São Paulo)	1	1	351
326	1960	4 December	Santos	6	Taubaté	1	2	353
327	1960	7 December	Santos	5	Ferroviária (Araraquara)	0	3	356
328	1960	11 December	Santos	1	São Paulo	2	0	356
329	1960	16 December	Santos	2	Palmeiras (São Paulo)	1	1	357
330	**1961**	8 January	Santos	6	Uberlândia	1	1	358
331	1961	10 January	Santos	10	Guarani (Campinas)	2	2	360

Match	Year	Date	Pelé's team	Goals for	Opposition	Goals against	Goals by Pelé	Total goals
332	1961	14 January	Santos	3	Colo Colo (Chile)	1	2	362
333	1961	18 January	Santos	2	Colombia	1	2	364
334	1961	22 January	Santos	7	Saprissa (Costa Rica)	3	1	365
335	1961	25 January	Santos	3	Herediano (Costa Rica)	0	1	366
336	1961	29 January	Santos	4	Guatemala	1	2	368
337	1961	2 February	Santos	3	Necaxa (Mexico)	4	0	368
338	1961	19 February	Santos	6	Guadalajara (Mexico)	2	0	368
339	1961	22 February	Santos	6	América (Mexico)	2	2	370
340	1961	24 February	Santos	2	Atlas de Guadalajara (Mexico)	0	0	370
341	1961	26 February	Santos	3	América (Guanabara)	3	0	370
342	1961	2 March	Santos	5	Vasco da Gama (Rio)	1	0	370
343	1961	5 March	Santos	3	Fluminense (Rio)	1	2	372
344	1961	11 March	Santos	7	Flamengo (Rio)	1	3	375
345	1961	15 March	Santos	1	São Paulo FC	0	0	375
346	1961	1 April	Santos	4	Botafogo (Rio)	2	2	377
347	1961	5 April	Santos	3	Atlético (Minas Gerais)	1	2	379
348	1961	10 April	Santos	6	América (Guanabara)	1	1	380
349	1961	13 April	Santos	1	Vasco da Gama (Rio)	2	0	380
350	1961	1 June	Santos	8	Basel (Switzerland)	2	3	383
351	1961	3 June	Santos	6	Wolfsburg (W. Germany)	3	2	385
352	1961	4 June	Santos	4	Antwerp (Belgium)	4	0	385
353	1961	7 June	Santos	6	Racing (France)	1	1	386
354	1961	9 June	Santos	6	Olympique Lyonnaise (France)	2	2	388
355	1961	11 June	Santos	3	Israel	1	1	389
356	1961	13 June	Santos	5	Racing (France)	4	1	390
357	1961	15 June	Santos	6	Benfica (Portugal)	3	2	392
358	1961	18 June	Santos	2	Juventus (Italy)	0	1	393
359	1961	21 June	Santos	5	Roma (Italy)	0	2	395
360	1961	24 June	Santos	4	Internazionale (Italy)	1	1	396
361	1961	26 June	Santos	8	Karlsruhe (W. Germany)	6	3	399
362	1961	28 June	Santos	3	AEK (Greece)	0	1	400
363	1961	30 June	Santos	3	Panathinaikos (Greece)	2	2	402
364	1961	4 July	Santos	1	Olimpiakos (Greece)	2	0	402
365	1961	23 July	Santos	0	Taubaté	0	0	402
366	1961	30 July	Santos	2	Palmeiras (São Paulo)	1	0	402
367	1961	6 August	Santos	4	Jabaquara	0	1	403
368	1961	9 August	Santos	3	Guarani (Campinas)	1	1	404
369	1961	13 August	Santos	7	Noroeste (Bauru)	1	3	407
370	1961	16 August	Santos	5	Corinthians (São Paulo)	1	1	408
371	1961	19 August	Santos	6	XV de Novembro (Piracicaba)	1	3	411
372	1961	25 August	Santos	0	Nacional (Uruguay)	1	0	411
373	1961	30 August	Santos	8	Olimpico (Blumenau)	0	5	416
374	1961	3 September	Santos	6	São Paulo FC	3	4	420

Appendix

Match	Year	Date	Pelé's team	Goals for	Opposition	Goals against	Goals by Pelé	Total goals
375	1961	6 September	Santos	10	Juventus (São Paulo)	1	5	425
376	1961	10 September	Santos	3	Botafogo (Ribeirão Preto)	0	1	426
377	1961	13 September	Santos	5	Guaratinguetá	1	4	430
378*	1961	17 September	Santos	6	Portuguesa de Desportos	1	4	434
379	1961	20 September	Santos	2	Londrina (Paraná)	1	0	434
380	1961	28 September	Santos	4	Racing (Argentina)	2	2	436
381	1961	1 October	Santos	1	Newell's Old Boys (Argentina)	1	1	437
382	1961	4 October	Santos	3	Colo Colo (Chile)	2	1	438
383	1961	8 October	Santos	3	Colo Colo (Chile)	1	1	439
384	1961	15 October	Santos	4	Botafogo (Ribeirão Preto)	1	1	440
385	1961	18 October	Santos	5	AA Portuguesa	2	2	442
386	1961	22 October	Santos	2	Guarani (Campinas)	1	0	442
387	1961	28 October	Santos	3	Portuguesa de Desportos	1	2	444
388	1961	1 November	Santos	3	Juventus (São Paulo)	1	1	445
389	1961	4 November	Santos	4	Taubaté	2	1	446
390	1961	8 November	Santos	4	Guaratinguetá	0	3	449
391	1961	11 November	Santos	6	América (Guanabara)	2	2	451
392	1961	15 November	Santos	1	Flamengo (Rio)	1	1	452
393	1961	19 November	Santos	0	América (Guanabara)	1	0	452
394	1961	21 November	Santos	6	América (Guanabara)	1	2	454
395	1961	26 November	Santos	4	Comercial (Ribeirão Preto)	1	1	455
396	1961	29 November	Santos	2	Palmeiras (São Paulo)	3	1	456
397	1961	3 December	Santos	1	Corinthians (São Paulo)	1	0	456
398	1961	6 December	Santos	4	Noroeste (Bauru)	2	2	458
399	1961	10 December	Santos	7	XV de Novembro (Piracicaba)	2	3	461
400	1961	13 December	Santos	6	Ferroviária (Araraquara)	2	2	463
401	1961	16 December	Santos	4	São Paulo FC	1	1	464
402	1961	19 December	AU (São Paulo)†	4	AU (Rio)	1	1	465
403	1961	22 December	Santos	1	Bahia	1	0	465
404	1961	27 December	Santos	5	Bahia	1	3	468
405	**1962**	3 January	Santos	0	Botafogo (Rio)	3	0	468
406	1962	7 January	Santos	6	Barcelona (Ecuador)	2	0	468
407	1962	14 January	Santos	6	Liga Universitaria (Ecuador)	3	3	471
408	1962	17 January	Santos	5	Alianza (Peru)	1	0	471
409	1962	20 January	Santos	5	Universitario (Peru)	2	1	472
410	1962	24 January	Santos	5	Sporting Cristal (Peru)	1	1	473
411	1962	27 January	Santos	3	Municipal (Peru)	2	1	474
412	1962	31 January	Santos	3	Nacional (Uruguay)	2	1	475
413	1962	3 February	Santos	8	Racing (Argentina)	3	1	476
414	1962	6 February	Santos	1	River Plate (Argentina)	2	0	476

*The end of a run in which he scored twenty-three goals in six matches.
†Athletes' Union.

Match	Year	Date	Pelé's team	Goals for	Opposition	Goals against	Goals by Pelé	Total goals
415	1962	9 February	Santos	2	Gimnasia y Esgrima (Argentina)	2	0	476
416	1962	14 February	Santos	3	Brazil	1	1	477
417	1962	18 February	Santos	4	Municipal (Bolivia)	3	0	477
418	1962	21 February	Santos	6	Municipal (Bolivia)	1	0	477
419	1962	28 February	Santos	9	Cerro Porteno (Paraguay)	1	2	479
420	1962	18 March	Santos	5	Palmeiras (São Paulo)	3	2	481
421	1962	21 April	Brazil	6	Paraguay	0	1	482
422	1962	24 April	Brazil	4	Paraguay	0	2	484
423	1962	6 May	Brazil	2	Portugal	1	0	484
424	1962	9 May	Brazil	1	Portugal	0	1	485
425	1962	12 May	Brazil	3	Wales	1	1	486
426	1962	16 May	Brazil	3	Wales	1	2	488
427*	1962	30 May	Brazil	2	Mexico	0	1	489
428	1962	2 June	Brazil	0	Czechoslovakia	0	0	489
429	1962	25 July	Santos	2	VW (São Bernardo do Campo)	0	0	489
430	1962	5 August	Santos	2	Prudentina	0	1	490
431	1962	8 August	Santos	2	Juventus (São Paulo)	0	0	490
432	1962	12 August	Santos	4	Palmeiras (São Paulo)	2	1	491
433	1962	19 August	Santos	5	Jabaquara	1	3	494
434	1962	26 August	Santos	1	Guarani (Campinas)	1	1	495
435	1962	30 August	Santos	3	Penarol (Uruguay)	0	2	497
436	1962	2 September	Santos	3	São Paulo FC	3	2	499
437	1962	5 September	Santos	5	Botafogo (Ribeirão Preto)	2	2	501
438	1962	16 September	Santos	7	Ferroviária (Araraquara)	2	4	505
439	1962	19 September	Santos	3	Benfica (Portugal)	2	2	507
440	1962	23 September	Santos	5	Corinthians (São Paulo)	2	1	508
441	1962	26 September	Santos	4	Noroeste (Bauru)	0	2	510
442	1962	30 September	Santos	3	Comercial (Ribeirão Preto)	1	1	511
443	1962	6 October	Santos	2	Portuguesa de Desportos	3	1	512
444	1962	11 October	Santos	5	Benfica (Portugal)	2	3	515
445	1962	17 October	Santos	5	Racing (France)	2	2	517
446	1962	20 October	Santos	3	Hamburg (W. Germany)	3	2	519
447	1962	22 October	Santos	4	Sheffield Wednesday (England)	2	1	520
448	1962	27 October	Santos	3	Taubaté	0	1	521
449	1962	31 October	Santos	5	Guarani (Campinas)	0	3	524
450	1962	4 November	Santos	2	Corinthians (São Paulo)	1	1	525
451†	1962	7 November	Santos	3	Juventus (São Paulo)	0	1	526
452	1962	11 November	Santos	1	Noroeste (Bauru)	1	0	526
453	1962	14 November	Santos	3	Palmeiras (São Paulo)	0	1	527
454	1962	18 November	Santos	1	XV de Novembro (Piracicaba)	1	0	527

*First match of the 1962 World Cup Finals, Chile.

†The end of a run in which he scored in twenty consecutive matches.

Match	Year	Date	Pelé's team	Goals for	Opposition	Goals against	Goals by Pelé	Total goals
455	1962	21 November	Santos	4	Portuguesa de Desportos	1	2	529
456	1962	25 November	Santos	1	Ferroviária (Araraquara)	1	0	529
457	1962	28 November	Santos	6	Comercial (Ribeirão Preto)	2	2	531
458	1962	2 December	Santos	8	Jabaquara	2	4	535
459	1962	5 December	Santos	5	São Paulo FC	2	1	536
460	1962	10 December	Santos	2	USSR	1	1	537
461	1962	12 December	Santos	1	Botafogo (Ribeirão Preto)	0	0	537
462	1962	15 December	Santos	4	Prudentina	0	2	539
463	1962	19 December	AU (São Paulo)	4	AU (Rio)	6	2	541
464	**1963**	9 January	Santos	3	Sergipe	2	2	543
465	1963	12 January	Santos	1	Recife	1	0	543
466	1963	16 January	Santos	4	Recife	0	0	543
467	1963	23 January	Santos	2	Colo Colo (Chile)	1	2	545
468	1963	30 January	Santos	8	Municipal (Peru)	3	3	548
469	1963	2 February	Santos	2	Alianza (Peru)	1	1	549
470	1963	6 February	Santos	3	Universidad (Chile)	4	2	551
471	1963	10 February	Santos	5	Clube Naval (Chile)	0	2	553
472	1963	16 February	Santos	2	Vasco da Gama (Rio)	2	2	555
473	1963	20 February	Santos	6	Portuguesa de Desportos	3	2	557
474	1963	3 March	Santos	2	Corinthians (Rio)	0	2	559
475	1963	7 March	Santos	6	São Paulo FC	2	3	562
476	1963	13 March	Santos	3	Palmeiras (São Paulo)	0	0	562
477	1963	16 March	Santos	5	Olaria (Rio)	1	3	565
478	1963	19 March	Santos	4	Botafogo (Rio)	3	0	565
479	1963	23 March	Santos	2	Fluminense (Rio)	4	1	566
480	1963	27 March	Santos	3	Flamengo (Rio)	0	1	567
481	1963	31 March	Santos	1	Botafogo (Rio)	3	0	567
482	1963	2 April	Santos	5	Botafogo (Rio)	0	2	569
483	1963	13 April	Brazil	2	Argentina	3	0	569
484	1963	16 April	Brazil	4	Argentina	1	3	572
485	1963	21 April	Brazil	0	Portugal	1	0	572
486	1963	28 April	Brazil	3	France	2	3	575
487	1963	2 May	Brazil	0	Netherlands	1	0	575
488	1963	5 May	Brazil	2	W. Germany	1	1	576
489	1963	12 May	Brazil	0	Italy	3	0	576
490	1963	29 May	Santos	3	Niedersachsen (W. Germany)	2	1	577
491	1963	2 June	Santos	2	Schalke (W. Germany)	1	1	578
492	1963	5 June	Santos	5	Eintracht (W. Germany)	2	4	582
493	1963	8 June	Santos	3	Stuttgart (W. Germany)	1	1	583
494	1963	12 June	Santos	0	Barcelona (Spain)	2	0	583
495	1963	15 June	Santos	4	Roma (Italy)	3	2	585
496	1963	19 June	Santos	0	Internazionale (Italy)	2	0	585
497	1963	22 June	Santos	0	Milan (Italy)	4	0	585

Match	Year	Date	Pelé's team	Goals for	Opposition	Goals against	Goals by Pelé	Total goals
498	1963	26 June	Santos	3	Juventus (Italy)	5	1	586
499	1963	21 July	Santos	4	Noroeste (Bauru)	3	4	590
500	1963	24 July	Santos	1	Portuguesa de Desportos	1	0	590
501	1963	28 July	Santos	5	Jabaquara	2	1	591
502	1963	31 July	Santos	2	Guaratinguetá	2	1	592
503	1963	4 August	Santos	2	Guarani (Campinas)	1	1	593
504	1963	7 August	Santos	1	Palmeiras (São Paulo)	1	0	593
505	1963	15 August	Santos	1	São Paulo FC	4	1	594
506	1963	18 August	Santos	0	XV de Novembro (Piracicaba)	0	0	594
507	1963	22 August	Santos	1	Botafogo (Rio)	1	1	595
508	1963	28 August	Santos	4	Botafogo (Rio)	0	3	598
509	1963	1 September	Santos	1	Ferroviária (Araraquara)	4	1	599
510	1963	4 September	Santos	3	Boca Juniors (Argentina)	2	0	599
511	1963	11 September	Santos	2	Boca Juniors (Argentina)	1	1	600
512	1963	18 September	Santos	2	Prudentina	2	1	601
513	1963	22 September	Santos	3	Corinthians (São Paulo)	1	3	604
514	1963	25 September	Santos	2	Juventus (São Paulo)	1	0	604
515	1963	29 September	Santos	3	Botafogo (Ribeirão Preto)	1	1	605
516	1963	2 October	Santos	4	Noroeste (Bauru)	2	1	606
517	1963	5 October	Santos	4	Prudentina	0	3	609
518	1963	16 October	Santos	2	Milan (Italy)	4	2	611
519	1963	24 October	Santos	2	Portuguesa de Desportos	3	1	612
520	1963	27 October	Santos	3	Comercial (Ribeirão Preto)	0	2	614
521	1963	30 October	Santos	2	São Bento (Sorocaba)	3	1	615
522	1963	2 November	Santos	0	Juventus (São Paulo)	0	0	615
523	**1964**	16 January	Santos	3	Grêmio (Porto Alegre)	1	1	616
524	1964	19 January	Santos	4	Grêmio (Porto Alegre)	3	3	619
525	1964	25 January	Santos	6	Bahia	0	2	621
526	1964	28 January	Santos	2	Bahia	0	2	623
527	1964	1 February	Santos	1	Independiente (Argentina)	5	0	623
528	1964	6 February	Santos	0	Penarol (Uruguay)	5	0	623
529	1964	22 February	Santos	3	Sport Boys (Peru)	2	2	625
530	1964	25 February	Santos	3	Alianza (Peru)	2	0	625
531	1964	28 February	Santos	2	Colo Colo (Chile)	3	0	625
532	1964	1 March	Santos	3	Godoy Cruz (Argentina)	2	0	625
533	1964	6 March	Santos	4	Colo Colo (Chile)	2	0	625
534	1964	8 March	Santos	2	Talleres (Argentina)	1	0	625
535	1964	18 March	Santos	3	Corinthians (São Paulo)	0	1	626
536	1964	22 March	Santos	1	Fluminense (Rio)	0	0	626
537	1964	25 April	Santos	3	Botafogo (Rio)	1	1	627
538	1964	1 May	Santos	2	Flamengo (Rio)	3	1	628
539	1964	5 May	Santos	4	Boca Juniors (Argentina)	3	1	629
540	1964	7 May	Santos	2	Racing (Argentina)	1	1	630

Appendix

Match	Year	Date	Pelé's team	Goals for	Opposition	Goals against	Goals by Pelé	Total goals
541	1964	10 May	Santos	1	Colon (Argentina)	2	1	631
542	1964	30 May	Brazil	5	England	1	1	632
543	1964	3 July	Brazil	0	Argentina	3	0	632
544	1964	5 July	Santos	1	América (Rio Preto)	2	1	633
545	1964	7 July	Brazil	4	Portugal	1	0	633
546	1964	19 August	Santos	6	Guarani (Campinas)	1	1	634
547	1964	23 August	Santos	2	Palmeiras (São Paulo)	1	1	635
548	1964	23 September	Santos	1	São Bento	1	1	636
549	1964	27 September	Santos	3	Portuguesa de Desportos	4	2	638
550	1964	30 September	Santos	1	Corinthians (São Paulo)	1	1	639
551	1964	4 October	Santos	3	América (Rio Preto)	1	1	640
552	1964	7 October	Santos	1	Colo Colo (Chile)	3	1	641
553	1964	11 October	Santos	3	São Paulo FC	2	0	641
554	1964	14 October	Santos	3	Comercial (São Paulo)	2	1	642
555	1964	18 October	Santos	4	Atlético (Minas Gerais)	1	1	643
556	1964	21 October	Santos	0	Guaratingueta	2	0	643
557	1964	25 October	Santos	5	Atlético (Minas Gerais)	1	2	645
558	1964	28 October	Santos	8	Prudentina	1	4	649
559	1964	1 November	Santos	6	XV de Novembro (Piracicaba)	3	3	652
560	1964	4 November	Santos	3	Palmeiras (São Paulo)	2	1	653
561	1964	7 November	Santos	2	Palmeiras (São Paulo)	3	0	653
562	1964	10 November	Santos	4	Palmeiras (São Paulo)	0	0	653
563	1964	15 November	Santos	0	Ferroviária (Araraquara)	0	0	653
564	1964	18 November	Santos	1	Guarani (Campinas)	5	0	653
565*	1964	21 November	Santos	11	Botafogo (Ribeirão Preto)	0	8	661
566	1964	29 November	Santos	3	Noroeste (Bauru)	0	1	662
567	1964	2 December	Santos	5	Juventus (São Paulo)	2	2	664
568	1964	6 December	Santos	7	Corinthians (São Paulo)	4	4	668
569	1964	9 December	Santos	6	São Bento (Sorocaba)	0	3	671
570	1964	13 December	Santos	3	Portuguesa de Desportos	2	0	671
571	1964	16 December	Santos	4	Flamengo (Rio)	1	3	674
572	1964	19 December	Santos	0	Flamengo (Rio)	0	0	674
573	**1965**	10 January	Santos	2	Botafogo (Rio)	3	0	674
574	1965	13 January	Santos	2	Universidad Cat6lica (Chile)	1	1	675
575	1965	16 January	Santos	6	Czechoslovakia	4	3	678
576	1965	22 January	Santos	2	River Plate (Argentina)	3	1	679
577	1965	29 January	Santos	3	Colo Colo (Chile)	2	1	680
578	1965	2 February	Santos	3	Universidad (Chile)	0	1	681
579	1965	4 February	Santos	1	River Plate (Argentina)	0	0	681
580	1965	9 February	Santos	4	River Plate (Argentina)	3	2	683

*Pelé scored eight of Santos' eleven goals in this match.

Match	Year	Date	Pelé's team	Goals for	Opposition	Goals against	Goals by Pelé	Total goals
581	1965	13 February	Santos	5	Universidad (Chile)	1	3	686
582	1965	19 February	Santos	2	Universitario (Peru)	1	0	686
583	1965	21 February	Santos	3	Galicia (Venezuela)	1	3	689
584	1965	23 February	Santos	4	Independiente (Argentina)	0	2	691
585	1965	26 February	Santos	1	Universidad (Chile)	0	1	692
586	1965	6 March	Santos	2	Universitario (Peru)	1	1	693
587	1965	8 March	Brazil	2	Gaúcha XI	0	0	693
588	1965	10 March	Santos	4	Portuguesa de Desportos	1	0	693
589	1965	25 March	Santos	5	Penarol (Uruguay)	4	1	694
590	1965	28 March	Santos	2	Penarol (Uruguay)	3	0	694
591	1965	31 March	Santos	1	Penarol (Uruguay)	2	1	695
592	1965	4 April	Santos	0	Vasco da Gama (Rio)	3	0	695
593	1965	11 April	Santos	2	Botafogo (Rio)	3	0	695
594	1965	15 April	Santos	4	Corinthians (São Paulo)	4	4	699
595	1965	18 April	Santos	5	Fluminense (Rio)	2	1	700
596	1965	21 April	Santos	2	América (Guanabara)	0	0	700
597	1965	29 April	Santos	9	Clube do Remo (Para)	4	5	705
598	1965	2 May	Santos	6	Bahia	1	1	706
599	1965	5 May	Santos	3	Bahia	1	0	706
600	1965	8 May	Santos	6	Dom Bosco (Cuiaba)	2	3	709
601	1965	11 May	Santos	4	Comercial (Campo Grande)	1	3	712
602	1965	14 May	Santos	2	Olimpia (Paraguay)	2	1	713
603	1965	16 May	Santos	11	Maringa (Parana)	1	2	715
604	1965	2 June	Brazil	5	Belgium	0	3	718
605	1965	6 June	Brazil	2	W. Germany	0	1	719
606	1965	9 June	Brazil	0	Argentina	0	0	719
607	1965	17 June	Brazil	3	Algeria	0	1	720
608	1965	24 June	Brazil	0	Portugal	0	0	720
609	1965	30 June	Brazil	2	Sweden	1	1	721
610	1965	4 July	Brazil	3	USSR	0	2	723
611	1965	14 July	Santos	6	Noroeste (Bauru)	2	5	728
612	1965	18 July	Santos	3	Ferroviária (Araraquara)	1	2	730
613	1965	21 July	Santos	5	Comercial (Ribeirão Preto)	3	3	733
614	1965	25 July	Santos	6	E. Club Brasil (Alagoas)	0	2	735
615	1965	28 July	Santos	3	Santo Antonio (Vitoria)	1	1	736
616	1965	1 August	Santos	1	São Paulo FC	1	0	736
617	1965	4 August	Santos	2	AA Portuguesa	0	1	737
618	1965	8 August	Santos	4	Boca Juniors (Argentina)	1	2	739
619	1965	12 August	Santos	2	River Plate (Argentina)	1	0	739
620	1965	15 August	Santos	3	Prudentina	1	3	742
621	1965	22 August	Santos	4	Portuguesa de Desportos	0	3	745
622	1965	28 August	Santos	4	Corinthians (São Paulo)	3	2	747
623	1965	4 September	Santos	7	Botafogo (Ribeirão Preto)	1	3	750

Appendix

Match	Year	Date	Pelé's team	Goals for	Opposition	Goals against	Goals by Pelé	Total goals
624	1965	8 September	Santos	3	Juventus (São Paulo)	1	2	752
625	1965	11 September	Santos	7	Guarani (Campinas)	0	4	756
626	1965	15 September	Santos	1	Minas Gerais	2	0	756
627	1965	19 September	Santos	0	Palmeiras (São Paulo)	1	0	756
628	1965	22 September	Santos	4	Ferroviária (Araraquara)	2	0	756
629	1965	3 October	Santos	3	Noroeste (Bauru)	0	1	757
630	1965	7 October	Santos	4	São Bento (Sorocaba)	2	1	758
631	1965	10 October	Santos	2	Comercial (Ribeirão Preto)	0	1	759
632	1965	13 October	Santos	3	AA Portuguesa	0	1	760
633	1965	16 October	Santos	0	São Paulo FC	0	0	760
634	1965	24 October	Santos	4	América (Rio Preto)	0	3	763
635	1965	27 October	Santos	1	Portuguesa de Desportos	0	0	763
636	1965	31 October	Santos	5	Prudentina	2	5	768
637	1965	3 November	Santos	4	Palmeiras (São Paulo)	2	0	768
638	1965	7 November	Santos	2	XV de Novembro (Piracicaba)	0	0	768
639	1965	10 November	Santos	1	Palmeiras (São Paulo)	1	1	769
640	1965	14 November	Santos	4	Corinthians (São Paulo)	2	1	770
641	1965	21 November	Brazil	2	USSR	2	1	771
642	1965	25 November	Santos	5	Botafogo (Ribeirão Preto)	0	4	775
643	1965	27 November	Santos	4	Juventus (São Paulo)	0	3	778
644	1965	1 December	Santos	5	Vasco da Gama (Rio)	1	0	778
645	1965	4 December	Santos	1	Guarani (Campinas)	0	1	779
646	1965	8 December	Santos	1	Vasco da Gama (Rio)	0	1	780
647	1965	12 December	Santos	0	Palmeiras (São Paulo)	5	0	780
648	**1966**	9 January	Santos	7	Stade Abidjan (Ivory Coast)	1	2	782
649	1966	13 January	Santos	2	San Martin / Atlético XI (Argentina)	0	0	782
650	1966	16 January	Santos	1	Alianza (El Salvador)	2	1	783
651	1966	19 January	Santos	1	Botafogo (Rio)	2	1	784
652	1966	22 January	Santos	0	Botafogo (Rio)	3	0	784
653	1966	26 January	Santos	2	Universitario (Peru)	2	1	785
654	1966	29 January	Santos	4	Alianza (Peru)	1	1	786
655	1966	6 February	Santos	1	Melgar de Arequipa (Peru)	1	0	786
656	1966	9 February	Santos	6	Universidad (Chile)	1	3	789
657	1966	11 February	Santos	1	Rosario Central (Argentina)	0	0	789
658	1966	13 February	Santos	1	Sarmiento (Argentina)	1	0	789
659	1966	17 February	Santos	2	Colo Colo (Chile)	2	1	790
660	1966	29 March	Santos	3	Cruzeiro (Minas Gerais)	4	1	791
661	1966	31 March	Santos	1	Atlético (Minas Gerais)	0	1	792
662	1966	19 May	Brazil	1	Chile	0	0	792
663	1966	4 June	Brazil	4	Peru	0	1	793
664	1966	8 June	Brazil	2	Poland	1	0	793
665	1966	12 June	Brazil	2	Czechoslovakia	1	2	795
666	1966	15 June	Brazil	2	Czechoslovakia	2	1	796

Match	Year	Date	Pelé's team	Goals for	Opposition	Goals against	Goals by Pelé	Total goals
667	1966	21 June	Brazil	5	Atlético Madrid (Spain)	3	3	799
668	1966	25 June	Brazil	1	Scotland	1	0	799
669	1966	30 June	Brazil	3	Sweden	2	0	799
670	1966	4 July	Brazil	4	AIK (Sweden)	2	2	801
671	1966	6 July	Brazil	3	Malmö (Sweden)	1	2	803
672*	1966	12 July	Brazil	2	Bulgaria	0	1	804
673	1966	19 July	Brazil	1	Portugal	3	0	804
674	1966	17 August	Santos	1	Juventus (São Paulo)	1	0	804
675	1966	21 August	Santos	4	Benfica (Portugal)	0	1	805
676	1966	24 August	Santos	1	AEK (Greece)	0	0	805
677	1966	28 August	Santos	1	Toluca (Mexico)	1	0	805
678	1966	30 August	Santos	2	Atlante (Mexico)	2	1	806
679	1966	5 September	Santos	4	Internazionale (Italy)	1	1	807
680	1966	11 September	Santos	3	Prudentina	1	2	809
681	1966	14 September	Santos	0	Portuguesa de Desportos	2	0	809
682	1966	8 October	Santos	3	Corinthians (São Paulo)	0	0	809
683	1966	13 October	Santos	7	Comercial (Ribeirão Preto)	5	0	809
684	1966	16 October	Santos	2	São Bento (Sorocaba)	2	1	810
685	1966	23 October	Santos	3	Portuguesa de Desportos	0	1	811
686	1966	26 October	Santos	4	Noroeste (Bauru)	1	2	813
687	1966	30 October	Santos	1	São Paulo FC	2	1	814
688	1966	5 November	Santos	3	Juventus (São Paulo)	0	1	815
689	1966	9 November	Santos	2	Nautico (Recife)	0	1	816
690	1966	13 November	Santos	3	Bragantino	2	3	819
691	1966	17 November	Santos	3	Nautico (Recife)	5	0	819
692	1966	19 November	Santos	4	Nautico (Recife)	1	0	819
693	1966	23 November	Santos	2	Palmeiras (São Paulo)	0	1	820
694	1966	26 November	Santos	2	Guarani (Campinas)	1	0	820
695	1966	30 November	Santos	2	Cruzeiro (Minas Gerais)	6	0	820
696	1966	4 December	Santos	3	Botafogo (Ribeirão Preto)	1	1	821
697	1966	7 December	Santos	2	Cruzeiro (Minas Gerais)	3	1	822
698	**1967**	15 January	Santos	4	Mar Del Plata (Argentina)	1	0	822
699	1967	19 January	Santos	4	River Plate (Argentina)	0	1	823
700	1967	22 January	Santos	1	Milionarios (Colombia)	2	0	823
701	1967	25 January	Santos	3	Atlético Juniors (Colombia)	3	0	823
702	1967	29 January	Santos	2	River Plate (Argentina)	4	2	825
703	1967	1 February	Santos	2	River Plate (Argentina)	1	1	826
704	1967	7 February	Santos	1	Universidad (Chile)	1	0	826
705	1967	10 February	Santos	2	Vazas (Hungary)	2	1	827
706	1967	17 February	Santos	2	Pefiarol (Uruguay)	0	0	827

*First match of the 1966 World Cup Finals, England.

Appendix

Match	Year	Date	Pelé's team	Goals for	Opposition	Goals against	Goals by Pelé	Total goals
707	1967	21 February	Santos	6	Universidad Catolica	2	4	831
708	1967	25 February	Santos	4	Alianza (Peru)	1	1	832
709	1967	28 February	Santos	2	Colo Colo (Chile)	1	0	832
710	1967	8 March	Santos	1	Atlético (Minas Gerais)	0	0	832
711	1967	12 March	Santos	1	Grêmio (Porto Alegre)	1	1	833
712	1967	15 March	Santos	5	Internacional (Porto Alegre)	1	1	834
713	1967	19 March	Santos	1	Flamengo (Rio)	0	0	834
714	1967	22 March	Santos	0	Botafogo (Rio)	0	0	834
715	1967	26 March	Santos	1	Vasco da Gama (Rio)	2	1	835
716	1967	1 April	Santos	1	São Paulo FC	1	1	836
717	1967	8 April	Santos	1	Palmeiras (São Paulo)	2	0	836
718	1967	15 April	Santos	2	Portuguesa de Desportos	2	2	838
719	1967	19 April	Santos	1	Cruzeiro (Minas Gerais)	3	0	838
720	1967	23 April	Santos	3	Bangu (Rio)	0	1	839
721	1967	30 April	Santos	0	Fluminense (Rio)	3	0	839
722	1967	3 May	Santos	3	Ferroviario (Coritiba)	0	1	840
723	1967	7 May	Santos	3	Ilhéus	1	1	841
724	1967	10 May	Santos	5	Santa Cruz (Recife)	0	1	842
725	1967	13 May	Santos	1	Corinthians (São Paulo)	1	1	843
726	1967	15 May	Santos	0	Olimpia (Paraguay)	0	0	843
727	1967	23 May	Santos	3	Portuguesa de Desportos	2	1	844
728	1967	25 May	Santos	5	Brasilia	1	1	845
729	1967	28 May	Santos	4	Senegal	1	3	848
730	1967	31 May	Santos	4	Gabon	0	1	849
731	1967	2 June	Santos	2	Congo	1	1	850
732	1967	4 June	Santos	2	Ivory Coast	1	1	851
733	1967	7 June	Santos	3	Congo	2	3	854
734	1967	13 June	Santos	5	TSV Munich (W. Germany)	4	2	856
735	1967	17 June	Santos	2	Mantova (Italy)	1	1	857
736	1967	20 June	Santos	1	Venice (Italy)	0	0	857
737	1967	24 June	Santos	5	Lecce (Italy)	1	3	860
738	1967	27 June	Santos	1	Fiorentina (Italy)	1	0	860
739	1967	29 June	Santos	3	Roma (Italy)	1	1	861
740	1967	9 July	Santos	4	São Bento (Sorocaba)	3	1	862
741	1967	15 July	Santos	4	Juventus (São Paulo)	0	1	863
742	1967	23 July	Santos	2	Guarani (Campinas)	1	0	863
743	1967	6 August	Santos	1	Palmeiras (São Paulo)	1	1	864
744	1967	19 August	Santos	4	Comercial (Ribeirão Preto)	1	1	865
745	1967	22 August	Santos	3	AA Portuguesa	1	0	865
746	1967	26 August	Santos	0	Internazionale (Italy)	1	0	865
747	1967	28 August	Santos	1	Deportivo Español (Spain)	4	0	865
748	1967	29 August	Santos	2	Malaga (Spain)	1	0	865
749	1967	8 October	Santos	3	América (Rio Preto)	2	1	866

Match	Year	Date	Pelé's team	Goals for	Opposition	Goals against	Goals by Pelé	Total goals
750	1967	15 October	Santos	2	São Paulo FC	2	1	867
751	1967	22 October	Santos	3	Prudentina	1	2	869
752	1967	29 October	Santos	4	Palmeiras (São Paulo)	1	1	870
753	1967	1 November	Santos	4	Juventus (São Paulo)	1	2	872
754	1967	4 November	Santos	1	Maranhão	0	0	872
755	1967	7 November	Santos	5	Fortaleza (Ceará)	0	1	873
756	1967	11 November	Santos	1	Comercial (Ribeirão Preto)	1	1	874
757	1967	19 November	Santos	1	São Bento (Sorocaba)	1	1	875
758	1967	26 November	Santos	0	Portuguesa de Desportos	0	0	875
759	1967	3 December	Santos	1	Guarani (Campinas)	1	1	876
760	1967	10 December	Santos	1	Corinthians (São Paulo)	1	1	877
761	1967	17 December	Santos	3	AA Portuguesa	1	1	878
762	1967	21 December	Santos	2	São Paulo FC	1	0	878
763	**1968**	13 January	Santos	4	Czechoslovakia	1	0	878
764	1968	23 January	Santos	4	Vazas (Hungary)	0	1	879
765	1968	2 February	Santos	4	Colo Colo (Chile)	1	0	879
766	1968	3 March	Santos	4	Ferroviária (Araraquara)	1	2	881
767	1968	6 March	Santos	0	Corinthians (São Paulo)	2	0	881
768	1968	9 March	Santos	5	Botafogo (Ribeirão Preto)	1	1	882
769	1968	16 March	Santos	3	Portuguesa de Desportos	0	1	883
770	1968	19 March	Santos	3	Goias	3	1	884
771	1968	23 March	Santos	4	Juventus (São Paulo)	0	2	886
772	1968	27 March	Santos	5	São Paulo FC	2	2	888
773	1968	31 March	Santos	4	América (Rio Preto)	3	2	890
774	1968	7 April	Santos	8	Comercial (Ribeirão Preto)	2	2	892
775	1968	10 April	Santos	2	Guarani (Campinas)	0	0	892
776	1968	13 April	Santos	1	Palmeiras (São Paulo)	0	0	892
777	1968	18 April	Santos	1	São Bento (Sorocaba)	0	0	892
778	1968	21 April	Santos	2	Corinthians (São Paulo)	0	1	893
779	1968	24 April	Santos	3	Juventus (São Paulo)	2	2	895
780	1968	28 April	Santos	1	XV de Novembro (Piracicaba)	0	0	895
781	1968	1 May	Santos	0	Ferroviária (Araraquara)	0	0	895
782	1968	4 May	Santos	1	Portuguesa de Desportos	0	0	895
783	1968	8 May	Santos	0	Flamengo (Rio)	0	0	895
784	1968	12 May	Santos	3	Botafogo (Ribeirão Preto)	1	0	895
785	1968	15 May	Santos	1	AA Portuguesa	2	0	895
786	1968	19 May	Santos	3	Palmeiras (São Paulo)	1	1	896
787	1968	23 May	Santos	0	Boca Juniors (Argentina)	1	0	896
788	1968	29 May	Santos	5	Comercial (Ribeirão Preto)	0	1	897
789	1968	1 June	Santos	3	São Paulo FC	1	0	897
790	1968	9 June	Santos	2	Cagliari (Italia)	1	0	897
791	1968	12 June	Santos	2	Alessandria (Italy)	0	1	898
792	1968	15 June	Santos	4	Zurich (Switzerland)	5	1	899

Match	Year	Date	Pelé's team	Goals for	Opposition	Goals against	Goals by Pelé	Total goals
793	1968	17 June	Santos	3	Saarbrücken (W. Germany)	0	1	900
794	1968	21 June	Santos	4	Napoli (Italy)	2	1	901
795	1968	26 June	Santos	6	Napoli (Italy)	2	2	903
796	1968	28 June	Santos	5	Napoli (Italy)	2	2	905
797	1968	30 June	Santos	3	St Louis Stars (USA)	2	1	906
798	1968	4 July	Santos	4	Kansas City Spurs (USA)	1	1	907
799	1968	6 July	Santos	4	Necaxa (Mexico)	3	1	908
800	1968	8 July	Santos	7	Boston Beacons (USA)	1	1	909
801	1968	10 July	Santos	1	Cleveland Stokers (USA)	2	0	909
802	1968	12 July	Santos	3	New York Generals (USA)	5	0	909
803	1968	14 July	Santos	3	Washington Whips (USA)	1	0	909
804	1968	17 July	Santos	4	Olimpic (Colombia)	2	1	910
805	1968	25 July	Brazil	4	Paraguay	0	2	912
806	1968	28 July	Brazil	0	Paraguay	1	0	912
807	1968	4 August	Santos	0	Ferroviária (Ceará)	0	0	912
808	1968	6 August	Santos	3	Paissandu (Para)	1	1	913
809	1968	9 August	Santos	3	Fast (Manaus)	0	1	914
810	1968	11 August	Santos	2	Fast (Manaus)	1	2	916
811	1968	15 August	Santos	2	River Plate (Argentina)	1	0	916
812	1968	18 August	Santos	4	Benfica (Portugal)	2	0	916
813	1968	20 August	Santos	2	Nacional (Uruguay)	2	1	917
814	1968	25 August	Santos	1	Boca Juniors (Argentina)	1	0	917
815	1968	28 August	Santos	6	Atlanta Chiefs (USA)	2	3	920
816	1968	30 August	Santos	3	Oakland Clippers (USA)	1	2	922
817	1968	1 September	Santos	3	Benfica (Portugal)	3	0	922
818	1968	15 September	Santos	2	Flamengo (Rio)	0	0	922
819	1968	18 September	Santos	0	Palmeiras (São Paulo)	0	0	922
820	1968	21 September	Santos	2	Fluminense (Rio)	1	1	923
821	1968	25 September	Santos	1	Bangú (Rio)	1	0	923
822	1968	29 September	Santos	2	Vasco da Gama (Rio)	3	0	923
823	1968	6 October	Santos	2	Corinthians (São Paulo)	1	1	924
824	1968	10 October	Santos	9	Bahia	2	3	927
825	1968	13 October	Santos	2	Cruzeiro (Minas Gerais)	0	1	928
826	1968	16 October	Santos	2	Portuguesa de Desportos	0	0	928
827	1968	20 October	Santos	0	São Paulo FC	0	0	928
828	1968	23 October	Santos	3	Internacional (Porto Alegre)	1	1	929
829	1968	27 October	Santos	3	Nautico (Recife)	0	1	930
830	1968	31 October	Brazil	1	Mexico	2	0	930
831	1968	3 November	Brazil	2	Mexico	1	1	931
832	1968	6 November	Brazil	2	FIFA XI	1	0	931
833	1968	10 November	São Paulo	3	Rio	2	1	932
834	1968	13 November	Brazil	2	Paraná	1	0	932
835	1968	19 November	Santos	2	Racing (Argentina)	0	1	933

Match	Year	Date	Pelé's team	Goals for	Opposition	Goals against	Goals by Pelé	Total goals
836	1968	21 November	Santos	1	Penarol (Uruguay)	0	0	933
837	1968	24 November	Santos	2	Atlético (Minas Gerais)	2	1	934
838	1968	27 November	Santos	3	Grêmio (Porto Alegre)	1	1	935
839	1968	1 December	Santos	2	Botafogo (Rio)	3	0	935
840	1968	4 December	Santos	2	Internacional (Porto Alegre)	1	1	936
841	1968	8 December	Santos	3	Palmeiras (São Paulo)	0	0	936
842	1968	10 December	Santos	2	Vasco da Gama (Rio)	1	1	937
843	1968	14 December	Brazil	2	W. Germany	2	0	937
844	1968	17 December	Brazil	3	Yugoslavia	3	1	938
845	**1969**	17 January	Santos	3	Pointe Noire (Congo)	0	1	939
846	1969	19 January	Santos	3	Congo	2	2	941
847	1969	21 January	Santos	2	Congo 'B'	0	0	941
848	1969	23 January	Santos	2	Congo 'A'	3	2	943
849*	1969	26 January	Santos	2	Nigerian FA	2	2	945
850	1969	1 February	Santos	2	Austria	0	0	945
851	1969	4 February	Santos	2	Middle W. Africa XI	1	0	945
852	1969	6 February	Santos	2	Hearts of Oak (Africa)	2	1	946
853	1969	9 February	Santos	1	Algeria	1	0	946
854	1969	14 February	Santos	6	XV de Novembro (Piradcaba)	2	2	948
855	1969	22 February	Santos	4	Portuguesa de Desportos	1	1	949
856	1969	26 February	Santos	3	Ferroviária (Araraquara)	0	2	951
857	1969	2 March	Santos	2	Paulista (Jundiaí)	1	0	951
858	1969	5 March	Santos	0	Guarani (Campinas)	1	0	951
859	1969	9 March	Santos	3	São Paulo FC	0	1	952
860	1969	12 March	Santos	4	São Bento (Sorocaba)	2	2	954
861	1969	15 March	Santos	2	Juventus (São Paulo)	1	1	955
862	1969	19 March	Santos	2	América (Rio Preto)	1	0	955
863	1969	22 March	Santos	2	Palmeiras (São Paulo)	3	2	957
864	1969	26 March	Santos	4	Botafogo (Ribeirão Preto)	1	1	958
865	1969	29 March	Santos	3	AA Portuguesa	1	3	961
866	1969	7 April	Brazil	2	Peru	1	0	961
867	1969	9 April	Brazil	3	Peru	2	1	962
868	1969	13 April	Santos	0	Corinthians (São Paulo)	2	0	962
869	1969	23 April	Santos	3	Portuguesa de Desportos	2	0	962
870	1969	27 April	Santos	1	América (Rio Preto)	1	1	963
871	1969	30 April	Santos	1	AA Portuguesa	2	1	964
872	1969	3 May	Santos	0	Palmeiras (São Paulo)	1	0	964
873	1969	1 May	Santos	1	Ferroviária (Araraquara)	2	1	965
874	1969	21 May	Santos	1	São Paulo FC	0	0	965
875	1969	25 May	Santos	1	Corinthians (São Paulo)	1	0	965

*The match that led to the 'ceasefire' in the Biafran civil war.

Appendix

Match	Year	Date	Pelé's team	Goals for	Opposition	Goals against	Goals by Pelé	Total goals
876	1969	28 May	Santos	3	Paulista (Jundiai)	2	1	966
877	1969	31 May	Santos	5	Botafogo (Ribeirão Preto)	1	4	970
878	1969	8 June	Santos	3	Corinthians (São Paulo)	1	2	972
879	1969	12 June	Brazil	2	England	1	0	972
880	1969	18 June	Santos	3	Palmeiras (São Paulo)	0	1	973
881	1969	21 June	Santos	0	São Paulo FC	0	0	973
882	1969	24 June	Santos	1	Internazionale (Italy)	0	0	973
883	1969	6 July	Brazil	4	Bahia	0	1	974
884	1969	9 July	Brazil	8	Sergipe	2	0	974
885	1969	13 July	Brazil	6	Pernambuco	1	1	975
886	1969	1 August	Brazil	2	Milionarios (Colombia)	0	0	975
887	1969	6 August	Brazil	2	Colombia	0	0	975
888	1969	10 August	Brazil	5	Venezuela	0	2	977
889	1969	17 August	Brazil	3	Paraguay	0	0	977
890	1969	21 August	Brazil	6	Colombia	2	1	978
891	1969	24 August	Brazil	6	Venezuela	0	2	980
892	1969	31 August	Brazil	1	Paraguay	0	1	981
893	1969	3 September	Brazil	1	Minas Gerais	2	1	982
894	1969	10 September	Santos	3	Red Star (Yugoslavia)	3	1	983
895	1969	12 September	Santos	1	Dinamo (Yugoslavia)	1	0	983
896	1969	15 September	Santos	4	Radnicki (Yugoslavia)	4	1	984
897	1969	17 September	Santos	3	Atlético Madrid (Spain)	1	0	984
898	1969	19 September	Santos	1	Zeljesnicar (Yugoslavia)	1	1	985
899	1969	22 September	Santos	3	Stoke City (England)	2	2	987
900	1969	24 September	Santos	7	Sampdoria / Genoa XI (Italy)	1	2	989
901	1969	28 September	Santos	1	Grêmio (Porto Alegre)	2	1	990
902	1969	12 October	Santos	1	Palmeiras (São Paulo)	2	1	991
903	1969	15 October	Santos	6	Portuguesa de Desportos	2	4	995
904	1969	22 October	Santos	3	Coritiba	1	2	997
905	1969	26 October	Santos	0	Fluminense (Rio)	0	0	997
906	1969	1 November	Santos	4	Flamengo (Rio)	1	1	998
907	1969	4 November	Santos	1	Corinthians (São Paulo)	4	0	998
908	1969	9 November	Santos	1	São Paulo FC	1	0	998
909	1969	12 November	Santos	4	Santa Cruz (Recife)	0	2	1000
910	1969	14 November	Santos	3	Botafogo (Paraiba)	0	1	1001
911	1969	16 November	Santos	1	Bahia	1	0	1001
912*	1969	19 November	Santos	2	Vasco da Gama (Rio)	1	1	1002
913	1969	23 November	Santos	0	Atlético (Minas Gerais)	2	0	1002
914	1969	29 November	Santos	1	Racing (Argentina)	2	0	1002
915	1969	2 December	Santos	1	Penarol (Uruguay)	2	1	1003

*Celebrated at the time as the 1,000th goal.

Match	Year	Date	Pelé's team	Goals for	Opposition	Goals against	Goals by Pelé	Total goals
916	1969	4 December	Santos	1	Estudiantes La Plata (Argentina)	3	0	1003
917	1969	6 December	Santos	1	Velez Sarsfield (Argentina)	1	1	1004
918	1969	9 December	Santos	0	Racing (Argentina)	2	0	1004
919	1969	11 December	Santos	2	Penarol (Uruguay)	0	1	1005
920	1969	14 December	São Paulo	2	Bahia	1	0	1005
921	1969	17 December	São Paulo	2	Minas Gerais	1	1	1006
922	1969	21 December	São Paulo	0	Rio	0	0	1006
923	**1970**	10 January	Santos	3	Coritiba	1	1	1007
924	1970	16 January	Santos	2	Boca Juniors (Argentina)	2	1	1008
925	1970	18 January	Santos	2	Talleres (Argentina)	0	0	1008
926	1970	21 January	Santos	3	Colo Colo (Chile)	4	1	1009
927	1970	24 January	Santos	4	Universitario (Peru)	1	2	1011
928	1970	28 January	Santos	2	Dinamo (Yugoslavia)	2	0	1011
929	1970	30 January	Santos	2	Universitario (Chile)	0	2	1013
930	1970	4 February	Santos	7	América (Mexico)	0	3	1016
931	1970	7 February	Santos	3	Universidad Catolica (Chile)	2	2	1018
932	1970	4 March	Brazil	0	Argentina	2	0	1018
933	1970	8 March	Brazil	2	Argentina	1	1	1019
934	1970	14 March	Brazil	1	Bangú (Rio)	1	0	1019
935	1970	22 March	Brazil	5	Chile	0	2	1021
936	1970	26 March	Brazil	2	Chile	1	0	1021
937	1970	5 April	Brazil	4	Amazon XI	1	1	1022
938	1970	12 April	Brazil	0	Paraguay	0	0	1022
939	1970	19 April	Brazil	3	Minas Gerais	1	0	1022
940	1970	26 April	Brazil	0	Bulgaria	0	0	1022
941	1970	29 April	Brazil	1	Austria	0	0	1022
942	1970	6 May	Brazil	3	Guadalajara (Mexico)	0	1	1023
943	1970	17 May	Brazil	5	León (Mexico)	2	2	1025
944	1970	24 May	Brazil	3	Irapuato (Mexico)	0	0	1025
945*	1970	3 June	Brazil	4	Czechoslovakia	1	1	1026
946	1970	7 June	Brazil	1	England	0	0	1026
947	1970	10 June	Brazil	3	Romania	2	2	1028
948	1970	14 June	Brazil	4	Peru	2	0	1028
949	1970	17 June	Brazil	3	Uruguay	1	0	1028
950†	1970	21 June	Brazil	4	Italy	1	1	1029
951	1970	5 July	Santos	2	Palmeiras (São Paulo)	0	0	1029
952	1970	8 July	Santos	0	Ferroviária (Araraquara)	1	0	1029
953	1970	12 July	Santos	2	São Paulo FC	3	0	1029
954	1970	15 July	Santos	2	São Bento (Sorocaba)	1	0	1029

*First match of the 1970 World Cup Finals, Mexico. It was in this match that Pelé attempted to chip the goalkeeper from the halfway line.

†1970 World Cup Final, Azteca Stadium, Mexico City.

Match	Year	Date	Pelé's team	Goals for	Opposition	Goals against	Goals by Pelé	Total goals
955	1970	19 July	Santos	5	Guarani (Campinas)	2	2	1031
956	1970	22 July	Santos	3	Goias	1	1	1032
957	1970	25 July	Santos	2	Portuguesa de Desportos	1	1	1033
958	1970	29 July	Santos	9	Sergipe	1	4	1037
959	1970	2 August	Santos	2	Corinthians (São Paulo)	2	1	1038
960	1970	5 August	Santos	5	Guarani (Campinas)	1	1	1039
961	1970	9 August	Santos	2	São Paulo FC	3	0	1039
962	1970	12 August	Santos	5	Ferroviária (Araraquara)	0	1	1040
963	1970	16 August	Santos	1	Ponte Preta (Campinas)	0	0	1040
964	1970	19 August	Santos	0	Botafogo (Ribeirão Preto)	0	0	1040
965	1970	22 August	Santos	0	Portuguesa de Desportos	1	0	1040
966	1970	26 August	Santos	2	São Bento (Sorocaba)	2	1	1041
967	1970	30 August	Santos	1	Corinthians (São Paulo)	1	0	1041
968	1970	2 September	Santos	2	Grêmio (Porto Alegre)	0	1	1042
969	1970	6 September	Santos	1	Palmeiras (São Paulo)	1	0	1042
970	1970	9 September	Santos	0	Cruzeiro (Minas Gerais)	0	0	1042
971	1970	12 September	Santos	5	Galicia (Venezuela)	1	1	1043
972	1970	15 September	Santos	4	All-Stars (USA)	3	0	1043
973	1970	18 September	Santos	7	Washington Darts (USA)	4	4	1047
974	1970	20 September	Santos	2	Guadalajara (Mexico)	1	1	1048
975	1970	22 September	Santos	2	West Ham United (England)	2	2	1050
976	1970	24 September	Santos	2	Santa Fé (Colombia)	1	0	1050
977	1970	30 September	Brazil	2	Mexico	1	0	1050
978	1970	4 October	Brazil	5	Chile	1	1	1051
979	1970	14 October	Santos	1	Atlético (Minas Gerais)	1	1	1052
980	1970	17 October	Santos	1	Vasco da Gama (Rio)	5	0	1052
981	1970	22 October	Santos	1	Ponte Preta (Campinas)	1	1	1053
982	1970	25 October	Santos	5	Alagoas	0	2	1055
983	1970	28 October	Santos	0	Atlético (Parana)	1	0	1055
984	1970	1 November	Santos	0	Corinthians (São Paulo)	2	0	1055
985	1970	8 November	Santos	2	Botafogo (Rio)	2	0	1055
986	1970	11 November	Santos	1	Palmeiras (São Paulo)	1	0	1055
987	1970	14 November	Santos	0	Flamengo (Rio)	2	0	1055
988	1970	18 November	Santos	1	Fluminense (Rio)	0	0	1055
989	1970	21 November	Santos	0	América (Guanabara)	0	0	1055
990	1970	25 November	Santos	2	Universitario (Peru)	3	0	1055
991	1970	29 November	Santos	3	São Paulo FC	2	1	1056
992	1970	2 December	Santos	5	Bahia	1	1	1057
993	1970	6 December	Santos	0	Santa Cruz (Recife)	1	0	1057
994	1970	10 December	Santos	4	Hong Kong	1	2	1059
995	1970	11 December	Santos	4	Hong Kong	0	3	1062
996	1970	13 December	Santos	5	Hong Kong	2	1	1063
997	1970	17 December	Santos	4	Hong Kong	0	2	1065

Match	Year	Date	Pelé's team	Goals for	Opposition	Goals against	Goals by Pelé	Total goals
998	**1971**	13 January	Santos	3	Cochabamba (Bolivia)	2	1	1066
999	1971	16 January	Santos	4	Bolivar (Bolivia)	0	2	1068
1000	1971	19 January	Santos	1	Atlético Marte (El Salvador)	1	0	1068
1001	1971	23 January	Santos	4	Martinica	1	1	1069
1002	1971	26 January	Santos	2	Guadeloupe	1	1	1070
1003*	1971	28 January	Santos	4	Transvaal (Surinam)	1	1	1071
1004	1971	31 January	Santos	1	Jamaica	1	0	1071
1005	1971	2 February	Santos	1	Chelsea (England)	0	0	1071
1006	1971	5 February	Santos	3	Milionarios (Colombia)	2	2	1073
1007	1971	7 February	Santos	3	Atlético Nacional (Colombia)	1	1	1074
1008	1971	10 February	Santos	1	Cali (Colombia)	2	1	1075
1009	1971	14 February	Santos	2	Alianza (El Salvador)	1	0	1075
1010	1971	17 February	Santos	2	Haiti	0	0	1075
1011	1971	3 March	Santos	4	Botafogo (Ribeirão Preto)	0	1	1076
1012	1971	7 March	Santos	1	Ferroviária (Araraquara)	4	0	1076
1013	1971	28 March	Santos	0	Palmeiras (São Paulo)		2	1078
1014	1971	31 March	Santos	0	Marseilles / St Etienne XI (France)	0	0	1078
1015	1971	4 April	Santos	2	Bahia	3	1	1079
1016	1971	7 April	Santos	2	Galicia (Bahia)	0	1	1080
1017	1971	11 April	Santos	2	Corinthians (São Paulo)	4	1	1081
1018	1971	18 April	Santos	0	Paulista (Jundiai)	0	0	1081
1019	1971	21 April	Santos	1	São Paulo FC	0	0	1081
1020	1971	25 April	Santos	0	Ponte Preta (Campinas)	0	0	1081
1021	1971	28 April	Santos	1	Juventus (São Paulo)	1	0	1081
1022	1971	2 May	Santos	2	Botafogo (Ribeirão Preto)	1	1	1082
1023	1971	9 May	Santos	1	Paulista (Jundiai)	0	0	1082
1024	1971	12 May	Santos	1	São Bento (Sorocaba)	0	0	1082
1025	1971	16 May	Santos	0	São Paulo FC	0	0	1082
1026	1971	20 May	Santos	1	Juventus (São Paulo)	1	0	1082
1027	1971	23 May	Santos	4	Oriente Petrolero (Bolivia)	3	1	1083
1028	1971	26 May	Santos	2	The Strongest (Bolivia)	0	1	1084
1029	1971	30 May	Santos	1	Palmeiras (São Paulo)	2	0	1084
1030	1971	2 June	Santos	1	Guarani (Campinas)	0	0	1084
1031	1971	6 June	Santos	1	Ferroviária (Araraquara)	0	0	1084
1032	1971	10 June	Santos	1	Portuguesa de Desportos	1	1	1085
1033	1971	13 June	Santos	2	Ponte Preta (Campinas)	1	1	1086
1034	1971	20 June	Santos	3	Corinthians (São Paulo)	3	1	1087
1035	1971	23 June	Santos	2	Bologna (Italy)	1	1	1088
1036	1971	27 June	Santos	1	Bologna (Italy)	1	0	1088
1037	1971	30 June	Santos	1	Bologna (Italy)	0	1	1089

*Celebrated at the time as the 1,000th match.

Appendix

Match	Year	Date	Pelé's team	Goals for	Opposition	Goals against	Goals by Pelé	Total goals
1038	1971	11 July	Brazil	1	Austria	1	1	1090
1039*	1971	18 July	Brazil	2	Yugoslavia	2	0	1090
1040	1971	24 July	Santos	1	Monterrey (Mexico)	1	0	1090
1041	1971	28 July	Santos	2	Jalisco (Mexico)	1	0	1090
1042	1971	30 July	Santos	3	Hanover (W. Germany)	1	0	1090
1043	1971	2 August	Santos	2	Cali (Colombia)	2	1	1091
1044	1971	4 August	Santos	5	All-Stars (USA)	1	2	1093
1045	1971	8 August	Santos	0	Bahia	0	0	1093
1046	1971	11 August	Santos	2	Recife	0	0	1093
1047	1971	14 August	Santos	3	São Paulo FC	1	0	1093
1048	1971	18 August	Santos	0	Botafogo (Rio)	0	0	1093
1049	1971	22 August	Santos	0	América (Guanabara)	0	0	1093
1050	1971	25 August	Santos	3	Boca Juniors (Argentina)	0	1	1094
1051	1971	29 August	Santos	0	Milionarios (Colombia)	1	0	1094
1052	1971	1 September	Santos	0	Grêmio (Porto Alegre)	1	0	1094
1053	1971	5 September	Santos	1	Atlético (Minas Gerais)	2	0	1094
1054	1971	18 September	Santos	0	Portuguesa de Desportos	0	0	1094
1055	1971	23 September	Santos	1	Atlético (Três Corações)	2	0	1094
1056	1971	26 September	Santos	1	Internacional (Porto Alegre)	1	0	1094
1057	1971	3 October	Santos	1	Cruzeiro (Minas Gerais)	0	0	1094
1058	1971	7 October	Santos	5	Nacional (Manaus)	1	1	1095
1059	1971	10 October	Santos	0	Ceará	0	0	1095
1060	1971	16 October	Santos	1	Palmeiras (São Paulo)	0	0	1095
1061	1971	24 October	Santos	2	Vasco da Gama (Rio)	0	0	1095
1062	1971	27 October	Santos	0	Coritiba	1	0	1095
1063	1971	30 October	Santos	1	Corinthians (São Paulo)	1	1	1096
1064	1971	20 November	Santos	1	Internacional (Porto Alegre)	1	0	1096
1065	1971	25 November	Santos	2	Atlético (Minas Gerais)	1	0	1096
1066	1971	28 November	Santos	0	Vasco da Gama (Rio)	0	0	1096
1067	1971	1 December	Santos	0	Atlético (Minas Gerais)	2	0	1096
1068	1971	5 December	Santos	0	Internacional (Porto Alegre)	1	0	1096
1069	1971	9 December	Santos	4	Vasco da Gama (Rio)	0	0	1096
1070	1971	12 December	Santos	3	América (Natal)	1	1	1097
1071	1971	15 December	Santos	2	Botafogo (Paraiba)	0	0	1097
1072	**1972**	8 January	Santos	2	América (Guanabara)	1	0	1097
1073	1972	12 January	Santos	0	Flamengo (Rio)	1	0	1097
1074	1972	15 January	Santos	0	Palmeiras (São Paulo)	4	0	1097
1075	1972	30 January	Santos	3	Deportivo Español (Honduras)	1	0	1097
1076	1972	2 February	Santos	1	Saprissa (Costa Rica)	1	0	1097
1077	1972	6 February	Santos	2	Medellín (Colombia)	2	0	1097

*Final game for Brazil.

Match	Year	Date	Pelé's team	Goals for	Opposition	Goals against	Goals by Pelé	Total goals
1078	1972	13 February	Santos	1	Comunicaciones (Guatemala)	1	1	1098
1079	1972	15 February	Santos	0	Olimpia (Honduras)	0	0	1098
1080	1972	18 February	Santos	5	Saprissa (Costa Rica)	3	1	1099
1081	1972	21 February	Santos	1	Aston Villa (England)	2	0	1099
1082	1972	23 February	Santos	2	Sheffield Wednesday (England)	0	0	1099
1083	1972	26 February	Santos	3	Bohemians / Duncondra XI (Ireland)	2	0	1099
1084	1972	1 March	Santos	0	Anderlecht (Belgium)	0	0	1099
1085	1972	3 March	Santos	2	Roma (Italy)	0	0	1099
1086	1972	5 March	Santos	3	Napoli (Italy)	2	2	1101
1087	1972	8 March	Santos	1	América (Rio Preto)	0	0	1101
1088	1972	12 March	Santos	1	Portuguesa de Desportos	0	0	1101
1089	1972	18 March	Santos	3	Juventus (São Paulo)	2	0	1101
1090	1972	26 March	Santos	1	Palmeiras (São Paulo)	2	0	1101
1091	1972	30 March	Santos	2	São Bento (Sorocaba)	1	0	1101
1092	1972	16 April	Santos	1	São Paulo FC	3	0	1101
1093	1972	23 April	Santos	0	Guarani (Campinas)	1	0	1101
1094	1972	25 April	Santos	2	Ferroviária (Araraquara)	0	1	1102
1095	1972	29 April	Santos	1	Napoli (Italy)	0	0	1102
1096	1972	1 May	Santos	3	Cagliari (Italy)	2	2	1104
1097	1972	3 May	Santos	6	Fenerbache (Turkey)	1	1	1105
1098	1972	5 May	Santos	5	Taj Sports Organization	1	3	1108
1099	1972	14 May	Santos	1	Corinthians (São Paulo)	1	0	1108
1100	1972	17 May	Santos	1	XV de Novembro (Piracicaba)	0	0	1108
1101	1972	21 May	Santos	3	Ponte Preta (Campinas)	2	1	1109
1102	1972	26 May	Santos	3	Japan	0	2	1111
1103	1972	28 May	Santos	4	South China (Hong Kong)	2	0	1111
1104	1972	31 May	Santos	3	Syu Fong (Hong Kong)	1	0	1111
1105	1972	2 June	Santos	3	South Korea	2	1	1112
1106	1972	4 June	Santos	4	Newcastle United (England)	2	3	1115
1107	1972	7 June	Santos	4	Caroline Hill (Hong Kong)	0	3	1118
1108	1972	10 June	Santos	6	Thailand	1	2	1120
1109	1972	13 June	Santos	2	Coventry City (England)	2	1	1121
1110	1972	17 June	Santos	2	Australia	2	0	1121
1111	1972	21 June	Santos	3	Indonesia	2	1	1122
1112	1972	25 June	Santos	7	Catanzaro (Italy)	1	2	1124
1113	1972	30 June	Santos	6	Boston Astros (USA)	1	3	1127
1114	1972	2 July	Santos	2	Universidad (Mexico)	0	2	1129
1115	1972	5 July	Santos	4	Toronto Metros (Canada)	2	1	1130
1116	1972	7 July	Santos	5	Vancouver (Canada)	0	0	1130
1117	1972	9 July	Santos	5	Universidad (Mexico)	1	2	1132
1118	1972	11 July	Santos	4	América (Mexico)	2	2	1134
1119	1972	23 July	Santos	0	São Paulo FC	2	0	1134
1120	1972	30 July	Santos	1	América (Rio Preto)	0	0	1134

Appendix

Match	Year	Date	Pelé's team	Goals for	Opposition	Goals against	Goals by Pelé	Total goals
1121	1972	2 August	Santos	4	Guarani (Campinas)	2	3	1137
1122	1972	6 August	Santos	3	Ferroviária (Araraquara)	0	1	1138
1123	1972	9 August	Santos	2	Juventus (São Paulo)	1	2	1140
1124	1972	13 August	Santos	0	Palmeiras (São Paulo)	1	0	1140
1125	1972	15 August	Santos	2	Avai EC (Parana)	1	0	1140
1126	1972	20 August	Santos	3	Portuguesa de Desportos	1	1	1141
1127	1972	27 August	Santos	0	XV de Novembro (Piracicaba)	1	0	1141
1128	1972	30 August	Santos	0	Corinthians (São Paulo)	1	0	1141
1129	1972	5 September	Santos	1	Trinidad and Tobago	0	1	1142
1130	1972	9 September	Santos	1	Botafogo (Rio)	1	0	1142
1131	1972	13 September	Santos	1	Sergipe	0	1	1143
1132	1972	17 September	Santos	0	Vitoria (Bahia)	1	0	1143
1133	1972	24 September	Santos	1	Fluminense (Rio)	2	0	1143
1134	1972	25 October	Santos	1	Palmeiras (São Paulo)	0	1	1144
1135	1972	29 October	Santos	2	Bahia	0	0	1144
1136	1972	12 November	Santos	0	Portuguesa de Desportos	2	0	1144
1137	1972	16 November	Santos	1	Atlético (Minas Gerais)	0	0	1144
1138	1972	19 November	Santos	4	Santa Cruz (Recife)	2	1	1145
1139	1972	23 November	Santos	0	Flamengo (Rio)	0	0	1145
1140	1972	26 November	Santos	4	Corinthians (São Paulo)	0	0	1145
1141	1972	29 November	Santos	2	ABC (Natal)	0	1	1146
1142	1972	3 December	Santos	1	Ceará	2	1	1147
1143	1972	9 December	Santos	2	Santa Cruz (Recife)	0	0	1147
1144	1972	14 December	Santos	0	Grêmio (Porto Alegre)	1	0	1147
1145	1972	17 December	Santos	1	Botafogo (Rio)	2	0	1147
1146	**1973**	2 February	Santos	2	Victoria (Australia)	0	0	1147
1147	1973	9 February	Santos	3	Riyadh (Saudi Arabia)	0	2	1149
1148	1973	12 February	Santos	1	Kuwait	1	1	1150
1149	1973	14 February	Santos	3	National Club (Doha)	0	1	1151
1150	1973	16 February	Santos	7	Bahrain	1	2	1153
1151	1973	18 February	Santos	5	National Club (Egypt)	0	2	1155
1152	1973	20 February	Santos	1	Hilal (Sudan)	0	0	1155
1153	1973	22 February	Santos	4	All Nasser Club (Egypt)	1	1	1156
1154	1973	27 February	Santos	0	Bavaria (W. Germany)	3	0	1156
1155	1973	4 March	Santos	2	Girondins (France)	2	1	1157
1156	1973	6 March	Santos	1	Royal Standard (Belgium)	0	0	1157
1157	1973	12 March	Santos	1	Fulham (England)	2	1	1158
1158	1973	14 March	Santos	2	Plymouth (England)	3	1	1159
1159	1973	25 March	Santos	2	São Paulo FC	2	1	1160
1160	1973	4 April	Santos	6	Juventus (São Paulo)	0	2	1162
1161	1973	8 April	Santos	1	Portuguesa de Desportos	0	0	1162
1162	1973	18 April	Santos	1	América (Rio Preto)	0	0	1162
1163	1973	22 April	Santos	1	Guarani (Campinas)	0	0	1162

Match	Year	Date	Pelé's team	Goals for	Opposition	Goals against	Goals by Pelé	Total goals
1164	1973	29 April	Santos	3	Corinthians (São Paulo)	0	2	1164
1165	1973	6 May	Santos	1	Palmeiras (São Paulo)	1	1	1165
1166	1973	13 May	Santos	2	Botafogo (Ribeirão Preto)	1	0	1165
1167	1973	20 May	Santos	5	Ponte Preta (Campinas)	1	2	1167
1168	1973	25 May	Santos	3	Lazio (Italy)	0	1	1168
1169	1973	28 May	Santos	4	Lazio (Italy)	2	2	1170
1170	1973	30 May	Santos	6	Baltimore Bays (USA)	4	3	1173
1171	1973	1 June	Santos	1	Guadalajara (Mexico)	0	1	1174
1172	1973	3 June	Santos	2	Guadalajara (Mexico)	1	1	1175
1173	1973	6 June	Santos	6	Miami Toros (USA)	1	1	1176
1174	1973	10 June	Santos	5	Arminia Bielefeld (W. Germany)	0	1	1177
1175	1973	15 June	Santos	7	Baltimore Bays (USA)	1	1	1178
1176	1973	17 June	Santos	2	Rochester Lancers (USA)	1	1	1179
1177	1973	19 June	Santos	4	Baltimore Bays (USA)	0	2	1181
1178	1973	1 July	Santos	1	União Tijucana (Rio)	0	0	1181
1179	1973	4 July	Santos	1	Goias	2	0	1181
1180	1973	8 July	Santos	2	Botafogo (Ribeirão Preto)	0	1	1182
1181	1973	15 July	Santos	1	São Bento (Sorocaba)	0	0	1182
1182	1973	22 July	Santos	1	Corinthians (São Paulo)	1	1	1183
1183	1973	26 July	Santos	0	Juventus (São Paulo)	0	0	1183
1184	1973	29 July	Santos	0	São Paulo FC	0	0	1183
1185	1973	5 August	Santos	1	América (Rio Preto)	0	0	1183
1186	1973	8 August	Santos	0	Portuguesa de Desportos	1	0	1183
1187	1973	12 August	Santos	0	Palmeiras (São Paulo)	1	0	1183
1188	1973	15 August	Santos	1	Guarani (Campinas)	0	1	1184
1189	1973	26 August	Santos	0	Portuguesa de Desportos	0	0	1184
1190	1973	29 August	Santos	0	Vitoria (Bahia)	2	0	1184
1191	1973	2 September	Santos	0	Palmeiras (São Paulo)	0	0	1184
1192	1973	9 September	Santos	1	Flamengo (Rio)	0	0	1184
1193	1973	12 September	Santos	0	Comercial (Mato Grosso)	1	0	1184
1194	1973	16 September	Santos	2	Atlético (Parana)	0	0	1184
1195	1973	19 September	Santos	0	Atlético (Minas Gerais)	0	0	1184
1196	1973	23 September	Santos	0	Ceará	2	0	1184
1197	1973	26 September	Santos	6	América (Natal)	1	3	1187
1198	1973	30 September	Santos	3	Nautico (Recife)	0	0	1187
1199	1973	3 October	Santos	3	Sergipe	0	1	1188
1200	1973	7 October	Santos	2	Santa Cruz (Recife)	3	1	1189
1201	1973	14 October	Santos	1	Vasco da Gama (Rio)	1	0	1189
1202	1973	17 October	Santos	0	Goias	0	0	1189
1203	1973	4 November	Santos	3	Portuguesa de Desportos	2	2	1191
1204	1973	11 November	Santos	1	Atlético (Parana)	0	1	1192
1205	1973	14 November	Santos	1	Guarani (Campinas)	1	1	1193
1206	1973	18 November	Santos	2	Coritiba	1	1	1194

Match	Year	Date	Pelé's team	Goals for	Opposition	Goals against	Goals by Pelé	Total goals
1207	1973	28 November	Santos	2	Internacional (Porto Alegre)	0	1	1195
1208	1973	5 December	Santos	4	Huracan (Argentina)	0	1	1196
1209	1973	9 December	Santos	1	Palmeiras (São Paulo)	1	0	1196
1210	1973	12 December	Santos	4	Grêmio (Porto Alegre)	0	2	1198
1211	1973	17 December	Santos	1	São Paulo FC	0	1	1199
1212*	1973	19 December	Brazil XI	2	Foreigners XI	1	1	1200
1213	**1974**	9 January	Santos	4	Palestra (São Bernardo)	0	1	1201
1214	1974	13 January	Santos	1	Santa Cruz (Recife)	1	0	1201
1215	1974	20 January	Santos	3	Botafogo (Rio)	0	1	1202
1216	1974	23 January	Santos	5	Fortaleza (Ceará)	1	2	1204
1217	1974	27 January	Santos	0	Grêmio (Porto Alegre)	1	0	1204
1218	1974	29 January	Santos	1	São Paulo FC	2	1	1205
1219	1974	31 January	Santos	1	Vitoria (Bahia)	0	0	1205
1220	1974	3 February	Santos	2	Guarani (Campinas)	0	1	1206
1221	1974	6 February	Santos	4	Goias	4	0	1206
1222	1974	10 February	Santos	0	Cruzeiro (Minas Gerais)	0	0	1206
1223	1974	22 February	Santos	2	Vila Nova (Goias)	1	0	1206
1224	1974	3 March	Santos	2	Uberaba	0	0	1206
1225	1974	6 March	Santos	1	AA Caldense	0	0	1206
1226	1974	10 March	Santos	1	Portuguesa de Desportos	2	0	1206
1227	1974	17 March	Santos	2	América (Minas Gerais)	0	0	1206
1228	1974	20 March	Santos	3	CEUB (Brasilia)	1	1	1207
1229	1974	24 March	Santos	2	Guarani (Campinas)	2	2	1209
1230	1974	30 March	Santos	1	Nautico (Recife)	1	1	1210
1231	1974	3 April	Santos	2	Guarani / Juazeiro XI (Ceará)	0	0	1210
1232	1974	6 April	Santos	1	Recife	1	1	1211
1233	1974	13 April	Santos	1	Cruzeiro (Minas Gerais)	0	0	1211
1234	1974	20 April	Santos	4	Palmeiras (São Paulo)	0	1	1212
1235	1974	24 April	Santos	0	AA Francana	0	0	1212
1236	1974	28 April	Santos	1	Nautico (Manaus)	0	1	1213
1237	1974	2 May	Santos	3	Rio Negro (Manaus)	0	1	1214
1238	1974	19 May	Santos	1	Corinthians (São Paulo)	1	0	1214
1239	1974	2 June	Santos	1	São Paulo FC	1	0	1214
1240	1974	9 June	Santos	1	Atlético (Minas Gerais)	2	0	1214
1241	1974	18 July	Santos	1	Fortaleza (Ceará)	1	0	1214
1242	1974	21 July	Santos	1	Vasco da Gama (Rio)	2	1	1215
1243	1974	24 July	Santos	2	Internacional (Porto Alegre)	1	0	1215
1244	1974	28 July	Santos	1	Cruzeiro (Minas Gerais)	3	0	1215
1245	1974	3 August	Santos	2	Noroeste (Bauru)	1	0	1215
1246	1974	11 August	Santos	0	Portuguesa de Desportos	1	0	1215

*Garrincha's farewell game.

Match	Year	Date	Pelé's team	Goals for	Opposition	Goals against	Goals by Pelé	Total goals
1247	1974	14 August	Santos	2	Botafogo (Ribeirão Preto)	1	0	1215
1248	1974	24 August	Santos	1	Saad	3	0	1215
1249	1974	31 August	Santos	0	Deportivo Español (Spain)	2	0	1215
1250	1974	1 September	Santos	1	Barcelona (Spain)	4	1	1216
1251	1974	3 September	Santos	3	Real Zaragoza (Spain)	2	2	1218
1252	1974	9 September	Santos	0	Palmeiras (São Paulo)	0	0	1218
1253	1974	15 September	Santos	1	São Paulo FC	1	0	1218
1254	1974	18 September	Santos	1	Comercial (Ribeirão Preto)	0	0	1218
1255	1974	22 September	Santos	2	Guarani (Campinas)	2	1	1219
1256	1974	29 September	Santos	0	Corinthians (São Paulo)	1	0	1219
1257*	1974	2 October	Santos	2	Ponte Preta (Campinas)	0	0	1219
1258	**1975**	26 March	All-Stars	3	Anderlecht (Belgium)	8	0	1219
1259	1975	15 June	Cosmos	2	Dallas Tornados	2	1	1220
1260	1975	18 June	Cosmos	2	Toronto Metros (Canada)	0	0	1220
1261	1975	27 June	Cosmos	3	Rochester Lancers	0	1	1221
1262	1975	29 June	Cosmos	9	Washington Diplomats	2	2	1223
1263	1975	3 July	Cosmos	1	Los Angeles Aztecs	5	0	1223
1264	1975	5 July	Cosmos	0	Seattle Sounders	2	0	1223
1265	1975	7 July	Cosmos	2	Vancouver Whitecaps (Canada)	1	0	1223
1266	1975	9 July	Cosmos	3	Boston Minutemen	1	0	1223
1267	1975	16 July	Cosmos	1	Portland Timbers	2	1	1224
1268	1975	19 July	Cosmos	0	Toronto Metros (Canada)	3	0	1224
1269	1975	23 July	Cosmos	2	San José Earthquakes	1	1	1225
1270	1975	27 July	Cosmos	2	Dallas Tornados	3	0	1225
1271	1975	10 August	Cosmos	1	St Louis Stars	2	0	1225
1272	1975	27 August	Cosmos	2	San José Earthquakes	3	1	1226
1273	1975	31 August	Cosmos	1	Malmö (Sweden)	5	1	1227
1274	1975	2 September	Cosmos	3	Alliansen (Sweden)	1	2	1229
1275	1975	4 September	Cosmos	2	Stockholm All-Stars (Sweden)	3	2	1231
1276	1975	11 September	Cosmos	4	Valarengen (Norway)	2	2	1233
1277	1975	13 September	Cosmos	1	Roma (Italy)	3	0	1233
1278	1975	18 September	Cosmos	2	Victory (Haiti)	1	0	1233
1279	1975	19 September	Cosmos	1	Violette (Haiti)	2	0	1233
1280	1975	21 September	Cosmos	0	Santos (Jamaica)	1	0	1233
1281	1975	26 September	Cosmos	12	Puerto Rico	1	1	1234
1282	**1976**	24 March	Cosmos	1	San Diego Jaws	1	0	1234
1283	1976	28 March	Cosmos	1	Dallas Tornados	0	1	1235
1284	1976	31 March	Cosmos	0	San Antonio Thunder	1	0	1235
1285	1976	5 April	Cosmos	0	Los Angeles Aztecs	0	0	1235
1286	1976	8 April	Cosmos	5	Honda (Japan)	0	4	1239

*Final game for Santos.

Appendix

Match	Year	Date	Pelé's team	Goals for	Opposition	Goals against	Goals by Pelé	Total goals
1287	1976	10 April	Cosmos	3	Seattle Sounders	1	2	1241
1288	1976	11 April	Cosmos	1	Los Angeles Aztecs	0	1	1242
1289	1976	18 April	Cosmos	1	Miami Toros	0	0	1242
1290	1976	2 May	Cosmos	1	Chicago Sting	2	1	1243
1291	1976	5 May	Cosmos	3	Hartford Bicentennials	1	1	1244
1292	1976	8 May	Cosmos	1	Philadelphia Atoms	2	1	1245
1293	1976	15 May	Cosmos	3	Hartford Bicentennials	0	0	1245
1294	1976	17 May	Cosmos	6	Los Angeles Aztecs	0	2	1247
1295	1976	19 May	Cosmos	2	Boston Minutemen	1	0	1247
1296	1976	23 May	USA All-Stars	0	Italy	4	0	1247
1297	1976	31 May	USA All-Stars	1	England	3	0	1247
1298	1976	3 June	Cosmos	2	Violette (Haiti)	1	1	1248
1299	1976	6 June	Cosmos	1	Tampa Bay Rowdies	5	0	1248
1300	1976	9 June	Cosmos	2	Minnesota Kicks	1	0	1248
1301	1976	12 June	Cosmos	3	Portland Timbers	0	0	1248
1302	1976	16 June	Cosmos	2	Boston Minutemen	3	1	1249
1303	1976	18 June	Cosmos	3	Toronto Metros (Canada)	0	0	1249
1304	1976	23 June	Cosmos	1	Chicago Sting	4	0	1249
1305	1976	27 June	Cosmos	2	Washington Diplomats	3	1	1250
1306	1976	30 June	Cosmos	2	Rochester Lancers	0	0	1250
1307	1976	2 July	Cosmos	3	St Louis Stars	4	0	1250
1308	1976	10 July	Cosmos	2	Philadelphia Atoms	1	1	1251
1309	1976	14 July	Cosmos	5	Tampa Bay Rowdies	4	2	1253
1310	1976	18 July	Cosmos	5	Washington Diplomats	0	1	1254
1311	1976	28 July	Cosmos	4	Dallas Tornados	0	0	1254
1312	1976	7 August	Cosmos	1	San José Earthquakes	2	0	1254
1313	1976	10 August	Cosmos	8	Miami Toros	2	2	1256
1314	1976	17 August	Cosmos	2	Washington Diplomats	0	1	1257
1315	1976	20 August	Cosmos	1	Tampa Bay Rowdies	3	1	1258
1316	1976	1 September	Cosmos	2	Dallas Tornados	2	0	1258
1317	1976	5 September	Cosmos	2	Dallas Tornados	1	0	1258
1318	1976	6 September	Cosmos	3	Dallas Tornados	2	1	1259
1319	1976	8 September	Cosmos	1	Canada	1	0	1259
1320	1976	10 September	Cosmos	1	Canada	3	0	1259
1321	1976	14 September	Cosmos	1	Paris St Germain (France)	3	0	1259
1322	1976	16 September	Cosmos	1	Royal Antwerp (Belgium)	3	1	1260
1323	1976	23 September	Cosmos	0	West Japan All-Stars (Japan)	0	0	1260
1324	1976	25 September	Cosmos	2	Japan	2	0	1260
1325	1976	6 October	Brazil XI	0	Flamengo (Rio)	2	0	1260
1326	**1977**	2 April	Cosmos	9	Victory (Haiti)	0	2	1262
1327	1977	3 April	Cosmos	2	Tampa Bay Rowdies	1	0	1262
1328	1977	9 April	Cosmos	0	Las Vegas Quicksilvers	1	0	1262
1329	1977	13 April	Cosmos	2	Team Hawaii	1	0	1262

Match	Year	Date	Pelé's team	Goals for	Opposition	Goals against	Goals by Pelé	Total goals
1330	1977	17 April	Cosmos	2	Rochester Lancers	0	1	1263
1331	1977	24 April	Cosmos	1	Dallas Tornados	2	0	1263
1332	1977	1 May	Cosmos	2	St Louis Stars	3	0	1263
1333	1977	8 May	Cosmos	3	Connecticut Bicentennial	2	0	1263
1334	1977	11 May	Cosmos	2	Chicago Sting	1	0	1263
1335	1977	15 May	Cosmos	3	Fort Lauderdale Strickers	0	3	1266
1336	1977	22 May	Cosmos	1	Chicago Sting	2	0	1266
1337	1977	29 May	Cosmos	2	Tampa Bay Rowdies	4	0	1266
1338	1977	1 June	Cosmos	2	Lazio (Italy)	3	0	1266
1339	1977	5 June	Cosmos	6	Toronto Metros (Canada)	0	0	1266
1340	1977	8 June	Cosmos	3	Fort Lauderdale Strickers	0	1	1267
1341	1977	12 June	Cosmos	2	Minnesota Kicks	1	0	1267
1342	1977	16 June	Cosmos	2	Toronto Metros	1	0	1267
1343	1977	19 June	Cosmos	3	Tampa Bay Rowdies	0	3	1270
1344	1977	23 June	Cosmos	0	St Louis Stars	2	0	1270
1345	1977	26 June	Cosmos	5	Los Angeles Aztecs	2	3	1273
1346	1977	30 June	Cosmos	3	Vancouver Whitecaps (Canada)	5	0	1273
1347	1977	2 July	Cosmos	1	Los Angeles Aztecs	4	0	1273
1348	1977	10 July	Cosmos	0	Seattle Sounders	1	0	1273
1349	1977	15 July	Cosmos	0	Rochester Lancers	1	0	1273
1350	1977	17 July	Cosmos	2	Portland Timbers	0	0	1273
1351	1977	27 July	Cosmos	8	Washington Diplomats	2	0	1273
1352	1977	31 July	Cosmos	3	Connecticut Bicentennials	1	1	1274
1353	1977	6 August	Cosmos	1	Washington Diplomats	2	1	1275
1354	1977	8 August	Cosmos	3	Tampa Bay Rowdies	0	2	1277
1355	1977	14 August	Cosmos	8	Fort Lauderdale Strickers	3	0	1277
1356	1977	17 August	Cosmos	3	Fort Lauderdale Strickers	2	1	1278
1357	1977	21 August	Cosmos	2	Rochester Lancers	1	0	1278
1358	1977	24 August	Cosmos	4	Rochester Lancers	1	1	1279
1359	1977	28 August	Cosmos	2	Seattle Sounders	1	0	1279
1360	1977	1 September	Cosmos	5	Caribe	2	1	1280
1361	1977	4 September	Cosmos	1	Portuguesa (Venezuela)	1	0	1280
1362	1977	10 September	Cosmos	4	Furukawa (Japan)	2	1	1281
1363	1977	14 September	Cosmos	3	Japan	1	0	1281
1364	1977	17 September	Cosmos	1	China	1	0	1281
1365	1977	20 September	Cosmos	1	China	2	1	1282
1366	1977	24 September	Cosmos	2	Mohum Bagan (India)	2	0	1282
1367*	1977	1 October	Cosmos	2	Santos	1	1	1283

*Final game for Cosmos; his last as a professional footballer.

PICTURE CREDITS

Section 1

1: Nelson Coelho/Editora Abril; 2, 4, 5, 10, 11, 12, 14, 15, 18, 29: Popperfoto; 3: Reprodução Alexandre Battibugli/Editora Abril; 6: AFP/Getty Images; 7: Keystone/Getty Images; 8, 9, 16, 24, 28: Empics; 13: Hulton Deutsch Collection/Corbis; 17: José Pinto/Editora Abril; 19, 20: Arquivo O Dia; 21, 25: Allsport/Getty Images; 22: Lamyr Martins/Editora Abril; 23: Colorsport; 26: Sebastião Marinho/Editora Abril; 27: Fernando Pimentel/Editora Abril

Section 2

30, 33: Manoel Motta/Editora Abril; 31, 39: Carlos Namba/Editora Abril; 32: Keystone/Getty Images; 34, 41: Bettmann/Corbis; 35, 36, 37, 38, 48: Empics; 40: Media Press International/ Rex Features; 42: Everett Collection/Rex Features; 43, 46: Antonio Milena/Editora Abril; 44: Sipa Press/Rex Features; 45: Roberto Jayme/Editora Abril; 47: Ira Wyman/Corbis Sygma; 49: Carlos Moraes/O Dia; 50: Reuters/Corbis; 51: Tim de Waele/Corbis; 52: Sergio Moraes/ Reuters/Corbis; 53: Juda Ngwenya/Reuters/Corbis

Hardback endpaper: Empics
Hardback endpaper verso: Popperfoto

INDEX

A

A Marcha, 245
AC Milan, 137, 214
Ademir, 46
Agnelli, Umberto, 121
AIK (Sweden), 77
Albert, Florian, 151
Albertosi, Enrico, 186
Alex, 294
Ali, Muhammad, 233
Allen, Woody, 225
Almeida, José de, 86
Almeida, Paulo, 294
Alonso, Luis *see* Lula
Altafini, José, 146
Amaral, Paulo, 87–8, 89, 124, 146
Amarildo, 127, 129, 145, 146
Ambrosina, Dona *see* Nascimento, Ambrosina
América (Mexico), 214
Américo, Mario, 83, 87, 91, 98, 123, 125, 178
Amériquinha (formerly Sete de Setembro), 49–50
Andrada, Edgardo, 170
Antoninho, 52, 200–1, 203
Antonio, Sr, 72
Ardiles, Osvaldo, 246
Argentina, 80, 210; playing style, 136; v. England in World Cup (1966), 194
Ari, 39
Ashe, Arthur, 229
Aston, Ken, 194
Atlético Mineiro, 15
Atlético of Três Corações, 14, 15
Augusto, 15
Austria: v. Brazil in World Cup (1958), 89
Avalone Jr, Nicola, 106
Ayers de Abreu, Olten, 117

B

Baggio, Roberto, 253, 298
Bahia, 169–70
Baltazar, 15–16, 38
Baltimore Bays, 203
Bangú, 56

Banks, Gordon, 180, 299; save from Pelé in 1970 World Cup, 181
Baquinho, 50, 51–5
Barbosa, Benedito Ruy, 247
Barbosa (goalkeeper), 46
Baresi, Franco, 298
Baroninho, 17
Barreto, Luiz Carlos, 245
Barros, Captain Antônia Dias de, 12
Batistuta, Gabriel, 298
Bauru, 12–13, 16, 17–18
Bauru Athletic Club (BAC), 18, 20, 41, 50
Beatles, 148–9
Beckenbauer, Franz, 231, 233, 234, 295, 297
Beckham, David, 299
Bellini, Luiz, 5, 87, 149, 151, 210, 232
Benedict XVI, Pope, 301
Benfica, 131, 157
Bertini, Mario, 186
Best, George, 207, 241
bicycle kick, 51
Bilé (José Lino), 44, 290
Boca Juniors, 136–7
Boninsegna, Roberto, 187
Bosman, Jean-Marc, 256
Bosman ruling, 202, 256, 258, 260
Botafogo, 109, 120, 168, 174
Bradley, Gordon, 221–2, 223, 227, 228, 231
Brazil (country), 160, 193, 281, 293
Brazil (football team), 6, 300; style of play, 136, 300; v. England (1959), 117; and World Cup *see* World Cup
Brazilian Coffee Institute, 289
Brazilian Football Confederation (CBF), 252
Brazilian Sports Confederation (CBD), 173
Breil, Giora, 206
Bremner, Billy, 210
Brito (player), 236, 179
Brito, Waldemar de, 197, 232; football career, 50–1; lessons taught to Pelé, 63; managing of Baquinho, 50, 52, 53–4, 55; and Pelé's Santos contract, 57–8, 61, 72, 73, 78
Bulgaria: v. Brazil in World Cup (1966), 149–50
Burgnich, Tarcisio, 155, 298

C

Café Pelé, 289
Caine, Michael, 245–6
Cameroon, 249
Carbajal, Antonio, 124
Carbone, 38
Cardoso, Fernando Henrique, 255, 259
Carlos Alberto Parreira, 177, 208–9, 253
Carlos Alberto Torres, 147, 162, 168, 176, 178, 179, 186, 191, 197–8, 231, 232, 266
Carter, President Jimmy, 217, 301
Carvalhaes, Dr João, 90
Carvalho, Dr Paulo Machado de, 82, 83–4, 90, 96, 123, 129, 146
Castilho, 87
Cavalcanti, Flávia, 242–3
Celeste, Dona *see* Nascimento, Celeste
Célio, 114
Charles, John, 93
Charlton, Bobby, 127, 133, 180, 295, 299
Chateaubriand, Senator Assis, 103–5
Chile: v. Brazil in World Cup (1962), 128
Chinaglia, Giorgio, 227, 231
Cholbi, Guilherme, 111, 141
Cholbi, Rosemeri *see* Nascimento, Rosemeri Cholbi
Cida, Dona, 21
Cidão, 39
Claudio, 38, 75

Clemente, Ari, 83
Clinton, President Bill, 301–2
Clodoaldo, 5, 179, 183, 185, 187, 209, 294
Collor, Fernando, 255
Colombia, 248
Coluna, Mario, 298
Cooper, Terry, 181
Copa Roca, 80
Corinthians, 68, 75–6, 83, 108, 109, 167
Cosmos, 204–5; (1976) season, 227–8; (1977) season, 230–2; European tour (1975), 223; Furphy's strategy at, 227–8; and Pelé *see* Pelé; players, 222, 223, 227, 231; record, 221–3
Coury, Dr Athiê Jorge, 121
Coutinho, Claudio, 109, 123, 131, 137, 177, 194, 203
criancinhas, 172
Cristensen, Carlos Hugo, 245
Cruyff, Johan, 210, 211, 299
Cruzeiro, 103–4
Cubatão, 211
Cubilla, Luís Alberto, 183, 184
Czechoslovakia: v. Brazil in World Cup (1962), 124–6, 128–9; v. Brazil in World Cup (1970), 179–80; v. Santos (1965), 140

D

De Sordi, 87, 96
Del Vecchio (Deo), 70, 73, 75, 77, 108
Delgado, Ramos, 294, 298
Deluca, Arthur, 275
Deluca, Kelly Cristina (née Nascimento), 159, 214, 275
Di Stefano, Alfredo, 298
Diário de Bauru, 54–5
Dias, Djalma, 147
Didi, 87, 89, 92, 94, 95, 122, 129, 145, 171, 182, 300
Diego, 294
Dimitrijevic, Vitomir, 231
Dino, 39, 146
Dom Pedro II, Emperor, 12
Domenghini, Angelo, 186
Dondinho (João Ramos do Nascimento), 13, 51, 104, 199, 227, 232, 286; death, 270; football career, 14, 15–16, 18, 33, 41–2; knee injury, 15, 18; and Pelé's football career, 57, 78; relationship with Pelé, 22, 33, 40, 64; smoking lesson given to Pelé, 64; teaching football skills to Pelé, 40–1; and World Cup (1950), 47–8
Dorval, 109
Dunga, Carlos, 254

E

East Germany, 210
Edinho *see* Nascimento, Edson Cholbi do
Edir, 52
Edison, Thomas, 14, 43
Edmundo, 260
Elizabeth II, Queen, 165–6, 259
Endler, Roland, 142
England, 203; playing style, 138; v. Argentina in World Cup (1966), 194; v. Brazil (1959), 117; v. Brazil in World Cup (1958), 89; v. Brazil in World Cup (1962), 127; v. Brazil in World Cup (1970), 180–1, 299; wins World Cup (1966), 152; and World Cup (1950), 220
Ernesto Monte primary school (Bauru), 21, 26–7
Ertegun, Ahmet and Nesuhi, 229
Escape to Victory (1981), 245–7
Esparrago, Victor, 183
Espinhel, Clayton, 290
Estevão, Jair, 169
Estranhos, Os, 163

Etherington, Gary, 231
Etzel Filho, João, 120
Eusébio, 131, 152, 298
Everaldo, 179

F

Fachetti, Giacinto, 186, 187, 298
Farkas, Janos, 151
Feijó, 77
Félix, 179, 184
Feola, Vicente, 82, 90–1, 96, 122, 146
Fernandes, João, 50
Field, Tony, 227
Fields, Freddie, 247
FIFA, 204, 206, 237–8, 238, 239, 296
Figo, Luis, 298
Filho, Romualdo Arppi, 71
Filomena, Dona, 54
Finney, Tom, 220
Fiolax, 158, 213
Firmani, Eddie, 230–1
Flamengo, 109
Flamenguinho, 55
Fluminense, 109, 119, 138
Fontaine, Just, 94, 101, 298
Fontana, 136
Fontes, Dagoberto, 184
Ford Lauderdale Strikers, 231
Formiga, 70
Frade, Henrique, 117
France: v. Brazil in World Cup (1958), 93–4
Friaça, Albino, 47
Furphy, Ken, 227–8
futebol de salão, 56

G

Garrincha, 5, 91–2, 109, 117, 145, 300; concern for Pelé's injury during World Cup (1962), 126; death, 207; and Elza Soares, 126–7, 130; injury from motor accident, 150; partnership with Pelé, 95; personal problems, 206–7; talent of, 128; testimonial at Maracanã (1973), 206; and World Cup (1958), 90, 94–5, 97, 98; and World Cup (1962), 122, 127, 128, 129; and World Cup (1966), 149, 150, 151
Geisel, Ernesto, 208
Gemima (Assíria's daughter) *see* Lemos, Gemima
Georgina, Dona, 28, 78, 135
Gerson, 147, 148, 175, 176, 179, 181, 186, 187, 300
Gil, Gilberto, 245
Gilmar, 5, 87, 88, 109, 122, 129, 145, 149, 151
Giresse, Alain, 298
Glória, Otto, 151
Gonzáles, José *see* Pepe Gordo
Gosling, Dr Hilton, 83, 84, 85–6, 87, 89, 90, 96, 123, 124, 126, 127, 148, 150
Graça Meneghel, Maria da *see* Xuxa
Greaves, Jimmy, 127, 299
Grellet, Celso, 252, 301
Guarani, 120
Guedes, Osmar, 52
Gullit, Ruud, 299
Gustav, King, 98

H

Hak, Abdul Samir, 254–5
Havelange, Dr João, 173, 175, 204, 208, 219, 238, 253; campaign for FIFA presidency, 204, 213, 238, 253; relationship with Pelé, 248, 253, 257
Helio, 70
Henry, Thierry, 298
Hepacaré, 15
Hermany, Bruno, 146

Holland, 210–11, 299; and World Cup (1994), 253
Howe, Don, 89
Hungary: playing style, 138; v. Brazil in World Cup (1954), 54; v. Brazil in World Cup (1966), 150–1
Hurst, Geoff, 152
Huston, John, 245, 246

I

Iarusci, Bob, 231
Idalina, Dona, 88, 111, 141
Ilena, 112, 223
Intercontinental Club Cup, 131, 137
International Youth Football Programme (Pepsi), 205–6, 209, 224, 228–9
Internazionale (Milan), 121, 157, 158, 167
Isto é Pelé, 245
Italy: defeat by Brazil in World Cup final (1994), 253–4; defeat by Brazil in World Cup final (1970), 185–8; playing style, 138

J

Jabaquara, 71
Jackson, Michael, 225
Jagger, Mick, 225
Jaír da Costa, 145, 146
Jáir da Rosa Pinto, 69, 70, 201
Jairzinho, 5, 147, 148, 179, 180, 181, 182, 185, 187, 209, 210, 300
Jatene, Adib, 259
John Paul II, Pope, 301
Josimar, 248
Julinho, 117
Junior, 247
Juventus (São Paulo), 120
Juventus (Turin), 121, 214

K

Kaká, 300
Kansas City Spurs, 220
Kelsey, Jack, 93
Kent, Duke of, 259
Kiki, 116
Kissinger, Henry, 203–4, 219, 235, 248
Kodja Neto, Miguel, 254
Kopa, Raymond, 298
Kurtz, Flávia Christina, 241
Kurtz, Lenita, 241

L

Laércio, 165
Lala, Jan, 126, 299
Lara, 114
Laurinda, Dona, 26, 27, 28
Lazaroni, Sebastião, 249
Leão, 175
Leleco, 52
Lemos, Assíria Seixas *see* Nascimento, Assíria
Lemos, Gemima 243, 249–50, 276
Lennon, John, 149
Libertadores Cup, 130, 136–7
Liedholm, Nils, 96–7
Lima, 158, 164, 303
Lineker, Gary, 238
Lino, José, 44
Litoral, 294, 295
'Little Prince' Pelé Institute, 293–4
Lorico, 114
Lourdes, Dona, 26
Luizinho, 82–3
Lula (Luis Alonso), 68–9, 70, 77–8, 203
Lula da Silva, Luis Inácio, 304
Lusitana (later Bauru Athletic Club), 18

M

McCabe, George, 152
McDonald, Colin, 89
Macedo, 276
Machado, Anísia, 240
Machado, Sandra Regina, 240
Mandela, Nelson, 302
Mandioca, Landão, 52
Manga, 151–2
Mangueira Samba School (Rio de Janeiro), 301–2
Maninho, 52
Mannion, Wilf, 220
Maracanã stadium, 46, 79, 80, 117, 119, 131, 170, 199, 206, 250
Maradona, Diego, 248, 298
Maravilha, Dada, 193
Maria (aunt), 19, 277
Maria, Manoel, 294
Marques, Armando, 207
Marsh, Rodney, 228
Masopust, Josef, 125, 299
MasterCard, 252, 253, 287
Matthews, Stanley, 298
Mauro, 38, 88, 109, 123, 129, 145, 200–1, 203, 232
Mazurkiewicz, Ladislao, 184
Mazzei, Maria Helena, 221
Mazzei, Professor Julio, 201, 203, 214, 215, 228; at Cosmos, 221, 227; and International Youth Football Programme, 205; relationship with Pelé, 139, 140; as Santos's technical instructor, 139; support of Pelé's studies, 196, 197, 198, 230
Mazzola, 87, 89–90
Médici, Emilio, 193, 202
Mendes, Sérgio, 245
Mexico, 248; v. Brazil in World Cup (1962), 124
Mifflin, Ramón, 223
Milla, Roger, 249
Mohammed, General, 229
Moore, Bobby, 127, 165, 180, 181, 232, 246, 299
Morais, João, 152
Morais, Nelsi, 223
Moreira, Aymoré, 122, 174
Müller, Gerd, 297

N

Naldinho, 269, 274
Nascimento, Ambrosina (grandmother), 13, 18, 62, 160, 277
Nascimento, Assíria (second wife), 243–4, 249–51, 271, 291
Nascimento, Carlos, 146, 148–9
Nascimento, Celeste (daughter), 251, 276
Nascimento, Celeste (mother), 13–14, 19, 24, 35, 40, 57, 72–3, 104, 107, 232, 270, 282
Nascimento, Edson Cholbi do (Edinho; son), 195, 224, 265–9; arrested over drugs allegation and imprisonment, 269–73; as goalkeeper for Santos, 265–6; knee injury and retirement, 266–7; prison sentence following illegal car race accident, 268; release from prison, 273–4
Nascimento, Edson Arantes do *see* Pelé
Nascimento, Jair (Zoca; brother), 14–15, 18, 25, 29, 34, 39, 40, 106, 117–18, 158, 266
Nascimento, Jennifer (daughter), 239, 275
Nascimento, João Ramos do (Dondinho; father) *see* Dondinho
Nascimento, Jorge (uncle), 13, 19, 40, 42, 62, 106
Nascimento, Joshua (son), 251, 276, 277

Nascimento, Kelly Cristina (daughter) *see* Deluca, Kelly Cristina
Nascimento, Maria Lúcia (sister), 15, 18, 106, 240
Nascimento, Rosemeri Cholbi (first wife), 110–12, 117, 121, 140–1, 143–4, 194–5, 215, 220–1, 239–41, 244
NASL, 220, 221, 228, 231, 233
Neuzinha, 65, 112
Neves, Tancredo, 255
New York, 225 *see also* Cosmos
Nigeria, 166–7, 229
Noroeste, 55–6, 117
Nunes de Souza, Deise, 242

O

O Rei Pelé, 245
Oberdã, 165
'Olympic Villages', 257–8
Olympico, 120
Orlando, 87, 145–6, 151
Osman, Colonel, 113, 115
Owen, Michael, 299

P

Pacheco, Nestor, 158
Paçoca, 52
Pagão, 109
Palmeiras, 108, 139, 167
paradinha, 171
Paris Match, 103
Parling, Sigge, 98
Passo, Antonio do, 178
Paul VI, Pope, 142, 301
Paulista, 108, 109, 207
Paulo Cesar, 209
Paulo, Dr *see* Carvalho, Dr Paulo Machado de
Pelé: The Master and His Method, 205–6
Pelé (Edson Arantes do Nascimento)
Business interests, 122, 158; advertising work, 163, 229; and Café Pelé, 289; endorsement of products, 122, 163, 287–9; finances, 122, 143–4, 158, 163; financial problems with Fiolax, 213; launching of Pelé brand, 289–90; mishandling of business affairs by Pepe Gordo, 143–5; and Pelé Physiotherapy, 158; and Pelé Sports & Marketing, 252, 292
Early years: behaviour at school and punishments meted out, 26–7, 28–9; birth and early childhood in Três Corações, 11–12, 13–15; and Brazil's loss in 1950 World Cup final, 46–8; childhood and upbringing in Bauru, 18–19, 23–5, 244; creation of Sete de Setembro club and playing for, 35–40; dead pilot incident, 22–3; education, 21–2, 24, 26–7, 51; girls and first sexual experience, 64–6; hide-out tragedy, 25–6; moves to Bauru, 16–18; name at birth, 14; nightmares and sleepwalking, 26, 28; origin of name Pelé, 43–5; part-time jobs, 54; passion for aeroplanes, 22; playing football on the street and developing skills, 33–5, 45; shoe-shining work, 19–20; and smoking, 64; swimming accident, 24; teaching of footballing skills by father, 40–1; wins local tournament playing for Sete de Setembro, 49–50

Pelé (Edson Arantes do Nascimento) – *cont.*
Football career: ability to anticipate what is going to happen, 53; approaches from European clubs, 121, 213–14; 'beautiful game' phrase, 225; and bicycle kicks, 51, 189; called up for national team, 80; called up for 1958 World Cup, 82–3; criticism of by Brazilian media, 202; decision not to play in 1974 World Cup, 207, 208, 209, 214; enjoyment at playing abroad, 138; fame and celebrity, 120–1, 122, 161; favourite goals, 97, 119; first World Cup goal, 93; and footballers' rights, 202–3; goal and match tally, 75, 199, 233; and goalkeeping, 169, 266; goalscoring career, 309–41; groin strain during World Cup (1962), 123–4, 125–6, 127, 128; injuries, 83–4, 86, 118–19, 123, 157, 222, 284; match schedule, 115, 167; partnership with Garrincha, 95; penalty-taking, 171; and Pepsi's International Youth Football Programme, 205–6, 209, 224, 228–9; players admired, 81, 297–9; playing for army, 113–14; playing position preferred, 41; plays indoor football for Radium, 56; popularity in New York, 224; pressure to resume international career after retirement, 207, 208; reaches 1,250th goal, 229–30; refusal of captain role, 149–50; retirement from national squad and farewell matches, 199–200; retirement from playing career and reasons for, 231–2, 233; sendings off, 164, 184; and shoulder feint, 41; signs and plays for Baquinho, 51–5; style of play, 41; support of Havelange in campaign for FIFA presidency, 204, 213, 238, 253; targeted by defenders when playing, 135–6, 137, 138–9; 1,000th goal target and reaching of, 167–71; tribute games played in, 233–4; and World Cup *see* World Cup (1958–1970)
at SANTOS, 61–82, 107–9, 303; shift in attitude towards after changes at, 200–1, 203; contract, 72–3, 78, 115, 144; decision to leave and farewell game, 211–12; European tours, 115–16, 119, 138–9; first goal scored, 75–6; first-team debut, 73–4, 75–6; first-team official debut, 77; goals scored for, 80, 108, 119, 120, 130, 131, 137, 140, 203, 207–8; leaves Bauru and arrival at, 61–3, 68–9; and Maracanã stadium, 79; matches played abroad (1963), 135; negotiation of new contract, 201–2, 203; playing in junior teams, 70, 71, 73; plays for Santos/Vasco all-stars, 79–80; relationship with Professor Mazzei, 140; social life at, 74–5; sub-Saharan Africa tour, 159–62; training sessions and building up of body, 69–70, 71, 73, 80; wages, 78; *see also* Santos
at COSMOS: announcement of signing, 221; contract negotiations, 219–20; decision to play for, 214–15; farewell game, 231–2; goals scored for and number of matches, 228, 231; league debut, 222; number of matches played for, 231;

publicity engagements, 224–5; signs one-year extension to contract, 230; training sessions, 226; *see also* Cosmos
Personal life: advice given to young people, 267; affair with Lenita Kurtz and birth of daughter, 241; anti-drugs message, 271–2; and arrest of son for drug trafficking, 269–73; awarded honorary knighthood by Queen, 259; beauty queen dates, 242–3; birth of children and fatherhood, 159, 195, 239, 251, 277; birth of daughter by Anísa Machado, 240; burial place, 277; character, 108, 130, 290–2, 293; charity work, 289, 293; 'Citizen of the World' honour, 237; competitiveness, 290–1; courtship with and marriage to Rosemeri, 110–12, 121, 140–2; divorce from Rosemeri, 239–40, 241; education message, 172–3; emotional, 293; experience of racism, 142; eyesight and vision, 53, 175; and family, 275–6; fiftieth birthday, 234; food tastes, 226–7; genealogy, 160; and grandchildren, 275; hairstyle, 286; health, 226, 230; homes, 275; interview with *Playboy*, 242, 252; living in New York, 225–6, 275; love of arts and music, 244–5; love of fishing, 75, 88; marriage to Assíria, 243–4, 249, 250–1; meeting fans, 302–3; meets Queen Elizabeth, 165–6; military service, 112–15; nicknames, 42–3, 83; parental background, 14; Pelé persona, 285–7; perfectionism, 8, 254, 291–2; and press, 63, 283–4; ranch in São Paulo, 276–7; relationship with father, 22, 33, 40, 64; relationship with Xuxa, 241–2; and religion, 12, 48, 74, 123, 178–9, 250, 273; return to Bauru after 1958 World Cup victory, 105–6; and Ronaldo, 284; signature, 289–90; songwriting, 245; stubbornness, 291; studies for Physical Education degree, 195–9; talking in sleep, 28; and tennis, 295; treatment of by Brazilians, 282
Post-football career: accuses CBF of corruption, 252–3; ambassadorial role for FIFA, 238; becomes a 'Goodwill Ambassador' for UNICEF, 238; commentator for World Cup, 239, 260; film-making involvement and acting, 245–7; as International Relations Adviser at Santos, 254–5; joins FIFA's Fair Play board, 238; as MasterCard's ambassador at World Cup (1994), 253; as Minister for Sport, 202, 283, 293, 255–60; not interested in coaching, 254; promotional work for Warner, 241; setting up kids' football team (Litoral), 294, 295; suggestions for improving the game, 296–7; training of youngsters at Santos, 294
Pelé Club, 289
Pelé Foundation, 289
'Pelé Law', 259–60
Pelé museum, 282
Pelé Physiotherapy, 158
Pelé Sports & Marketing, 252, 292
Peñarol (Uruguay), 130
Pepe, 5, 28, 69, 70, 87, 105, 109, 131, 165, 201, 203

Pepe Gordo, 122, 143–4
Pepsi International Youth Football Programme *see* International Youth Football Programme
Pernambucano, Juninho, 300
Peru: v. Brazil in World Cup (1970), 182
Petronilho, 51
Pfizer, 288
Philadelphia Atoms, 221
Philip, Prince, 166
Piantoni, Roger, 94, 298
Piazza, 178, 179
Pinheiro, 54
Pitico, 269
Platini, Michel, 295, 298
Playboy, 242, 252
Pluskal, Suatopluk, 299
Ponte Preta, 211, 212
Popluhar, Jan, 125
Portugal: v. Brazil in World Cup (1966), 151–2
Portuguesa, 207
Professional Athletes' Union, 258
Puskas, Ferenc, 54, 297

R

Radium, 56
Raimundo, Senhor, 28, 78
Ramos de Oliveira, Mauro, 77
Ramsey, Sir Alf, 180, 220
Ramundini, Marby, 163
Rattin, Antonio, 194
Reagan, President Ronald, 301
Real Madrid, 116, 214
Redford, Robert, 226
referees, 238
Regina, Elis, 245
Rildo, 152, 231
Rio de Janeiro, 79
Rivelino, 5, 176, 179, 182, 185, 186, 209, 300
Rivera, Gianni, 298
Robinho, 294
Rodrigues, Jair, 245
Rodrigues, José Fornos (Pepito), 158
Rogério, 178
Romania: v. Brazil in World Cup (1970), 182
Romário, 253, 284
Rome, 85
Ronaldinho, 300
Ronaldo, 260, 284, 300
Rooney, Wayne, 299
Rosemeri *see* Nascimento, Rosemeri Cholbi
Ross, Steve, 219, 229, 292
Rossi, Paolo, 247

S

Sabuzinho, 71–2, 75
Saddam Hussein, 289
Saldanha, João, 174–5, 176
Sampaio, Oswaldo, 245
San José Earthquakes, 222
Sani, Dino, 87
Sanitária Santista, 122, 143, 158
Santana, Telê, 234
Santos, 13, 57–8; African tours, 159–62, 166–7; American tours, 157–8, 220, 290; appointment of Pelé as International Relations Adviser, 254–5; benefits of World Cup victory, 115; changes in structure of, 200–1; European tours, 115–16, 138–9; financial difficulties, 254; hiring of Julio Mazzei as technical instructor, 139; Intercontinental Club Cup victory (1962), 131; Intercontinental Club Cup victory (1963), 137; matches played abroad (1963), 135; Pelé at *see* Pelé; players, 70, 109; record and tournaments won, 70, 108, 109, 167, 207; success in

(1968), 163; tours abroad (1973), 203–4; training of youngsters by Pelé, 294; v. Czech national team (1965), 140; wins Libertadores Cup (1962), 130; wins Libertadores Cup final against Boca Juniors (1963), 136–7
Santos, Djalma, 87, 96, 122, 129, 149, 151
Santos, Nilton, 88, 89, 97, 122, 124, 129, 145, 298, 300
São Cristóvao, 15
São Paulino, 48
São Paulo, 62, 74
São Paulo FC, 81, 108, 120, 167
São Paulo Sporting Gazette, 55
Sarney, José, 255
Scotland: and World Cup (1974), 210
Scullion, Stewart, 228
Seattle Sounders, 231
Seeler, Uwe, 209, 297
Senna, Ayrton, 243
Senna, Viviane, 243
Servílio, 147
Sete de Setembro, 34–40, 48, 49
Simões Neto, Pedro, 268
Simonal, Wilson, 245
Simonian, Nikita, 91
Simonsson, Agne, 97
Sinatra, Frank, 225
slavery, 160
Smith, Bob, 231
Soares, Elza, 126–7, 129–30
Socrates, 247
Sono, Jomo, 231
Sormani, 146
South American Military Championships, 114
Spain: v. Brazil in World Cup (1962), 127
Spielberg, Steven, 225
Stallone, Sylvester, 246, 247
Stewart, Rod, 225
Sweden, 86; defeat by Brazil in World Cup (1958), 96–9

T

Tampa Bay Rowdies, 228, 231
Tebaud, François, 120
Teixeira, Ricardo, 252–3, 257, 260–1
throw-ins, 296–7
Tigana, Jean, 298
Tim (Elba de Pádua Lima), 56–7
Tinnian, Brian, 227
Toronto Metros, 222
Tostão, 5, 151, 176, 178, 179, 181, 182, 185, 300
Toye, Clive, 204–5, 214, 223
Trapattoni, 297
Três Corações, 11–12, 13, 14
Trigo, Dr Mario, 84–5
Trombadinhas, Os (1979), 245

U

UNICEF, 238, 239, 292
United States, 300; and football, 220, 233; hopeful of staging 1986 World Cup, 248; tour of by Santos, 157–8; *see also* Cosmos
Urubatão, 70
Uruguay: v. Brazil in World Cup (1950), 47, 183; v. Brazil in World Cup (1970), 183–5
USSR: v. Brazil in 1958 World Cup, 89, 91–3

V

Vadinho, 39
Valdir, 147
van Basten, Marco, 299
Vancouver, 221
Vasco da Gama, 46, 79, 109, 136, 170
Vasconcelos, 69, 73, 77, 122, 202
Vavá, 92, 94, 97, 122, 128, 129, 300

Velazquez, Guillermo 'Chato', 164–5
Veloso, Caetano, 232
Viana, Hélio, 252, 292
Viktor, Ivo, 180
Vila Belmiro, 68, 69, 76, 77, 109, 206, 211
Vila Falcão, 52
Vogts, Berti, 297

W

Waldemar de Brito *see* Brito, Waldemar de
Wales: and World Cup (1958), 93
wall at free kicks, 296
Warhol, Andy, 225, 279
Warner Communications, 219, 222, 225, 241, 246
Washington Diplomats, 228
West Germany, 185–6
World Cup: (1930), 220; (1950), 15, 46–7, 183, 220; (1954), 54;
(1958), 82, 84–99, 103, 115, 145; based at Hindas hotel, 86–7; bonding of team and spirit, 87–8; formation used, 94; goals scored by Pelé, 93, 94, 97; Pelé's knee injury and treatment, 85–6, 89, 92; practice friendlies, 85–6; preparations, 87–8; v. Austria, 89; v. England, 89; v. France, 93–4; v. USSR, 89, 91–3; v. Wales, 93; victory celebrations on return to Brazil, 103–7; wins final against Sweden, 96–9
(1962), 122–30, 140, 145, 178–9; devastation felt by Pelé at not playing in final, 128–9; formation played, 124; goals scored by Pelé, 124; Pelé's groin strain, 123–4, 125–6, 127, 128; players, 122–3; preparations and training, 123, 124; v. Chile, 128; v. Czechoslovakia, 124–6; v. England, 127; v. Mexico, 124; v. Spain, 127; wins final against Czechoslovakia, 128–9
(1966), 145–53, 157, 194, 238; defeated by Portugal, 151–2; friction amongst team, 146–7; goals scored by Pelé, 150; player selection, 145, 147, 151; preparations and training, 145, 146, 147, 148; v. Bulgaria, 149–50; v. Hungary, 150–1
(1970), 173–89, 208, 299; Banks' save, 181; goals scored by Pelé, 180, 182, 186; innovations, 194; Pelé's decision to play at, 173; player selection, 176, 179; and prayer, 178; preparations, 174, 177–8; v. Czechoslovakia, 179–80; v. England, 180–1, 299; v. Peru, 182; v. Romania, 182; v. Uruguay, 183–5; victory celebrations, 193–4; wins final against Italy, 185–9
(1974), 208–11, 214; (1978), 239; (1982), 247; (1986), 248; (1990), 248–9; (1994), 253–4; (1998), 260; (2002), 233, 239; (2006), 300
Wright, Billy, 89, 220

X

Xuxa (Maria da Graça Meneghel), 241–2, 243

Y

Yashin, Lev, 91, 93
Young, Dick, 224

Z

Zagallo, Mario, 5, 208; technical co-ordinator at World Cup (1994), 253; and World Cup (1958), 87, 97; and World Cup (1962), 122, 124, 129; as World Cup coach, 175–6, 177, 181, 209, 260
Zaluar, 76
Zé Leite, 49, 50
Zé Porto, 36, 39
Zé Roberto (Toquinho), 39
Zhechev, Dobromir, 150
Zidane, Zinedine, 298
Zinho, 65
Zito, 17, 43, 69, 87, 89–90, 105, 109, 122, 129, 144, 162, 203
Zizinho, 46, 81–2, 302
Zoca *see* Nascimento, Jair
Zoff, Dino, 298
Zózimo, 129